RED STORM ON THE REICH

RED STORM ON THE REICH

THE SOVIET MARCH ON GERMANY, 1945

Christopher Duffy

DA CAPO PRESS

Library of Congress Cataloging in Publication Data

Duffy, Christopher, 1936–
    Red storm on the Reich: the Soviet march on Germany, 1945 / Christopher
Duffy.—1st Da Capo Press ed.
        p.   cm.
    Originally published: New York: Atheneum: Maxwell Macmillan Interna-
tional, 1991.
    Includes bibliographical references and index.
    ISBN 0-306-80505-7
    1. World War, 1939–1945—Campaigns—Eastern. 2. World War, 1939–
1945—Campaigns—Germany. 3. Soviet Union. Raboche -Krest'ianskaia
Krasnaia Armiia History. I. Title
    [D764.D797 1993]   92-43696
    940.54'2131—dc20   CIP

First Da Capo Press edition 1993

This Da Capo Press paperback edition of *Red Storm on the Reich* is an
unabridged republication of the edition published in New York in 1991.
It is reprinted by arrangement with Atheneum Publishers, an imprint of
Macmillan Publishing Company.

3 4 5 6 7 8 9 10   02010099

Published by Da Capo Press, Inc.
A member of the Perseus Books Group

CONTENTS

CONTENTS

MAPS
by the author

INTRODUCTION

This book is the story of a decisive but as yet little-understood episode in the most terrible war in history—the Soviet assault on the historic lands of Germany between the middle of January and the middle of April 1945. We trace the events from the opening of the offensive on the Vistula, and follow them up to, but not through, the Berlin Operation, on which very many works have already been published.

Red Storm on the Reich has a curious history of its own. It began life (if that is not an inappropriate term) as a technical analysis of the Vistula-Oder Operation, which I wrote as teaching material for the British Army's Junior Command and Staff Course. My dissatisfaction with this booklet impelled me to start work on a much wider ranging strategic study. The 'Vistula-Oder Operation,' as I soon grasped, never existed as such, but formed a chapter which was related in complex ways with the course of European war and politics in the early months of 1945. Here my immediate problems were not connected with high-flown historical interpretations, but with establishing basic chronologies and tracing the most important sequences of cause and effect. No single account had yet attempted to match the Soviet accounts with the German in any convincing detail, or to present an overview of how operations on any given theatre were related with those on others.

It has often been observed that works of history tell us as much about the period in which they were written as about the time they purport to explain. The composition of *Red Storm on the Reich* coincided with some remarkable international developments—the disintegration of Communism over wide areas of Europe, and, far sooner than expected, the reunification of Germany. What I venture to call the 'Yalta Period of German History' emerged as a recognisable entity, and it gave a new relevance to the strategic calculations of 1945. Likewise I had to take cognizance of certain historical themes which have already acquired fresh interest for the new Germans, namely the loss of extensive territory to eastern neighbours, and the slaughter and suffering of German civilians in 1945, which reached dimensions that are still little understood in Western Europe.

In this sense *Red Storm on the Reich* became a partial response to the formidable challenge set by Andreas Hillgruber:

> The mighty happenings between the autumn of 1944 and the spring of 1945 still demand a description and treatment which keeps in view the events on the world historical stage, and yet illustrates the sufferings, deeds, ambitions and failings of men as individuals. This must be one of the most difficult tasks which lie before historians.
>
> With stupendous effort historians have researched the decline of the democratic Republic, the rise of the National Socialist movement and its Führer, and the foundation of the Third Reich and its structures. Perhaps the last great demand on this historiography will be to form a comprehensive picture of the collapse of the battle fronts, the conquest of eastern Central Europe, and the shattering of the Third Reich and the fall of the Germanic east, together with all the things that these developments mean. (*Zweierlei Untergang: Die Zerschlagung des Deutschen Reiches und das Ende des europäischen Judentums*, Berlin, 1986)

In its completed form *Red Storm on the Reich* stands as an atrocious book, in the literal sense of that term. I have limited the story of destruction as far as I could to that of landscape and machines, and I hope that I have given no satisfaction to lovers of the pornography of violence, but I cannot conceal the fact that I found many of the passages difficult to write, and difficult to live with after they had been set down on paper.

I must acknowledge my debt to Charles Dick of the Soviet Studies Research Centre, based at Sandhurst. Directly through his advice, and indirectly through his good cheer, he enabled me to carry this book through to completion. Count von Brühl (16th Panzer Division) provided very encouraging hospitality and information, and further assistance came from veterans who prefer to remain anonymous.

NOTES:

Distances on the maps are given in kilometres.

Colonel-general is a German and Soviet rank coming between full general and field-marshal.

PART I

Total War

CHAPTER 1

The Evolution of Total War

The Berlin Sportpalast, 18 February 1943
GOEBBELS: 'Do you desire total war?'
AUDIENCE: '*Ja!*'

ESSENTIALLY, the Second World War was won and lost on the Eastern Front. Only nations which were spared the experience of that holocaust have been able to regard the Second World War as somehow more light-hearted than the Great War, and a fit subject for adventure stories and comedies.

Statistics by their nature carry little emotional impact, but a few figures bear some repetition. Russian deaths in the Great Patriotic War exceed 27 million. This makes up about 40 per cent of all the people killed in the Second World War, and equates to at least ten souls for every metre of ground between Moscow and Berlin. At least seven million of the Russians who died were civilians, and 3.25 million were soldiers who perished in German captivity.

On its side, the Soviet military effort accounted for the greater part of the 3.25 million German military fatalities in the war. Approximately 3 million further German troops were captured by the Russians, and about one-third of them did not survive the ordeal. Altogether the German human sacrifice on the Eastern Front came to around 10 million killed, missing, wounded or captured, and the loss of equipment amounted to some 48,000 tanks, 167,000 artillery pieces and nearly 77,000 aircraft.

Historians have striven to explain how humanity could have

come to this pass. They have identified a first turning point in the late eighteenth century, when the young French Republic, at war with most of Europe, created a mass army through the mechanism of conscription. The French had three-quarters of a million men under arms in 1794, and by 1815 literally millions of troops had been mobilised by Napoleonic France and by the successive enemy alliances. Just as important was the impulse of nationalism, which powered the ragged armies of the French Revolution and then provoked a spirited reaction among the other peoples of Europe, especially in Spain, Russia and a number of the states of Germany.

Altogether the continual fighting between 1792 and 1815 established that warfare had ceased to be the exclusive affair of kings, the ruling circles and the professional armies. In former times defeated states had been able to buy off their victors by making over frontier fortresses, trading concessions or other small coinage of the currency of international relations. Now the price of defeat could amount to the extinction of a regime or state.

The next two centuries brought important social and economic advances, and many of them had a significant military dimension. Seemingly unlimited cannon fodder for the *Millionenheeren*—the mass conscript armies—was provided by five- or tenfold increases in population. These probably had less to do with burgeoning fertility than with simple improvements in the conditions of everyday life, which caused infant mortality to fall.

The accompanying Industrial Revolution went through two phases. The first was a 'heavy' revolution, which bore images of coal, coke, jets of steam and the grinding and clanking of pieces of heavy metal. By the middle of the nineteenth century the process of industrialisation was spreading fast from Britain to many areas of continental Europe, and 1849 saw the first operational movement of troops by rail, when the tsar of Russia sent forces to help the Austrian emperor to put down a rebellion in Hungary.

The Industrial Revolution furnished armies with mass-produced weapons that were at once precisely manufactured and cheap. In the second half of the century almost every span of five years brought radical changes in the technology of killing: the first rifled small arms and artillery gave unprecedented increases in accuracy and range in the 1850s; and over the next three decades single-shot breech-loaders, magazine rifles and the Maxim gun produced successive and significant increases in the rate of fire. By the end of the century high explosives, 'smokeless' powders and barbed wire were all available for military use.

We associate the second, or 'light' Industrial Revolution with oil, the internal-combustion engine and electricity. In warfare the effect was felt in the dimensions of speed, range and control. The first man-carrying mechanical aircraft took to the air in 1903, and within eight years the Italians were employing bomber aircraft in Libya. The first tanks were seen in 1916. They were slow, thin-skinned and unreliable, but they were used with increasing force and effect, and by the end of the Great War they had established a claim to be considered, at the very least, as an important adjunct of modern warfare.

In the Great War it was still very difficult to coordinate the action of the new weapons and forces. However, a solution was at hand by the 1930s, and it was provided by compact, reliable and long-range field radios—which became a vital ingredient of the blitzkrieg style of warfare. It was probably no coincidence that Heinz Guderian, the creator of the German Panzer arm, had specialised experience of signals. Taken together, the products of the 'light' Industrial Revolution gave skilled commanders the means of overcoming the defensive firepower which had dominated most battlefields in the Great War.

Notions about the purpose and general conduct of warfare were strongly influenced not just by increases in technical potential but by the example of Napoleon and the reading, or rather the misreading, of the writings of the Prussian military philosopher Karl von Clausewitz (1780–1831). Military activity focused on a search for victory in the big battle—finding the main body of the enemy and destroying it in short order by the maximum application of force.

Spontaneous popular nationalism, which we have noted at the beginning of the nineteenth century, was increasingly taken under political guidance, and it assumed a particularly potent form when it was reinforced by military victories. These processes were harnessed by Piedmont-Sardinia and Prussia to form the new united nations of Italy (1870) and Germany (1871).

Still more disquieting in the long term was the rise of totalitarian ideologies of the left and the right in the twentieth century. These were secular religions that overthrew traditional notions of authority which had represented continuity and had been willing to allow some limitation on the power of the state. No such restraints were observed in Leninist-Stalinist Russia, or in Nazi Germany, where the old certitudes were overset by defeat in the Great War, the harsh Versailles peace settlement, and subsequent financial crises which destroyed the economic order twice over.

Early in the Great War statesmen and generals learned to familiarise themselves with a scale of 'acceptable' casualties which far exceeded anything previously known in Western warfare. Another psychological barrier was crossed at the same time, when in 1915 the Turks massacred about 1.5 million Armenians, which proved that it was technically possible to take action against an entire racial stock. Hitler referred specifically to this episode on 22 August 1939, in his instructions to SS units for the imminent campaign in Poland: 'Who now talks of the Armenians?'

Such was the background of technical advance and moral regression which shaped the war on the Eastern Front between 1941 and 1945. Seeking to convey the character of that struggle, commentators have compared it with a combat between tribes of insects, or creatures from warring planets. The images differ, but they all remind us that we are touching on an episode of unprecedented scale and ferocity.

CHAPTER 2

The War Until 1945

The Little War, 1939–41

THE SECOND WORLD WAR took some time to assume its global character. For the Germans the first campaigns were a series of expeditions from an invulnerable heartland. They invaded and defeated Poland in the autumn of 1939 with the collusion, and later the active participation, of the Soviet Union. In the West the 'Phoney War' gave way on 10 May 1940 to an all-out German offensive, and within eleven days the leading forces of Army Group A carved their way to the English Channel. The greater part of the British Expeditionary Force escaped by way of the port of Dunkirk, at the price of abandoning its heavy weapons and equipment, and the French gave up the fight on 25 June.

It is instructive to see the uncut version of the German film *Triumph in the West*, which was released after this second blitzkrieg. The editors hark back repeatedly to the monuments and grievances of the Great War, and there is relief as well as jubilation in the welcome that was given to the returning troops. The impression is that of closing an old book rather than opening a new one.

The Great Patriotic War, 1941–45

1941

The fighting continued in the early months of 1941 because the British unaccountably refused to come to terms, and the Germans intervened in south-eastern Europe and North Africa, not least because Hitler's Italian allies had run into difficulties. These were small items of unfinished business compared with the great enterprise which Hitler now had in mind, which was a single crushing blow against his Soviet associates, whereby he intended to destroy the Bolshevik system, throw the surviving Russian forces into the emptiness beyond the Urals and open European Russia to German exploitation and colonisation. Europe would then indeed become a single geopolitical heartland, in which Russian oil, grain, coal and iron would sustain the German population and industries.

What the Russians call their 'Great Patriotic War' began on 22 June 1941, when the Germans attacked from their start lines in occupied Poland on the first day of Operation Barbarossa. The Soviet forces, unprepared and maldeployed, went on to suffer the most severe losses ever recorded in military history up to that time. No less than 660,000 Russian troops were lost in one of the episodes, when in September the Second Panzer Army cut south and isolated the Russian forces in the northern Ukraine. The Germans fell short of total victory only by the narrowest margins of time and space. Their forces were fighting on the immediate approaches to Moscow and Leningrad when they were overtaken by the first Soviet counteroffensives and the arrival of the Russian winter.

Five days in December 1941 probably have a better claim than any other span of time to be considered the turning point of the Second World War. On 6 December the Russians launched the first of their major counteroffensives outside Moscow. On 7 December Japan attacked the American base at Pearl Harbor, and five days later Hitler declared war on the United States.

Within less than a week, therefore, Germany was faced not only with the immediate reality of a winter campaign on the Eastern Front, but with the prospect of a multi-front war with two economic and military giants. This was why Winston Churchill, after a run of almost unrelieved British reverses, could look forward to an ultimate victory over Germany. Inevitably, the form, timing and cost of that victory remained in doubt.

1942

Having stabilised their lines just in front of Moscow and Leningrad, the Russians began to rebuild their army and relocate their vital war industries to the east of the Urals. For most of 1942, however, the initiative still lay in the hands of the Germans. This time they put the weight of the attack on the southern flank of that vast theatre of war. The fronts outside Moscow and Leningrad were still deadlocked, but in the summer of 1942 two German army groups coursed across the open fields of the Ukraine, one of them veering right and lodging in the Caucasus Mountains, while the other, which was spearheaded by the Sixth Army, made for the industrial city of Stalingrad on the Volga.

The obstinate defence which the Russians put up at Stalingrad is one of the most famous passages of the Second World War. Less well known is the technical skill with which the Soviet commanders managed their resources—they held the Germans frontally at Stalingrad with the necessary minimum of troops while they built up reserves for counterattacks from both flanks. The Russian counteroffensive broke on 19 November. On 23 November the jaws of the pincers closed behind the Sixth Army and elements of the Fourth Panzer Army and two Romanian armies. The Germans, from having been on the attack, were now besieged in the western part of Stalingrad, and General Friedrich von Paulus with 94,000 survivors finally surrendered on 2 February 1943.

9

1943

The Russians still had to prove that they were superior in mobile warfare, and in February and March a spirited counteroffensive by General Erich von Manstein forced the Soviets to give up some of the ground they had gained in the south, and left them holding a potentially vulnerable salient, or bulge, around the city of Kursk.

The Germans chose the Kursk salient as the target of a concerted attack (Operation Citadel) by their main armoured forces, and they now had some excellent tanks—the Tigers and the Panthers—to pit against 'those little beasts,' the Russian T-34s. This time the Soviets acted on good intelligence of what was coming, and a lull of sixty-six days gave them the opportunity to create deep zones of anti-tank defences on all three sides of the Kursk bulge. The German armoured wedges attacked on 5 July, but within ten days they had been ground down by the Soviet armour, static defences and massed batteries of anti-tank guns. On 12 July the Russians opened a counteroffensive from the flanks. This time they did not manage to encircle the enemy forces, as had happened at Stalingrad, but the Germans suffered such heavy losses in tanks and assault guns that they were never again able to bring together such a powerful theatre-level reserve on the Eastern Front. From now on the Soviets were almost invariably on the attack, and by October they exploited their success as far as the Dnieper River.

1944

On 17 January the Russians relieved the city of Leningrad, which broke a siege which had lasted more than two years. On the southern flank the 2nd Ukrainian Front opened the Uman-Botosumi Operation in the spring, and pushed the Germans out of the western Ukraine. All the Soviet vehicles bogged down in the mud, except for the tanks, and even these were sliding on their bellies, yet the Germans were not merely defeated, they fled from the Ukraine naked, without their artillery, Panzers and motor transport. They fled on oxen, cows, even on foot, and abandoned all their equipment. (Konev, 1969, 16)

The main campaigning season of 1944 was remarkable for a series of Soviet operations which cleared Russian territory, carried the war into south-eastern Europe and central Poland, and established the Soviets in the positions from which they were going to assault the German Reich in 1945. These campaigns are therefore directly relevant to our story, and they deserve to be examined in some detail.

First of all, we turn to the breakthrough in the centre. This was a sequence of two hammer blows which smashed the Germans in western Russia and eastern Poland, and brought the Soviets as far as the Vistula River. The Belorussian Operation opened on 22 June 1944. It was a day of great heat, and the anniversary of the German attack on Russia three years before. Before the sun had set the 1st Belorussian Front had broken through the left wing of German Army Group Centre, and within three weeks the Germans had lost about 350,000 troops, amounting to twenty-eight of their forty divisions, and the breach in their front attained a width of three hundred kilometres. The 1st Belorussian Front kept up the impetus of its advance into central Poland, and between 27 July and 4 August it won two bridgeheads on the far side of the great natural barrier of the Vistula.

Now that liberation appeared so close, the Polish Home Army took up arms against the Germans in Warsaw on 1 August. The Home Army was a nationalist resistance movement which owed allegiance to the government in exile in London, and not to the Polish 'Lublin government' which was sponsored by the Soviets, and it is a moot point whether the 1st Belorussian Front could have done more than it did to bring help to the battling Poles in Warsaw. By 20 September the last Russian attack in this area was beaten off, and the uprising was finally suppressed on 2 October. The Germans began to destroy the historic centre of Warsaw eight days later.

The 1st Ukrainian Front began a parallel offensive to the south on 13 July. This 'Lvov-Sandomierz Operation' smashed the German Army Group North Ukraine, cleared the western Ukraine and south-eastern Poland, and gained an extensive bridgehead on the left bank of the Vistula at Sandomierz.

In terms of distance the Russian gains in the centre of the theatre were outclassed by still more spectacular progress in south-eastern Europe. Here Stalin and his staff detected important opportunities, for the Germans depended to some degree on the help of inherently weak allies or associates (Romania, Bulgaria, Hungary, Croatia and Slovakia). There was an incipient left-wing guerrilla movement in Slovakia, and a pitiless partisan struggle, or rather civil war, was raging in Yugoslavia. Altogether three Russian fronts (army groups) were committed in this promising direction.

The Yassy-Kishinev Operation started on 19 August 1944. Romanian troops at once deserted to the Russians in large numbers, and four days later the Romanian government abandoned the German alliance. The Germans lost sixteen of their own divisions, and the military and political setbacks combined to make the outer bulwarks of south-eastern Europe untenable. The Germans relinquished the beech-clad ridges of the eastern Carpathians, and they made no serious attempt to defend the plains of the lower Danube to the south. Bucharest, the capital of faithless Romania, was occupied by the Russians on 1 September, and on the eighth Bulgaria too declared war on Germany.

By now the original Soviet push generally south from the Ukraine had been converted into a giant wheel, progressing westward through the Balkans. Belgrade and the north Yugoslavian plain were overrun in October, and on the fifteenth of that month Hungarian Regent Admiral Miklós von Horthy asked the Soviets for an armistice. On the next day Hitler divested Horthy of his powers and installed in his place the Hungarian fascist Ferenc Szálasi.

By the end of October 1944 the runaway Soviet progress had come to an end. Against all likelihood, a number of Hungarian troops continued to fight alongside the German Army Group South, so helping to form a core of five German and two Hungarian divisions, and a three-and-a-quarter-month struggle opened for the Hungarian capital of Budapest. Behind the city the natural obstacles of Lake Balaton and the Bakony Forest formed a base where Army Group South could cover the approaches to Austria and support, or try to relieve, Budapest.

To the north-east the grain of the land strongly favoured the Germans and the loyal Hungarians, for the mountain systems of the Carpathians, the Beskids and the Tatras ran along the axis of the Soviet right wing, and presented the luckless Russian Thirty-Eighth Army with some particularly difficult fighting. This mountainous region was defended by the command of Colonel-General Gotthard Heinrici (First Panzer Army and First Hungarian Army), which will play a significant part in our narrative as the link between the southern and central sectors of the Eastern Front.

Thanks to the advantages of the terrain, and their own proficiency, Heinrici's troops held a salient which jutted well to the east of the rest of the German lines in Hungary and southern Poland. Their frontage came to more than three hundred kilometres, and ran all the way from the main body of their parent Army Group A in Poland down to the boundary with Army Group South in northern Hungary.

We end the review with a survey of developments on the northern flank of the Eastern Front. The Germans were standing firm in Hungary for both military and economic reasons, since Hitler needed to hold the Soviets away from the Danubian flank of the Reich and to retain the oilfields in north-western Hungary. On the Baltic flank, however, symbolic and emotional considerations also came into play, for the littoral lay on the way to the historic heartland of the old Prussian monarchy, and this region had been under heavy German cultural influence for centuries. Compared with the grand sweeps further south, the Russian offensives in the Baltic coastlands were slow-moving and limited in scale, but they imposed Soviet rule in Estonia, Latvia and Lithuania, and they penned up significant German forces along the shore.

On this theatre the Soviet 2nd Baltic Front opened its offensive on 11 July 1944, and the 3rd Baltic Front followed suit on 24 July. Estonia was cut off when the 2nd Baltic Front reached the Gulf of Riga on 8 August, and on 18 September the Germans began to evacuate their troops from the city-port of Riga, which was finally abandoned on 16 October. The forces which the Germans retrieved from Riga helped to build up the strength of the main body of Army Group North further south in Kurland, which was itself cut off by land on 13 October. There was a small bridgehead further south again at Memel, which had a tenuous communication with Königsberg. Both Kurland and Memel were valued by Hitler, who prized them for the way he supposed they tied down superior forces. He always hated giving up ground.

Between 16 and 28 October one of the Soviet offensives penetrated a short way into outermost East Prussia, which was the first time the Russians had reached sovereign German territory in the course of the war. The Germans recovered the area of Goldap on 5 November and found that the enemy had massacred the entire population of the little town of Nemmersdorf—this was an inkling of what was in store for the rest of the Reich in the coming year.

Germany's one associate in the northern theatre had been Finland, which cut its ties on 4 September and joined the Russians in attacking the three German corps standing on its territory. Only with difficulty did Colonel-General Dr. Lothar Rendulić extricate his forces from the danger of encirclement, and he reached northern Norway at the beginning of November after a lengthy retreat.

CHAPTER 3

Instrument of Vengeance

Stalin as War Leader

SOVIET HISTORIANS are only now beginning to penetrate the secrets of the darkest regime of the twentieth century, that of Stalin. One estimate has put the number of people killed or imprisoned by him at 40 million, and it is already clear that he was a murderer on a scale surpassing Hitler. By the same token, Soviet military historians no longer seek to palliate Stalin's responsibility for the disasters of 1941, which derived not just from the way he was taken so badly off guard by the Germans, but from the wholesale purge of the Russian officer corps in the late 1930s.

Possibly the revisionists will be kinder when they come to reassess Stalin's performance in the final, victorious stages of the Great Patriotic War. As military leader, he was immediate head of a personal staff, STAVKA. Operational planning was carried out in concert with the army's General Staff, and Stalin managed the war effort as a whole through the State Defence Committee (GKO), a cabinet made up of members of the Politburo.

Stalin now orchestrated forces on a massive scale, and coherent planning had progressed beyond Fronts (groups of armies) to embrace whole groups of Fronts at a time, from the two Fronts which had attacked in western Russia and Poland in June and July 1944 to the four Fronts which were going to be committed against the historic Reich in January 1945. At this level we are talking of assets on the order of 200 divisions—2.5 million men—40,000 guns and heavy mortars, and 6,000 tanks and assault guns.

It is important to establish the character of Stalin's military interventions, which were different in kind from those of Hitler in this phase of the war. While Stalin allowed the Fronts a good margin of operational freedom, he believed that it was vital for STAVKA to keep the coordination of the various Fronts under constant control, and to this end he was in regular telephone conversation with the individual Front commanders. The reason was that the war in Europe was drawing to a close, 'and it was natural that the military-political leadership strove to participate directly in conducting operations' (Larionov et al., 1984, 374).

Political and economic considerations certainly loomed large, for Stalin was now staking out claims to Eastern and Central Europe ahead of the Allied victory. Between 9 and 18 October 1944 a series of outwardly cordial talks in Moscow between the Soviets and Churchill reached a general accord on degrees of 'predominance' in Eastern Europe. In fact, many crucial issues remained unresolved, and the Soviets pressed ahead with their twofold strategy of sponsoring 'national liberation fronts' while planning for the outright military victory which would enable them to deal with the West from a foundation of *uti possidetis*.

A sort of political agency for Hungary was set up at Szegedin at the end of October, and it evolved into an allegedly representative provisional government. No agreement on the political future of Poland had been made with the West, which continued to support the Polish government in exile in London. A rival Provisional Government of the Polish Republic came into being in Russian-controlled eastern Poland, as we have seen, and the Soviet Union was the first state to give it diplomatic recognition, which was 'a serious blow to the reactionary émigré group and its Anglo-American patrons' (Larionov et al., 1984, 374).

Within the boundaries planned for the new Poland the chief economic prize was in the south-west, in the Upper Silesian Industrial Region, which was still occupied by the Germans. When Marshal I. S. Konev reported on the preparations for his 1st Ukrainian Front at the end of November, he noticed how the area of the map which commanded Stalin's particular attention was that great concentration of factories and mines: 'Even on the map the scale and power of the Silesian area looked impressive. Stalin, as I realised very well, was emphasising the fact when he pointed at the map and, circling this area with his finger, said: "Gold!" ' (Konev, 1969, 5).

The image of Stalin as the ikon-like supreme commander was transmitted by film, radio, the press and the military Orders of the Day. Among his everyday working companions Stalin occasionally displayed an avuncular joviality. General S. M. Shtemenko recalls how he was invited with his wife, the members of the Politburo and a number of generals to make up a party to celebrate New Year's Eve at Kuntsevo, outside Moscow. The supper was laid out on tables for the guests to help themselves. At midnight Stalin proposed a toast to the armed forces, after which the party broke up into small and increasingly merry groups. The Bolshevik veteran Marshal Semyon Budenny produced an accordion on which he gave renderings of folk songs, waltzes and polkas, and then, when Stalin put a record on the gramophone, the old cavalryman flung himself into a Cossack dance.

It was about three in the morning when we returned from Kuntsevo. This first celebration of the New Year in an informal atmosphere had set us thinking. Everything seemed to indicate that the end of the war was near. We could breathe more freely these days although we knew, if anyone did, that in a few weeks a new offensive would begin and much hard fighting lay ahead. . . . Moscow still retained its wartime appearance. We drove along the dark, deserted streets, past freezing houses with closely curtained windows and an

17

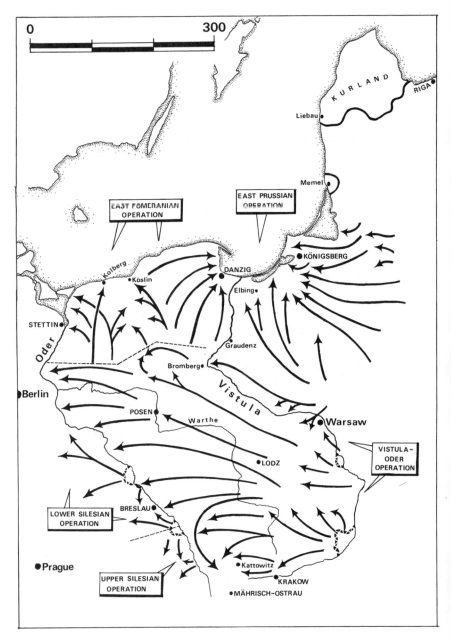

1. Overview of operations, January–April 1945

occasional timid gleam showing through a chink. (Shtemenko, 1985, 375)

The private face of Stalin was less accessible. It was not long
since he had been found at his desk, unconscious from illness
and exhaustion. When Marshal G. K. Zhukov was summoned
to Stalin's country house in March 1945, he too found that the
supreme commander's appearance, voice and walk all betrayed
weariness. Zhukov ventured to ask whether anything more had
been heard of Stalin's son Yakov, a pilot who had fallen into
the hands of the Germans. 'Stalin did not answer at once. We
had made a good hundred steps before he answered in a kind
of subdued voice: "Yakov won't be able to get out of captivity.
They'll shoot him, the killers!" ' (Zhukov, 1971, 582).

The Soviet Commanders

The leaders of the Soviet ground forces were products of the
hardest of hard schools of generalship. They were officers who
had survived Stalin's purge of the military leadership between
1937 and 1940. Their next ordeal was the national emergency
of 1941 and early 1942, when to the danger of being killed or
captured by the Germans was added the very real risk of being
shot for failure by one's own side. Thereafter, the more promising commanders were allowed to learn and improve, and the
result was that by early 1945 Stalin could draw on a considerable
depth of talent at the higher and middle levels of command.

Ideological soundness was secured through a hierarchy of
political deputies ('commissars'), and although bodies of security troops were at hand to enforce obedience where necessary, the Soviets did not divert resources into setting up a front-
line Party army like the Nazi SS. On 15 March 1945 Goebbels
told Hitler that he had read a staff study on the Russian system
of promotion, and that he had

gained the impression that we are totally unable to compete with such a method of selecting commanders. The Führer shares our view entirely. Our generals are too old and worn out and they are complete aliens to our National-Socialist ways of thought and behaviour. Many of our generals do not even want a National-Socialist victory. Soviet generals, on the other hand, are fanatical adherents of Bolshevism and so they will fight fanatically for its victory. (Goebbels, 1977, 145–46)

Within the Soviet formations a degree of military self-expression was possible as far down the chain of command as the tank and mechanised brigades, which frequently operated well ahead of their parent bodies. Full tank armies in their turn were capable of executing dramatic moves which could change the course of a campaign, and in Konev's experience none of their commanders had a greater insight into the potential of tank forces than Pavel Semenovich Rybalko. Another Russian officer testifies that

Colonel-General Rybalko's Third Guards Tank Army enjoyed a well-earned reputation. Its commanding officer was a masterly tactician and a brave soldier. Whenever this army went into action he rode in the leading tank and took direct charge in the field, maintaining radio contact with the other tanks, the infantry, and the planes in the air. (Koriakov, 1948, 63)

Significantly enough, it was Rybalko who, almost alone among the generals, had the moral courage to protest when Marshal Zhukov was sent to the doghouse after the war.

The all-arms armies were inherently slower-moving, but some of these formations entered the final campaigns of the war with an impressive reputation, and were endowed with the honorifics of 'Guards' or 'Shock.' Colonel-General Chuikov's Eighth Guards Army was outstanding. Vasilii Ivanovich

Chuikov was a perceptive and independent-minded officer, and he did not permit himself to be browbeaten even by the formidable Marshal Zhukov.

In the opening section of our story two of the Front commanders will claim our attention. The Georgii Konstantinovich Zhukov (1896–1974) just mentioned came with an authority which far transcended his nominal level of command. He was born into a poor rural family, and he did service as an ordinary cavalryman in the old tsarist army before he rose to prominence as an organiser of the Soviet mounted and mechanised forces before the Second World War. He showed his gift for managing operations on a large scale by defeating the Japanese in the battle of Khalkhin-Gol in Mongolia (August 1939), and he went on to direct the defence of Moscow (October–December 1941) and the defeat of the Germans at Kursk (July 1943). He had been made marshal of the Soviet Union in January 1943. Zhukov was idolised by the troops, but he had a brusque way with the political commissars, and his very popularity and brilliance served to distance him from the suspicious Stalin.

In June 1944 Zhukov took over the responsibility of coordinating the Belorussian Operation, in the capacity of the representative of STAVKA. Later in the year Stalin himself assumed the role of theatre coordinator, as we have noted, and in November Zhukov was appointed commander of the 1st Belorussian Front, one of the two army groups which were going to execute the grand offensive on the Berlin axis in January the next year.

Zhukov's style of leadership was direct and inspiring, and he set great store by personal reconnaissances and briefings. Just before the offensive opened, the senior officers of the Fifth Shock Army were told that Zhukov was about to descend on them, and

> not long afterwards we saw that two vehicles were moving at speed across the unmade track in our direction. They ar-

rived at the top of the hill and came to a halt. The door of the first car opened and out stepped a thick-set military man in a short khaki overcoat. He strode confidently towards us.

General Nikolai Erastovich Bezarin reported that all the senior officers were present. The marshal called him to one side, and as they talked, Colonel V. S. Antonov noted that Zhukov was smiling. The conversation terminated with a few gruff exclamations from Zhukov: 'Well, whatever happens, we won't lose time! Let's get down to work!'

The divisional commanders were summoned one by one to make their reports. Antonov's turn was first. When he had finished, the marshal demanded to know why he had deployed the regiments of his second echelon (i.e. wave) further to the rear than had been laid down in the instructions. Antonov explained that in this location they could take advantage of the cover afforded by a reverse slope, but that he would bring them forward when the attack began. 'That's an intelligent report, anyway,' commented Zhukov in a quiet voice. 'It all makes sense. Just remember, Colonel, don't lose those second-echelon regiments for me!'

Finally, Zhukov had all the divisional commanders called to him once more, and he asked each in particular about his career at the staff academy. He went on his way after shaking their hands. Antonov had the impression that Zhukov was recalling his own younger days (Antonov, 1975, 195–96).

The other army group committed on the central axis was the 1st Ukrainian Front, commanded by Marshal Ivan Stepanovich Konev (1897–1973), the favorite of Stalin. Like his rival Zhukov, Konev was a man of iron will, but he did not hail from such a disadvantaged background, and he was unique among Soviet high commanders in having begun his military career as a political officer, switching to the corps of regular officers only in the middle 1920s. In the Great Patriotic War Konev did not show his potential for offensive operations until comparatively late, in the counterattack at Kursk, but he cleared large areas of the Ukraine in a most efficient manner in the course of 1944. He was appointed marshal in February of that year.

Konev's war memoirs are more analytical and literary in tone than the more workmanlike product of Zhukov. His political instincts remained highly attuned, and his almost nightly telephone conversations with Stalin helped to keep him in the graces of the supreme commander. Konev took pride in the meticulous detail which went into the planning of his operations, and the precision with which he conveyed his meaning through his briefings, but he

> always felt indignant when, in my presence, senior commanders assigned missions to their subordinates in a formal manner, without realising that they were dealing with living, breathing men. . . . Formally everything appears to be correct, and yet there is no soul in it, no contact with one's subordinates. (Konev, 1969, 42)

Here, at least, Konev was at one with Zhukov.

Soviet Resources

The Soviet war industry was well into the second of the developments it experienced during the Great Patriotic War. The first had been to build up production behind the shelter of the Urals, but now the Soviets were reopening mines and metallurgical installations in the Donets Basin and other liberated regions of Russia. These augmented the already considerable output in the Urals and Siberia.

According to the calculations of John Erickson, the Soviet Union in 1944 manufactured 29,000 tanks and assault guns, 40,300 aircraft, 122,500 artillery pieces and mortars, and 184 million shells, mines and aircraft-delivered bombs (Erickson, 1975–83, II, 405). The quality as well as the quantity must be taken into account, for the figures include 2,000 of the new IS-

2 Stalin tanks, more than 11,000 T-34 tanks upgunned to 85 mm (T-34/85s), and over 3,000 new models of 100-mm, 122-mm and 152-mm assault guns mounted on tank chassis. Like Spartan warriors, or the grenadiers of Frederick the Great, the Soviet machines inspired as much awe when they were dead as when they were alive. On 8 March 1945 Joseph Goebbels went to the scene of a battle in Silesia and saw how

> both the market place at Lauban and the road in and out of the town were littered with burnt-out enemy tanks. Our anti-tank guns had really done a good job here. Privately one is seized with horror at the sight of the monstrous, robot-like steel colossi with which Stalin wants to subjugate Europe. (Goebbels, 1977, 81)

Less outwardly daunting but no less important was the Soviet fleet of soft-skinned vehicles, which amounted to 665,000 by the end of the war, 427,000 of them being of American manufacture. These machines helped to give mobility to the infantry elements of the armoured and mechanised forces.

The total size of the Soviet armoured forces was of an equally impressive order. The personnel amounted to some 7,109,000, of whom about 6,000,000 troops were employed on the Eastern Front (against a German figure in the same theatre of approximately 2,100,000).

This overall superiority was compounded by the skilful way the Soviets built up concentrations on the sectors where they made their main efforts. Thus the two-Front offensive in central Poland brought together nearly one-third of all the infantry formations and 43 per cent of the armour. These gave Konev and Zhukov 163 divisions, with

2,203,000 troops
4,529 tanks

2,513 assault guns
13,763 pieces of field artillery (76 mm or more)
14,812 mortars
4,936 anti-tank guns
2,198 Katyusha multiple rocket launchers
5,000 aircraft.

The vision of robotic force begins to disintegrate, however, once we discover the composition of these hosts. The Soviet resources of manpower were great, but not inexhaustible, and by now only the best of the tank armies and all-arms armies approached anything like their paper establishments. Individual divisions had been worn down to 40 or 50 per cent of their complement, and were the equivalent of brigades, while companies took the field with thirty or forty men instead of seventy-five. Increasingly, the ranks were being filled out with untrained peasants, and liberated prisoners of war and slave labourers, and the presence of these people contributed to some bad breakdowns of discipline.

The veterans were all the more valuable because they had undergone a tough but purposeful training. Beatings and cruel practical jokes often played a part in the conditioning process, and a survivor recalls how he and his fellow recruits were encouraged to steal from neighbouring units if anything of their own had gone missing: 'It was a method of education—to become courageous up to a point of being insolent' (Tarassuk, 1986, 55).

Punishments in the field were harsher still. No initiative at all was allowed to commanders at the unit level, and any officer who failed to carry out orders literally and successfully was liable to be shot without more ado, or assigned to a penal company alongside criminals and bandits. The men in such outfits were sent out to clear minefields or absorb German firepower, and their best hope of survival lay in being shot in the arm or leg and being carried to relative safety in the rear.

The Plan

Already in October 1944 the Russians began to consider how they were going to bring the war to a triumphant close. The plan evolved through three stages.

At the start General Sergei Matveeich Shtemenko, as Chief of the Operations Branch of the General Staff, called together his deputies and section chiefs to fix a preliminary scheme. They built on the knowledge that the Russians were superior in numbers and equipment, and that Germany was effectively encircled by the Soviets and their Western allies. 'Now it was a matter of completing the last swift attacks that would end in the enemy's final defeat' (Shtemenko, 1985, 380). They identified the central sector, on the 'Berlin axis,' as the decisive one, and the General Staff concluded that the Soviets must divert and hold German forces on the two flanks before and during the main attack.

The staff estimated that the activity on the flanks in the course of November and December persuaded the Germans to concentrate twenty-six divisions in East Prussia, and fifty-five near Budapest in Hungary, leaving only forty-nine in the central sector in Poland. The fighting around Budapest went on without respite into the New Year, but the staff believed that it was important to develop further offensives on the northern flank early in 1945, so as to make sure of isolating and beating the German forces in East Prussia and thereby give the two central Fronts a clear run to Berlin. The attack on East Prussia was the business of two army groups:

- The 2nd Belorussian Front was to execute a thrust from the south and south-west, in order to cut off East Prussia and cover the right flank of the advance on Berlin.
- The 3rd Belorussian Front was to carry out a frontal, or fixing, attack from the east against Königsberg.

All of this effort, it must be stressed, was intended to facilitate the blow on the central axis, where it was hoped that the 1st

Ukrainian Front and the 1st Belorussian Front would destroy the Wehrmacht in forty-five days of consecutive action. 'Finally, the plan was put down in graphic form. It was plotted on the map with all its calculations and argumentation, after which it was again subjected to what one might call almost hair-splitting discussion' (Shtemenko, 1985, 381).

The second stage in the planning process began early in November 1944, when the outline from the staff was passed to the commanders and staffs of the individual Fronts. These officers filled in the fine detail, at least as far as it concerned the initial objectives, and they made adjustments in the light of their local circumstances. On 25 November, for example, Marshal Zhukov was able to persuade the Supreme Command to divert the offensive of the 1st Belorussian Front away from a due westerly direction, where it would have run into a heavily fortified region, and into a push north-west by way of Lodz and Posen (Poznan).

The planning reached its final phase at the end of December, when the designs were reviewed and approved. Before the earlier operations it had been the practice for the Front commanders to settle the definitive details in a grand conference, but now they reported individually to Stalin, in deference to his role as Front coordinator.

The last point they had to resolve was the exact timing. The Russians had long before settled on the general principle of a midwinter offensive, not least because the ground would be frozen hard and permit the armoured and mechanised forces to move cross-country. The sources give the original date for the opening of the offensive variously as 20 January, or some time in the overall span between 15 and 20 January. At the end of the first week in January, however, Stalin moved quickly to bring forward the attack by a number of days. Ostensibly, he acted in response to a telegram which was transmitted by Winston Churchill on 6 January, asking him as a matter of urgency to launch a major attack as a means of relieving pressure on the Allies in the West. Stalin replied on the following day:

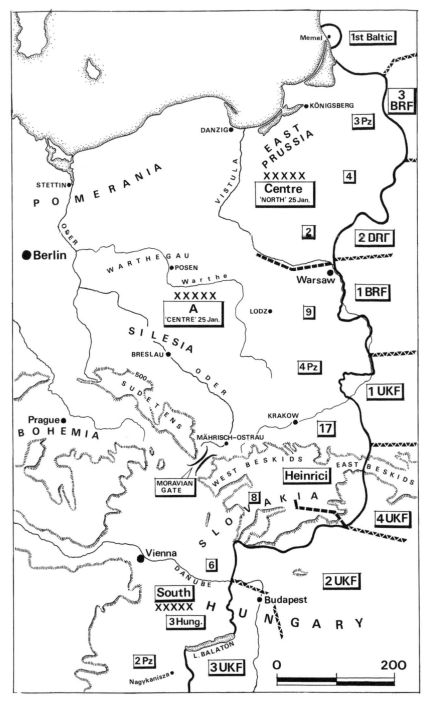

2. Formations on the Eastern Front, early January 1945

GHQ of the Supreme Command [i.e. STAVKA] have decided to complete preparations at a rapid rate and, regardless of weather, to launch large-scale offensive operations along the entire Central Front not later than the second half of January. Rest assured we shall do all in our power to support the valiant forces of our Allies. (Larionov, et al., 1984, 373)

The episode is a little puzzling. The German offensive in the Ardennes had long spent its force, and its successor in Lorraine (Operation Nordwind) was a small affair. Probably, Stalin agreed so readily to shorten his timetables because the Allied leaders were due to confer in February at Yalta, and he wished to make sure that he had Poland in his pocket and that the Soviet forces were well advanced on the way to Berlin. This would lodge the Red Army deep in Central Europe, and give the Soviet Union an important role in ordering the world after the war.

The Russians rescheduled the offensive as a sequence of staggered blows on widely separated theatres, so as to keep the Germans off balance. Konev's 1st Ukrainian Front was to take the lead on 12 January. Up in northernmost East Prussia the 3rd Belorussian Front (Chernyakovskii) was to attack on the thirteenth. Last of all on the fourteenth the Germans in northern Poland and southern East Prussia were going to be hit by the 1st Belorussian Front (Zhukov) and the 2nd Belorussian Front (Rokossovskii) at the same time.

Preparations for the Vistula-Oder Operation in Detail

The theatre of operations which lay in front of Konev and Zhukov was a plain which measured five hundred kilometres in breadth and more than five hundred in depth, and extended from the Vistula to beyond the Oder—in other words across western Poland to the regions of Silesia and Brandenburg in

Germany. The conditions in general favored fast-moving offensive action, for the earth was like iron under a thin blanket of snow, the rivers and canals were frozen and the terrain was flat and open, apart from the hilly region of the Lisaya Gora north of Kielce and a dense old forest along the Pilica. Throughout the operation one of the first priorities for the Russians was to keep their armoured spearheads on the move, thrusting around Kielce and the other cities, and rushing the passages over the Pilica, Radomka and Nida rivers before the Germans could utilise them as defensive lines.

The shape of the joint offensive was conditioned by the three bridgeheads which the Russians had won on the far side of the Vistula in central Poland in the late summer of 1944, namely:

- The extensive Sandomierz (Baranow) bridgehead on the sector of the 1st Ukrainian Front.
- The smaller Pulawy and Magnuszew bridgeheads on that of the 1st Belorussian Front.

The Germans held the river bank between these three isolated bridgeheads, and to have attacked them on these sectors would have involved the Russians in making assault crossings of the Vistula, a barrier which was about one kilometre wide. Essentially, therefore, the Vistula-Oder Operation was developed from the three bridgeheads. Only after the offensive had opened was the Forty-Seventh Army on Zhukov's far right to cross the river below Warsaw. Another general feature of the operation was its north-westerly trend, which drew the spearheads away from the most direct routes to the Reich but carried them around the northern flanks of some awkward strongpoints and built-up areas.

The Sandomierz bridgehead measured seventy-five kilometres in breadth along the Vistula and nearly sixty kilometres in depth. It was by far the largest of the bridgeheads over the Vistula, but it was packed almost to bursting point with about 90 per cent of the forces of the 1st Ukrainian Front, comprising five complete all-arms armies and both the tank armies. Konev planned to make his breakthrough on a frontage of thirty-nine kilometres and exploit along two axes in particular—that of Rybalko's Third Guards Tank Army in the south (which was going to swing by way of Radomsko and around the north of the Upper Silesian Industrial Region), and that of Lelyushenko's Fourth Tank Army in the north (ordered to cooperate with the southern flank of Zhukov's Front in a pincer movement against the German forces in the region of Kielce and Radom).

The Pulawy bridgehead on Zhukov's left was the smallest of the three bridgeheads under consideration, and it had room for only two of the all-arms armies. Here the role assigned to full tank armies in the other bridgeheads was assumed by two tank corps (the IX and XI), which were to assist the 1st Ukrainian Front to destroy the German Kielce-Radom group of forces in the way already indicated.

Zhukov's main strength was concentrated in and near the larger Magnuszew bridghead. It was deep (up to twenty-three kilometres) but narrow (about twenty), which produced a stacking-up effect of two all-arms armies, part of a third which was deployed astride the Vistula, and two tank armies standing close behind in the right bank.

In detail the planned offensive of the 1st Belorussian Front consisted of multiple thrusts, as on Konev's Front, and again the two component tank armies were expected to take the lead in the exploitation phase. On the left flank the First Guards Tank Army was going to advance west-north-west on the Lodz-Posen axis, while on the right flank the Second Guards Tank Army turned Warsaw from the south and advanced roughly parallel with the Vistula, following the north-west trend of that river downstream from the Polish capital—this axis would take the army through the area of Bromberg, near where the Vistula turned sharply to the north-east.

On both Fronts the detailed planning did not extend beyond the first few days, and the initial objectives seem to have followed a line which stretched roughly from Czestochowa through Posen to Bromberg. The offensive was hurriedly designated the 'Vistula-Oder Operation' only after the Soviet forces had outrun the original phase lines and were well on their way to the Reich and the Oder.

A degree of the unexpected is of great help in all military operations, and surprise was particularly important for the success of the Soviet offensives in the later stages of the Great Patriotic War, when frontages were cramped by the narrowing of the great European peninsula. By now the Russians had brought the appropriate techniques of *Maskirovka* (loosely translated as 'deception') to a fine art. Both of the Fronts instituted measures of *Maskirovka*, and they included variations of hoary old ruses which are part of the basic vocabulary of war.

By night, under the cover of darkness, units were moved up bit by bit to their genuine deployment areas, avoiding populated localities, while a show of activity was kept up in other sectors through ostentatious road and radio traffic and by warning householders that they were about to be turned out of their accommodation to make way for troops. Security was observed on a strict 'need to know' principle—regimental commanders were not aware of the task of their parent division; company and platoon commanders were left in ignorance of the regimental mission; the ordinary soldiers were told that the offensive was due to begin only one, two or three hours before it started.

Probably the great single effort of *Maskirovka* went into building up dummy forces on the sector of the Sixtieth Army, which was on the far left of Konev's Front and to the south of the upper Vistula. Colonel Samoilov and his parties of engineers and infantrymen set to work on 21 December, and they soon finished building mock-ups of 320 T-34s, 250 other vehicles and 600 artillery pieces. With the help of the IV Guards Tank Corps, which made a short visit from the area of the Sandomierz bridgehead, these fraudulent articles were deployed for the benefit of the Germans early in January. The guiding principle was to keep the items well concealed, but not *too* well concealed.

The standard dummy of the T-34 was a well-tried design made of wire and sacking, but care was taken to site more accurate models at important points. Further dummies were cranked up and down by ropes and windlasses, and a few specimens of the genuine article cruised around to lend an air of verisimilitude.

The Germans were almost completely taken in. Their intelligence firmly located that IV Guards Tank Corps in the area of the Sixtieth Army, and they feared a major thrust in the direction of Krakow. On a larger scale the Germans gravely underestimated the genuine concentrations of force which faced them in the three bridgeheads, and they missed the movement of nine full armies and a tank corps which arrived to take part in the central Polish offensive from STAVKA's reserve, where they had been standing at the immediate disposal of Stalin. The STAVKA reserve (RVGK) included all the tank armies, and had become 'the principal source of the forces needed to create powerful strike groupings at the most important axes at crucial times' (Dick, 1990, 108).

The logistic preparations were very thorough. Both Fronts were well stocked with supplies when the offensive began, and the example of Zhukov's army group indicates the kind of quantities involved. Ammunition was given top priority, but the 1st Belorussian Front also had to provide fuel for its 2,000-odd tanks and assault guns, 7,000 trucks, 3,000 heavy artillery tractors and 2,500 supporting aircraft, as well as a daily consumption of 1,500 tons of bread and 220 tons of meat. The dumps were filled with the help of 1,200 trains (with 68,000 individual waggon-loads), and thousands of trucks were overhauled to carry the supplies beyond the railheads.

The railway tracks through eastern Poland had been widened to the Russian gauge, which was a heroic undertaking in itself, and it was particularly difficult to transport the supplies on the final stage across the Vistula to the bridgeheads, for the bridges had only just been built by the Russian military engineers, and they were few and not especially strong. In December the water level rose and burst the ice, revealing that the Vistula was a treacherous river: 'It carries ice not only on the surface, but on the bottom too. Ramming the bridge piles the floes form invisible dams, and then the force of the current builds up and washes away the banks and the river-bed around the piles' (Chuikov, 1978, 79). The Russians ended up by towing the floes away by tractor, smashing them with explosive charges or bombarding them with batteries of 120-mm mortars.

The Soviets had reached the far side of the Vistula in July and August 1944, and although the bridgeheads contracted somewhat under German pressure in the weeks immediately following, the enemy effort fell away in September and the Russians were left with almost four clear months to prepare for their next offensive. This was a long period of grace, and they turned it to good account.

Now that they were fighting on foreign soil, the Russians had no network of agents in place behind enemy lines, and they had to put an intensive effort into building up a detailed intelligence picture of German defences, deployments and movements. Surveillance in depth was carried out by scouting patrols (ancestors of the *Spetsnaz*) and by reconnaissance aircraft which ranged as far as five hundred kilometres in the German rear, as well as making repeated photographic sorties over the forward positions.

Marshal Konev (perhaps seeking to establish his credentials as a fighting soldier) claims that he did not consider it below his dignity to reconnoitre the terrain in person, crawling about on all fours:

> Some theoreticians are inclined to overestimate the operational art and hold that the rough work on the spot is, so to speak, the business of the lower commanders, not the operational planners. My opinion, however, is that thorough preparation on the spot and the subsequent practical realisation of the theoretical postulates go very well together. (Konev, 1969, 9)

The main Russian ground forces kept the German lines under constant surveillance, and occasionally mounted reconnaissances in some force. Late in November Colonel Antonov was ordered to probe with his division in the direction of Warsaw:

It was a clear and frosty day. We followed the road as it led westwards across a plain with scattered woodlands, and it brought us to the neighbourhood of Praga, a suburb of Warsaw. In front of us there was a heap of ruins, and from the summit it was possible to take in the surroundings—the terrain to the south of Praga was open and flat, but to the north and east extended the dark woods of the Vistula valley. Through binoculars you could make out the smoking ruins of Warsaw. Bodies were littered on the western side of the Vistula, and along the river bank itself—some of them were in civilian clothing and some in uniforms. The skeletons of blocks of buildings were outlined in a dismal way against the background of smoke. We were stunned by this dreadful sight. (Antonov, 1975, 181)

From Antonov's report Zhukov concluded that it was impossible to send the Fifth Shock Army in a direct cross-river assault against Warsaw.

The Russians incorporated the findings of the reconnaissances in the detailed operational and tactical plans, which were in turn tested and rehearsed in war games and briefings that were held at every level down to the regiment. A number of these sessions extended over several days, and they turned out to be particularly useful for uncovering hidden snags and for perfecting liaison between the different arms of the service.

The final details and the fundamental principles were rammed home by the Front commanders in the days immediately before the offensive. Amazasp Khachaturovich Babadzhanyan was commander of the IX Guards Tank Corps, and he was summoned with the other tank and mechanised corps commanders to a briefing which had been organised by Zhukov:

I must say that the reports concerning Zhukov's bad temper were not without foundation. But it would be untrue to say that he was gratuitously boorish, or that he insulted the dignity of his subordinates. The qualities that appealed to him in his officers were courage and activity, energy and daring.

This was not known to Babadzhanyan at the time, and it was with some trepidation that he, as a mere colonel, made his report to Zhukov, who was seated among the generals. Zhukov satisfied himself as to the state of readiness of the corps, and then he suddenly changed tack:

'There are two kinds of men—the ones who dream of expiring in bed surrounded by their friends and relations, and the others who prefer to die on the field of battle. To which category do you belong?'
'To the second, naturally.'
'I did not expect any other answer.'

Zhukov went on to outline the task of the tank formations:

'The tank forces must cleave through the enemy defences, and strive to penetrate to the greatest possible depth in the enemy rear. They must spread panic and confusion. Don't allow the enemy to establish themselves on defensive lines or create new centres of resistance. Press on regardless!' (Babadzhanyan, 1981, 227–28)

For many of the Russian soldiers the 'lull' in the bridgeheads was a period of back-breaking labour, spent in digging positions and helping to bring up supplies and equipment. The forces were packed closely together, and despite camouflage and other forms of *Maskirovka* the Germans exacted a heavy toll when they worked over the area with their methodical artillery strikes and their fighter-bombers bombed and strafed the cowering Russians.

The political officers did what they could to keep up morale and motivation into the New Year. The Party-political meetings and the articles in the newspapers were mostly dull stuff, but the commissars sought out veterans who could tell about earlier Russian victories, and on some sectors they gave further point to the training when they took the soldiers on tours of the scenes of Nazi atrocities. The sights and smells of the death camp at Maidanek made an especially deep impression on the men of the First Guards Tank Army.

The business of working up the units culminated, where possible, in live firing exercises. Lelyushenko's Fourth Tank Army had the stimulating experience of testing the performance of their new IS-2 Stalin tanks and the 152-mm M-43 assault guns against the hulks of captured German vehicles. One of the political officers noticed that a veteran tank man had led a group of soldiers to a Tiger. It was pierced by numerous shot holes, but he pointed out that the frontal armour was 100 mm thick, and he advised his listeners to aim for the sides or rear —it was no use looking for trouble for its own sake (Krainyukov, 1979, 57).

Altogether few forces in military history have been better prepared for their task than the army groups of Konev and Zhukov on the eve of the Vistula-Oder Operation.

CHAPTER 4

The Reich Before
the Storm

The Higher Leadership

ADOLF HITLER was not a great man, if we are inclined to link that term with things that are of lasting good. But Hitler was undoubtedly a man of great attributes, who thrilled and energised a nation, and established a personal domination over men who were his intellectual, social and moral superiors.

To all outward appearances Hitler installed himself as total master of the German war machine by the end of January 1945. The process had begun much earlier, and the year 1938 was decisive, for that was when the chief of staff (Colonel-General Ludwig Beck) resigned in despair at Hitler's expansionist schemes, and the war minister (Field-Marshal Werner von Blomberg) and the commander-in-chief of the army (Colonel-General Werner von Fritsch) were forced from office through sexual blackmail.

The new commander-in-chief, the incompetent Field-Marshal Walter von Brauchitsch, was deposed in December 1941 when Hitler chose to take direct control of the armies in the East. After the abortive Bomb Plot of 20 July 1944, officers were aware that any recalcitrance on their part might be construed as treason. Finally, on 19 January 1945 Hitler ordered that the proposed movements of every formation down to corps and division had to be cleared with him personally before they could be put into effect.

Hitler was fond of emphasising, among his military qualifications, his service as a front-line soldier in the Great War. His celebrated 'intuition' brought Germany a number of incontestable triumphs in international affairs in the 1930s and on the field of battle early in the Second World War. He had a remarkable memory for factual detail, and his grasp of military technology impressed such an expert as Lieutenant-Colonel Hans Ulrich Rudel, the dive-bomber hero, who was summoned to the western headquarters at Ziegenberg. The Führer led him into his private study, which was furnished in 'good taste and utilitarian simplicity,' and Hitler's conversation ranged from updating the Ju-87 across the whole range of modern weapons development, all of which was conveyed with the 'same astonishing knowledge' (Rudel, 1952, 203).

Hitler's sense of historical destiny suggested many encouraging precedents. He was inspired above all by the embattled life of the Prussian soldier-king Frederick the Great (ruled 1740–80). A portrait of Old Fritz was set above his desk, and he used to explain: 'When bad news threatens to crush my spirit I derive fresh courage from the contemplation of this picture. Look at those strong, blue eyes, that wide brow. What a head!' (Guderian, 1952, 416).

Hitler was delighted to hear that Frederick had been very tough with his generals, for this justified his own dealings with those gentry. Frederick too had struggled against seemingly hopeless odds, and it was in the blackest year of all, in 1759, that Prussia had been saved by disunity among her enemies. Was it not reasonable to hope that the alliance of Bolsheviks and capitalists, which made up Germany's present enemies, might not also fall apart through its own contradictions? Hitler explained his present situation to Major-General Thomale in December 1945:

> There is no forseeable end to reorganisation. Everything is in a process of flux—our national production, the state of training, the competence of the commanders. But this is noth-

ing new in history. Only just now I was reading through a volume of the letters of Frederick the Great. This is what he writes in one of them, in the fifth year of the Seven Years War: 'There was a time when I went on campaign with the most magnificent army in Europe. Now I have a heap of rubbish—I possess no more commanders, my generals are incapable, my officers are no longer proper leaders, and my troops are of appalling quality.' You can't imagine a more devastating indictment, and yet this man stuck it out through the war. (Schramm, ed., 1982, IV, 1,647)

Under this illusion of tyrannical mastery, the German war effort lacked purpose and coordination. Goebbels perceived that in 'neither the military nor the civilian sector have we strong central leadership, because everything has to be referred to the Führer, and that can only be done in a small number of cases' (Goebbels, 1977, 71). The result was what historians term the Hitlerian 'weak dictatorship'—a polyocracy in which branches of the government and the armed forces went their own ways and vied for resources and prestige.

Hitler had always been difficult to reach as a social animal:

He was a vegetarian, a teetotaller and a non-smoker. These were, taken independently, very admirable qualities which derived from his personal convictions and from his ascetic way of life. But, connected with this, was his isolation as a human being . . . his path through the world was a solitary one, and he followed it alone, with only his gigantic plans for company. (Guderian, 1952, 440–41)

By this late stage in the war Hitler's capacity to follow rational arguments was severely affected by his neurological state. The bomb explosion in his old eastern headquarters at Rastenburg on 20 July 1944 had left him in the grip of uncontrollable twitches and tremblings, and his feverish excitement was sustained only by the crazy regime of pills prescribed by his doctor, the sinister Theodor Morell.

Hitler was also isolated in the geographic sense. On 16 December 1944 he moved his headquarters to the Adlerhorst at Ziegenberg, in the wooded Hessian hills near Giessen, to coincide with the opening of the German offensive in the Ardennes. In the middle of January he was back at Berlin, where the concrete of his bunker and the massive Chancellery above gave him protection against bombs of 1,000 kilograms or more. 'Zossen [i.e. the headquarters of the General Staff] is insecure—not because it was impossible to make it secure, but because it was built by the army and not a private construction firm. . . . Everything the Wehrmacht puts up is a fraud' (Hitler, 23 March 1945, Schramm, ed., 1982, IV, 1,657).

Hitler stirred from his lair less and less frequently, and it required a crippling effort on the part of the chief of staff, Colonel-General Heinz Guderian, to supply the Führer with the detailed briefings he required twice daily—at noon, and again after midnight. Guderian writes that the drive from Zossen took forty minutes, making three hours lost on the road for the two round trips, to which was added the time spent in preparing the material, and the duration of the briefings themselves, which often lasted two hours each. Even when relays of staff officers took on some of the briefings in January, they still had to be rehearsed in the presence of Guderian.

The main visual material for the Führer briefings was provided by situation maps which were updated constantly by the Operations Branch of the General Staff. 'Enemy attacks were clearly plotted on the maps by means of red arrows, so that one could not fail to see them. Moreover, there was a legend provided at the side of the maps displaying, clearly arranged in graphic form, the current status of the individual units' (Humboldt, 1986, 93). The scale of the briefing maps was 1:300,000, a significantly small scale which was capable of displaying only one theatre of war at a time. General Hans Krebs, who succeeded Guderian as chief of staff on 29 March 1945, made so bold as to provide a map on the scale of 1:1,000,000. The effect was appalling. Both the Eastern and Western fronts for the first time appeared on the same map, showing the enormous gains made by the Allies. Hitler was outraged, and reproached Krebs for being defeatist.

The Competition for Power

Beyond the Führerbunker we encounter not so much a recognisable hierarchy of command as a number of disassociated centres of influence and responsibility—the two things by no means coincided.

Next to Hitler four men in particular stood out in the leadership of the Reich. Largest in physical mass and popular stature was Reichsmarschall Hermann Göring (1893–1946), who was chief of the Luftwaffe and minister of the interior of Prussia. He had been a swashbuckling fighter ace in the Great War, and he became one of Hitler's right-hand men in the Nazi Party's fight for power. He was rewarded with the command of the Luftwaffe, which he built into a formidable modern air force in the 1930s. In the course of the war, however, Göring lost all standing with Hitler on account of the unfulfilled promises which he made on behalf of himself and the Luftwaffe—to destroy the British at Dunkirk, to supply the encircled Sixth Army at Stalingrad, and to deny the German skies to enemy bombers.

Men of taste despised Göring for the ostentation of his country house, Karinhall, which was stuffed with plundered treasures, and for his painted face and the extravagance of his garb—from vast tent-like uniform jackets and coats to his own version of the hunting dress of the ancient Teutons. Vulgar, cruel and incompetent though he was, Göring owed his ultimately unassailable position to the affection of the Party masses, who saw him as a man of the world who knew how to enjoy himself.

Göring occasionally prized himself free of Karinhall to visit nearby operational formations. Late in January 1945 he manifested himself to the astonished staff officers of the II Fliegerkorps at Schorfheide on the middle Oder:

> He was wearing a fur hat, and on top of his long greatcoat he sported a gigantic pistol in a holster of curious design. The staff officers were accustomed to Göring's style of uniform, but they had never before seen him wear that pistol. In some amazement they asked him where he had got it. Göring answered that it had been presented to him in 1938 by German industrialists.
>
> It was explained to him on the map that the Russian spearheads were at Kunersdorf. Göring jabbed his index finger at the map table . . . and replied: 'Kunersdorf, Kunersdorf, that's where I'll give them a kick in the balls!' (Paul, 1978, 75–76)

This was a quotation from one of the less urbane sayings of Frederick the Great.

If he had served any master other than Hitler, the career of Dr. Joseph Goebbels (1897–1945) might now be remembered as one of inspired dedication. The contrast with Göring was total. His slight frame, his pinched features and his elongated head bore resemblances to an ancient Egyptian mummy, and his relative importance in the Nazi scheme of things grew when the war neared its end. Already the minister of propaganda, responsible for all aspects of communications, Goebbels became Reich commissar for Total War Mobilization on 24 July 1944, and began to introduce the German people to the disciplines of a national fight to the death. Lies, fantasies and self-delusion were part of Goebbels' makeup, but his work as gauleiter of Berlin gave him a direct insight into the day-to-day existence of the suffering capital, and his messages to the German nation, delivered in his beautiful actor's voice, were informed with a new sense of urgency and realism. By their massacres in East Prussia in October 1944, the Russians had shown that they would give little mercy, and Goebbels also tried to persuade the public that not much more could be expected from the Western Allies, to judge by their terror bombing and the demand for unconditional surrender which emanated from the Casablanca Conference in January 1943.

Martin Bormann (1900–45?) was a thick-set, sweating thug who was secretary to Hitler and national organiser (*Reichsleiter*) of the Nazi Party. In the first of these capacities this 'sinister guttersnipe' (Guderian, 1952, 449) controlled all access to Hitler. As national organiser, Bormann was head of the political and administrative structure of the Reich, whose representatives at the provincial level were the gauleiters, or governors, exercising responsibility for local defence as well as local administration.

The gauleiters were frequently in conflict with the military authorities, and they often fell out among themselves. Late in 1944 Gauleiter Bracht of Upper Silesia began to set up fortifications along his borders. On some sectors the barbed wire and other defences spilled onto the soil of German-occupied Poland. Governor-General Hans Frank of Poland sought to deny all access to Bracht's men, and then relented only as far as to put the working parties under police control and levy customs duties on the trucks which crossed the border with building materials. Bracht appealed to Hitler and had the border advanced temporarily to the outer wire. Frank lodged a new protest, and he was still awaiting the outcome when the Russian troops arrived and imposed a solution of their own.

It is possible to link Göring, Goebbels and Bormann with recognisable human characteristics, however distorted. The same does not apply in the case of Heinrich Himmler (1900–45), who seemed like 'a man from another planet' (Guderian, 1952, 447). Only an extraordinarily ruthless and ambitious man could have become creator and head (*Reichsführer*) of the SS

(Schutzstaffel), chief of the German Police, and in the last two years of the war successively commander of the Training Army, commander of Army Group Upper Rhine, and on 25 January commander of the new Army Group Vistula.

The difficulty comes in trying to relate this career to what is known of Himmler the individual. This man of personal kindness was head of the Allgemeine-SS of the death camps. Likewise the lean young warriors of the Waffen-SS owed their allegiance to a person of timid disposition whose chief physical characteristics were a receding chin, heavy jowls, and eyes which appeared not so much bespectacled as glazed in: 'For the Waffen-SS Himmler was an alien being who was tolerated but not esteemed. We knew from manifold experience that his notions of military affairs were devoid of any real solidity. Indeed, the most junior lieutenant could have put him right' (SS General Steiner, in Murawski, 1969, 68).

The German armed services lacked any kind of coordinating body which might have spoken to Hitler with a united voice. The fault, as Guderian conceded, lay largely with the staff of the Wehrmacht, which in the 1930s had resisted the notion of giving up any of its independence. The joint-services Armed Forces Command Staff consequently had no real authority, and its sessions became still more pointless towards the end of the war, by which time the Luftwaffe had lost many planes and was virtually out of fuel.

The management of the ground forces was split into two parts on geographic, not functional, grounds. This arrangement bolstered the power of Hitler as supreme commander of the Wehrmacht, but otherwise defied all logic.

The OKW

Most directly under the thumb of Hitler was the OKW (Oberkommando der Wehrmacht, or High Command of the Wehrmacht) which was responsible for the Scandinavian, Western European, Mediterranean and Balkan theatres. The dividing line between this area and that under the command of the other organisation, the OKH, ran through a village between Belgrade and Budapest, and therefore made it difficult for the Germans to conduct the war on the Danube as a unified theatre. The chief of the OKW was the colourless Field-Marshal Wilhelm Keitel (1882–1946), who functioned in effect as head of Hitler's private military office. Most of the real work was taken on by Colonel-General Alfred Jodl (1890–1946), who was a more active individual, but was disinclined to argue further with Hitler after a great falling-out they had experienced at the time of the Stalingrad campaign.

The OKH

By 1945 the only man to put a coherent view of the war in front of Hitler was Colonel-General Heinz Guderian (1888–1954), who from 21 July 1944 to 29 March was chief of staff, as head of the OKH (Oberkommando des Heeres), responsible for conducting the war on the Eastern Front. Guderian had been Germany's leading theorist, organiser and practitioner of armoured warfare, and he carried all his creative energy and independence of mind into his new post. He spoke without reserve whenever he believed the war was being mismanaged, and he concluded that Hitler the Austrian and Jodl the Bavarian were incapable of perceiving the mortal danger to the north-eastern provinces of the Reich: 'For us Prussians it was our immediate homeland that was at stake, that homeland which had been won at such cost and which had remained attached to the ideals of Christian, Western culture through so many centuries, land where lay the bones of our ancestors, land that we loved' (Guderian, 1952, 389).

It must be said, however, that not all the proceedings of the OKH were conducted in such a sense of historical perspective. Major-General Mueller-Hillbrand claimed that every evening the officers of OKH, including the Operations Branch, were as drunk as lords, and he remembered in particular a conference on 5 December 1944: 'First of all there was a tremendous grubfest with enough food to burst, and then a binge. Guderian stayed until 2 A.M. By which time they were standing on the tables. I was revolted' (Irving, 1977, 741).

The German Economy

In some respects the German war industry was still capable of some remarkable achievements. Production of fighters reached a wartime peak of 3,375 machines in September 1944, and in the following December a total of 1,854 tanks, assault guns and self-propelled guns was manufactured, which was another monthly record. Technically, many of the weapons were at least as advanced as anything in the hands of the Allies. These feats were accomplished under the weight of the Allied bomber offensive, and the credit goes largely to Albert Speer (1905–81), the *Reichsminister* for armaments and production. In the overall context of the war, however, the German efforts were the equivalent of the last feverish rally of a dying consumptive, and Speer himself pointed out that on economic grounds alone the war had become unwinnable.

It is extraordinary to reflect that in spite of its totalitarian trappings, and the ruthless conduct of some of its forces, the Reich was never fully geared up for total war. The commitment of material resources to military ends was very great, but all the long-term planning had been designed to produce a military-economic superpower by the middle 1940s, and not to supply the campaigns which were actually fought from 1939. There was still a great deal of the atmosphere of craft industry about the teams of designers and skilled workers who produced weapons which were superb in quality but rarely available in sufficient quantity to meet the demands of the armed forces. Significant shortages were already noted during Operation Barbarossa in 1941, and they got much worse.

Until late in the war the availability of 4 million foreign workers encouraged the Germans to enjoy some of the conditions of peacetime society. Goebbels delivered his energising Total War speech on 18 February 1943, and yet by July the next year half a million domestic servants were still in employment, and 3.2 million men were locked in office work. Suddenly, the armed forces, the public facilities and the industries found that they were in competition for manpower. As commissar for Total War, Goebbels proceeded to withdraw half a million men from the economy between August and October 1944. He made further heavy drafts in 1945, and he wrote proudly in March that great numbers were still being offered up for front-line duty by the most diverse agencies of the Reich, from the Post Office to the forestry service. This was in the same month that Albert Speer complained that he had just 180,000 men to repair the railways, when 2 million were needed.

Some of the most economically productive areas of the Reich were now falling to the Allies as they closed in from east and west. A sudden crisis in the provision of coal was reported on 26 January 1945, when trains ceased to arrive from the Upper Silesian Industrial Region. By February half the Reichsbahn (National Railway) was compelled to resort to the use of brown coal, which was dirty and inefficient, and the locomotives laboured between their coaling stops (now every seventy to eighty kilometres instead of two hundred), punching sparks and clouds of sulphurous smoke into the frosty air. The coal and iron of the Saar were lost in March, after which the Reich could draw only upon the mangled mines and factories of the Ruhr, and the beleaguered south-western rump of the Upper Silesian Industrial Area around Mährisch-Ostrau.

A severe shortage of oil had set in earlier still, after Romania was abandoned in August 1944. The Reich now had to depend on synthetic oil plants (which were vulnerable to air attack), and the sources of natural oil at Zistersdorf in Lower Austria, and Nagykanizsa and other locations near Lake Balaton in Hungary, which were threatened by the Russian ground forces. Now that vital regions were in immediate danger, Hitler was more convinced than ever that he had been right to defy his military critics—'and yet they are the same people who used to keep up a sustained attack on my "insane" policy of holding large tracts of ground' (January, undated, Schramm, ed., 1982, IV, 1,652).

Compounding all these problems was the unrelenting American and British offensive from the air. As Hitler put it, 'The bombers are our destruction' (10 January, Schramm, ed., 1982, IV, 649). Air attacks caused a temporary but complete stoppage of synthetic oil production in September 1944. There were further damaging strikes in December and near-total destruction in a series of raids between 13 and 15 January 1945. A German report on 27 February confirms that production of synthetic oil had ceased altogether.

Industrial output was also hit by the Anglo-American attacks on the railways. Between July and December 1944 the number of railway waggons available to the Reichsbahn fell from 136,000 to 87,000. In February 1945 the Germans calculated that they needed 36,000 waggons to sustain just 80 per cent of public facilities and 25 per cent of industrial production—in other words, a mere semblance of civil and economic life. By then only 28,000 waggons had survived. The proportionate losses in locomotives were at least as severe, and 104 were destroyed on 14 February alone. By the end of the month the activity of the armaments factories was largely confined to producing ammunition and to completing work on vehicles and weapons which were already on the production line. Even when they were finished, many of these precious items were stranded in the factory yards because the railways had collapsed.

Germany had large stocks of the heavy diesel oil which powered the surviving vessels of the Kriegsmarine (navy), which were therefore able to keep up a high rate of operations in the Baltic in support of the army and the civilian refugees. The Luftwaffe, however, was very badly hit when the RAF destroyed the synthetic oil plant at Pölitz near Stettin on 8 February 1945, and the manoeuvrability and effectiveness of the ground forces were degraded by shortages of fuel and ammunition. Thus most of the tanks lost by the 7th Panzer Division, for example, were simply abandoned from lack of petrol (gasoline), and not because they had been shot up by the Russians. In January the Panzer and Panzer-Grenadier divisions as a whole were overtaken by an enforced policy of demechanisation, which reduced the truck establishment by 25 per cent and forced many of the infantrymen to go about on foot or bicycle.

The destructive effects of the bombing reached throughout the decision-making processes of the Reich. Goebbels mourned the destruction of the 'lovely building' of the Propaganda Ministry on the Wilhelmstrasse on 13 March 1945, and his nerves and those of the Berliners were worn ragged by the light and fast British Mosquito bombers, which ranged unchecked over the capital almost every night. In the middle of January the move of the location of the OKH from Friedberg eastwards to Zossen was delayed by fourteen hours because of damage to the railways. Two months later, on 15 March, the OKH became the target of a direct attack, and the key personnel were probably saved only through the presence of mind of Guderian's wife (a refugee from the Warthegau), who was watching an NCO while he tracked the progress of a bombing raid on his radar screen at Zossen. She saw the blips turn aside from the direct path to Berlin, and perceiving the danger to headquarters, she telephoned her husband, who immediately ordered all his people to the shelters. The Operations Branch ignored the warning, and its chief, General Hans Krebs, sustained a wound in his temple which took him away from work for one or more days (the accounts differ).

The sheer danger of moving anywhere in the Reich during this period was brought home by the death of the gifted Lieutenant-General Wolfdietrich von Xylander, the chief of staff of Army Group A, whose aircraft strayed into the air raid on Dresden on 14 February and was shot down.

The German Armed Forces

By 1945 the German ground forces were as severely stressed as the German economy. In the final months of 1944 the German strength on the Eastern Front sank to a level estimated at 3,700,000 troops by Soviet historians and at 1,840,000 by some of their West German counterparts. The odds were in any case stacked heavily in favour of the Russians, with their 6,000,000 men. In the areas of the Vistula bridgeheads the German disadvantage was on the order of 1:5, and some of the formations faced superiorities of 1:30 or 1:40. 'It was no wonder that those divisions were oftentimes simply vaporized by the Soviet assault' (Glantz, 1986, 507).

The German army in general was a backward organisation from the aspect of mechanical transport. Horsepower in the literal sense was still vital to the Germans for moving guns and military supplies. About nine out of ten German divisions in the East were still unmechanised (see p. 365), and on 12 January 1945 the Wehrmacht had on its books no fewer than 1,136,318 horses, of which 923,679 were on active service with the field army.

Mechanisation was largely confined to the original divisions of the Waffen-SS, and the comparable Panzer (armoured) and Panzer-Grenadier (mechanised) divisions of the Wehrmacht proper. In this sense the German phenomenon of blitzkrieg was exactly what the Soviet historians say it was, namely a 'bourgeois elitist' concept, depending on the prowess of a minority of well-equipped forces, and not mass mechanised armies after the Soviet style. Otherwise the brunt of the fighting was borne by the long-enduring *Landser* of the ordinary infantry divisions.

In the autumn of 1944 and over the following winter, the political leadership of the Reich threw itself into the task of raising fresh forces from the last available reserves of manpower. In general terms the Nazis were impelled by the need to confront the near-certainty of invasion, but they were also attracted, after the generals' Bomb Plot of 20 July 1944, by the notion of creating units and formations which owed everything to themselves and nothing to the military hierarchy of the Wehrmacht.

The new levies were of two kinds. The Volksgrenadiers were raised by Himmler and Goebbels, wearing their respective hats as commander of the Training Army and commissar for Total War, and they were destined from the first to form active combat divisions. Half a million Volksgrenadiers were mobilised within a few months, and one of their divisions, the 6th, had an unenviable place in the front line facing the Magnuszew bridgehead when the 1st Belorussian Front opened its attack at 0630 on 14 January 1945.

The Volkssturm was a militia summoned in virtue of a decree of 25 September 1944 from all non-serving males aged sixteen to sixty. The relevant lists were compiled by the local Party organisation, and the officers were appointed (largely on grounds of political reliability) by the gauleiters and their subordinate kreisleiters. The size of the Volkssturm ultimately reached 1.5 million, and it is not included in the figures of German forces which have been outlined above.

It is characteristic of the chaotic state of Germany at that time that nobody can establish the precise occasion of the founding of the Volkssturm. In September 1944 Guderian had to yield up most of the one hundred battalions of fortress infantry with which he had intended to hold the prepared positions behind the Eastern Front. He writes that he then fell back on a proposal by General Adolf Heusinger's Operations Branch of the OKH, to the effect that men should be withdrawn from hitherto reserved civilian occupations and formed into a *levée en masse*. This, according to Guderian, was the origin of the Volkssturm. In 1956 (two years after Guderian died) Guderian's account was contested by Heusinger, who pointed out that his proposal had just been to evacuate the population of East Prussia, for he was convinced that there was no place for armed civilians in modern warfare.

Veterans of the Grossdeutschland Panzer Corps saw one of the Volkssturm battalions spill into a factory yard:

> Some of these troops with Mausers on their shoulders must have been at least sixty or sixty-five, to judge by their curved spines, bowed legs, and abundant wrinkles. But the young boys were even more astonishing. . . . They had been hastily dressed in worn uniforms cut for men, and were carrying guns which were often as big as they were. They looked both comic and horrifying, and their eyes were filled with unease, like the eyes of children at the reopening of school. Not one of them could have imagined the impossible ordeal which lay ahead. . . . We noticed some heart-wringing details about these children, who were beginning the first day of their tragedy. Several of them were carrying school satchels their mothers had packed with extra food and clothes, instead of schoolbooks. A few of the boys were trading their saccharine sweets which the ration allowed to children under thirteen. (Sajer, 1971, 395)

In fact, some of the baby-faced boys of the Volkssturm turned out to be its most effective elements, when they hailed from the Hitlerjugend and were armed with anti-tank Panzerfaust rocket launchers. The Mausers mentioned by our soldier were the standard service rifles, which were something of a rarity, and many of the Volkssturm had to be content with Russian or Italian rifles or the Carl Walther *Volksmaschinenpistole*, (a German version of the British Sten). Preparation was largely confined to drill, on account of the lack of proper materials or facilities, and the allowance of practice ammunition often consisted of a handful of cartridges.

The Volkssturm were not employed for local defence *per se*, let alone as guerrillas, but were formed into battalions which (however badly armed) found themselves holding gaps in the line, static positions and built-up areas. Those who fought on the Eastern Front usually stood their ground much better than those in the West, many of whom were concerned only about how to arrange to surrender to the Americans or the British.

Morale and Proficiency

Germany's war was lost, by any rational calculation of the material and human resources. Already in 1942 well-informed staff officers at the OKH were aware that a disaster of great proportions was taking shape. The outlines became much clearer at the time the German Sixth Army surrendered at Stalingrad in February 1943, and from the middle of 1944 it was evident that the army was burnt out and the cause was hopeless. We are left with the paradox that at the beginning of 1945 the Soviets detected no signs of fading morale among the Germans, and all the Russian plans 'proceeded from the knowledge that we would have to fight a battle-wise, strong and stubborn enemy' (Zhukov, 1971, 562). For an explanation we must look to the technical skills, cohesion and motivation of the German troops.

By the end of 1944 it was possible for the Grossdeutschland Panzer Corps to have suffered losses which equated to 192 per cent of its original strength and still fight on to the following spring without any obvious signs of strain. Grossdeutschland was admittedly an elite formation, but in 1944 the German army as a whole was still killing or wounding four Russian soldiers for every casualty of its own, and only the Soviet advantage in replacement (6:1) permitted the Russians to sustain and improve their decisive numerical advantage until the end of the war (Magenheimer, 1976, 47).

Among the reasons why the Germans held together and fought so well was the legacy of the old Prussian tradition of *Auftragstaktik* ('mission-directed command'), which set out objectives clearly but left subordinates on a loose rein when it came to deciding just how those tasks were to be achieved. The *Heeres Dienstvorschrift* of 1936 put it in the following terms:

> Above all, orders are to avoid going into detail when changes in the situation cannot be excluded by the time they are carried out. In the case of larger operational situations, involving orders for several days in advance, this problem is to be taken into account. . . . In such cases the overall objective gains overriding importance. (Van Creveld, 1983, 37)

The influence of *Auftragstaktik* was by no means always good (see p. 362), but it undeniably encouraged initiative, and its survival (although degraded by the heavy losses among commanders) gave German officers and NCOs an almost unique facility to meet unexpected emergencies. Scratch forces were thrown together at a moment's notice, which permitted the Germans to deliver counterattacks or fight their way to safety when other troops might have broken or surrendered.

Auftragstaktik was itself built on the 'small-unit cohesion' which is prized by military sociologists. This too was fostered by the German military ethos:

> The soldiers felt at home in their company, and it was the only protection which they had—to keep together as closely as possible, which they did. It was the same thing with the wounded personnel who tried everything to get out of the hospital within a four-week period, in order to be authorised to return to their parent unit. This was their home. And this also explains a little bit how the units of a battalion held together in cooperation throughout the war. In larger units, like divisions or regiments, there was the same kind of feeling. The artillery belonged to the infantry and the infantry belonged to the artillery. There was interdependence and trust. This is the only explanation. (Condne, 1986, 658)

The point of view of the individual *Landser* was put particularly well by a first lieutenant of the 21st Panzer Division. By early 1945 the high hopes which had been invested in the Ardennes offensive had been dashed, and little confidence now remained in the effectiveness of the 'miracle weapons':

> Even the last soldier was aware that the war was lost. He was aiming to survive, and the only sense he could see was to protect the front in the East to save as many refugees as possible. He felt bitter to have to fight on German soil for the first time in this century, and he could not foresee any alternative but to stay with his unit and to stick to his oath of allegiance. He realised that the attempt of 20 July against Hitler had failed and, despite the obvious facts, he was hoping for a political solution for ending the war, not knowing however what kind of solution. Last but not least the demand for unconditional surrender left in the light of self-respect no alternative but to continue the hopeless fighting. (Liebeskind, 1986, 646)

The Ardennes Offensive

Germany could not afford a single mistake at the strategic or operational level, now that the war was fast approaching a decisive stage and material and human resources were so short. Towards the end of 1944 the German war managers had to resolve two basic questions—to weigh up the balance of priorities between the Eastern and Western fronts, and (given that the Eastern Front was much longer than the Western) to determine in detail how the forces facing the Russians were going to be deployed.

On the first issue Hitler was increasingly drawn from August onwards to the notion of assembling a striking force for some great pre-emptive effort in the West. He hoped that the thrust would sow dissension among the Allies, for he could not imagine how the Russians would be willing, as he put it, to 'pull the chestnuts out of the fire' for the Americans and the British (Magenheimer, 1976, 22). The plan was determined in detail on 10 November, when Hitler rejected the generals' 'Small Solution' of pinching out the American salient at Aachen and instead opted for an offensive through the Ardennes that was intended to smash its way to the city-port of Antwerp and to lead to the destruction of the Anglo-American forces north of the breakthrough.

On 16 December Field-Marshal Walter Model's Army Group B (twenty-eight divisions) opened the attack from the Eifel Mountains in a period of snowy and misty weather. The offensive was brilliantly conceived and executed at a tactical level, and it took the Americans by surprise on a weakly held sector of their front. Up in the far north Battle Group Peiper of the Sixth SS Panzer Army effected a deep penetration along the narrow ice-bound roads, but the most significant progress was made in the centre by General Hasso von Manteuffel's Fifth Panzer Army, where one of the Panzer divisions reached the heights above the Meuse.

It was not good enough. The OKW was unwilling to reinforce success by putting its main effort behind Manteuffel's army, which was a Wehrmacht and not a SS formation. Cut-off American forces held out obstinately at the road junctions of St. Vith (until 21 December) and Bastogne, which interfered with the German schedules, and worst of all the skies cleared on 23 December, enabling the Allied air forces to intervene after days of enforced inactivity.

By 24 December the effort was breaking down. From 30 December the Germans had to face a threat to their own left flank, where Patton's Third Army was pushing north in the direction of besieged Bastogne. On 8 January Hitler authorised the first withdrawals, and five days later the Germans began a full-scale retreat. The last German effort on the Western theatre was

Operation Nordwind, a brainchild of Jodl, whereby the Germans tried to regain the initiative by opening an attack in northern Alsace (1–9 January).

The Last Decisions

Altogether about 250,000 troops and 1,700 tanks and assault guns had been committed to the gamble in the West, including possibly the most potent of the German mobile reserves, namely General Sepp Dietrich's Sixth SS Panzer Army with its core of four SS Panzer divisions. The offensive in the Ardennes had already passed its Clausewitzian 'culminating point' when Colonel-General Guderian, as manager of the war in the East, drove to Ziegenberg on 24 December to try to impress on Hitler the imminent danger posed by the Russians. He was primed with the latest figures and assessments from Colonel Reinhard Gehlen, the head of the 'Foreign Armies East' intelligence department of the OKH, and he hoped to persuade Hitler to transfer the main defensive effort to the East, where the Soviets were expected to make their great move by the middle of January at the latest.

Guderian could have spared himself the trouble. Dismissing Gehlen's calculations as 'rubbish,' the Führer belittled the threat on the Vistula, and refused to pull out the forces stranded on the Baltic coast in Kurland or to consider a 'timely evacuation' of Norway and the Balkans. Jodl afterwards broached the subject of the forthcoming Operation Nordwind in Alsace, which seemed to Guderian to be another misapplication of resources, now that the bombed-out Ruhr was paralysed, whereas the invaluable Upper Silesian Industrial Region was still in full production and was vital to the survival of the Reich: 'All of this was of no avail. I was rebuffed and spent a grim and tragic Christmas Eve in those most unchristian surroundings. The news of Budapest's encirclement, which reached us that evening, did not tend to raise anyone's spirits. I was dismissed

with instructions that the Eastern Front must take care of itself'
(Guderian, 1952, 384).

Affairs were in a still sorrier state than Guderian had sus-
pected. Gehlen's figures made gloomy enough reading as they
stood, but they missed the movement of armies from STAVKA
reserve, underestimated the number of Russian formations concentrated in and immediately behind the three Vistula bridgeheads by a very wide margin, and represented German Army
Group A in Poland as facing odds of 1:3, whereas the true
proportion by January was an altogether overwhelming 1:5.

On Christmas Day, when Guderian was travelling by train
back to Zossen, Hitler ordered Herbert Gille's IV SS Panzer
Corps to move from the area north of Warsaw all the way to
Hungary, where it was to be thrown into action in a bid to
reach Budapest. This was just the latest of the diversions which
had weakened the German forces facing the Soviets in Poland.

The main task of holding the Polish theatre lay with Army
Group A under Colonel-General Josef Harpe, whose area of
responsibility stretched for more than seven hundred kilometres from the Carpathians to north of Warsaw. By January
1945 he had at his disposal 400,000 troops, 5,000 field guns and
heavy mortars and 1,136 tanks and assault guns, and the support of 515 tactical aircraft. These were arranged in three commands, which we shall follow in sequence from south to north:

- Army Group Heinrici (First Panzer Army and Hungarian First
  Army), and Seventeenth Army. These three armies guarded
  a defensively strong sub-theatre on the highland flank, to
  the south of the main 'Berlin axis.'
- Fourth Panzer Army.
- Ninth Army (lost to the new Army Group Vistula on 27
  January). The Fourth Panzer Army and the Ninth Army together formed a very thin line strung out along the Vistula,
  and they were very weak in armour, since they had only four
  Panzer divisions and two Panzer-Grenadier divisions at their
  disposal.

Beyond Harpe's left, the Germans held what Guderian called a 'balcony' along the Baltic coastlands, where the misleadingly named Army Group Centre (Colonel-General Hans Reinhardt) covered north-eastern Poland, the area of Danzig and the ancient German territory of East Prussia. Army Group Centre was relatively strong, with its 580,000 troops and three Panzer and four Panzer-Grenadier divisions.

Guderian believed that Army Group Centre posed a standing threat to the northern flank of the Soviet forces operating on the Berlin axis, but he was dismayed to find that Hitler insisted on keeping significant formations locked up further along the coast in the isolated bridgehead of Kurland (Colonel-General Ferdinand Schörner's Army Group North—thirty divisions on 9 October, reducing slowly to twenty-two by 1 March).

In Guderian's view the greatest maldeployment of all was the weighting in favour of the Hungarian theatre, where the German efforts around Budapest absorbed some of the most valuable armoured assets. Gille's IV SS Panzer Corps was ordered from Poland on Christmas Day, as we have seen, and the process assumed still larger dimensions in 1945.

Having failed to carry his point on his visit to Ziegenberg on Christmas Day, Guderian returned to the charge on 31 January. This time his first call was on the theatre commander in the West, Field-Marshal Gerd von Rundstedt, and his chief of staff General Siegfried Westphal. These men were under no illusion as to the desperate state of affairs in the East, and they ordered three divisions on the Western Front and one in Italy to hold themselves in readiness to move. Guderian could now address himself to Hitler and Jodl with more confidence. The Führer reluctantly agreed to transfer these four divisions, but he insisted that they must be deployed in Hungary, and not on the threatened front in Poland.

In the New Year Guderian made a rapid tour of the Eastern Front to see what might yet be done on the ground. On 5 January he was at the headquarters of Army Group South at Eszterhaza in Hungary, and he learned in detail how the newly arrived IV SS Panzer Corps had failed to break through to Budapest at the beginning of the month. On the night of 5–6 January Guderian's command train took him to Poland and the headquarters of Army Group A at Krakow. Here the chief of staff Lieutenant-General von Xylander presented him with detailed and well-considered proposals for an Operation Schlittenfahrt (Sleighride). The army group had calculated that if its forces remained in their present deployments the enemy would be able to break through to the German border by the sixth day of the offensive. To avert this danger, and especially to prevent the army group from being encircled by concentric thrusts from the Sandomierz and Magnuszew bridgeheads, Harpe and von Xylander proposed to pull back their main forces two days before the anticipated attack to a rearward position, the Hubertuslinie, which was a hundred kilometres shorter than the present defences facing the Vistula bridgeheads. This move was expected to yield two advantages. It would cushion the Germans against the initial Soviet bombardment, which would now fall on defences that were thinly held or abandoned altogether. Second, it would permit the Germans to create a mobile reserve, by grouping the four Panzer divisions in two pairs for a pincer attack of their own against a thrust from the Magnuszew bridgehead. According to von Xylander it was reasonable to hope that the Russian advance would be turned back at the Hubertuslinie, or at least at the Silesian border: 'That is the extent of what we may do by such means. However, the Upper Silesian Industrial Region will remain in production, the enemy will be held away from German soil, and the higher leadership of the Reich will gain time to turn the military situation, as created by us, to advantage in political negotiations' (Ahlfen, 1977, 39).

Guderian telephoned Colonel-General Reinhardt and found that Army Group Centre was thinking of a limited retreat in the same style, in this case from the position along the Narew River in northern Poland to the borders of East Prussia. Guderian agreed that these proposals were sensible, and he decided to lay them before Hitler, although with no great hope of success.

On 9 January Guderian visited Ziegenberg for the third time. As had happened before, Hitler flared up when Guderian produced maps and diagrams which had been compiled by 'Foreign Armies East.' Tempers calmed a little, but the session was completely unproductive, and nothing could persuade Hitler and Jodl that it was important to create adequate reserves behind the front line.

> To console me Hitler said, at the end of the conference: 'The Eastern Front has never before possessed such a strong reserve as now. That is your doing, and I thank you for it.' I replied 'The Eastern Front is like a pack of cards. If the front is broken through at one point all the rest will collapse, for twelve and a half divisions are far too small a reserve for so extended a front.' . . . With Hitler's parting remark—'The Eastern Front must help itself and do with what it's got'—I returned, in a very grave frame of mind, to my headquarters at Zossen. (Guderian, 1952, 387–88)

On the express orders of Hitler the main forces of Army Group A remained packed into what the Soviets termed the German 'tactical zone of defence,' which consisted of an outer belt of positions extending to a depth of five to seven kilometres from the forward edge of the battle area, and a second line a further twelve or fifteen kilometres to the rear. The four precious Panzer divisions could hardly be counted as operational reserves at all, for most of their forces were deployed within twenty-five kilometres or very much less of the front line.

Meanwhile the doom of the German forces on the Vistula drew measurably nearer. The twentieth of December came and went without producing the offensive which some analysts had predicted. On 4 January 1945 the interrogation of prisoners led German intelligence officers to expect the attack in the middle of the month. On 9 January Guderian had his final interview with Hitler. It turned out badly, as we have seen, but early the next morning the news had still not reached the commander of Army Group A, Colonel-General Josef Harpe, who was returning from the positions which faced the Sandomierz bridgehead. A biting wind whipped across the Polish plain, but Harpe drew the fur collar of his coat around his face, and he comforted himself further by reflecting that Hitler's luck and intuition would not allow him to leave the German forces in Poland exposed and defenceless. The command car sped through the streets of Krakow and came to a halt in front of the school where the staff had been established. A slim and youthful-looking figure stepped forward to meet him. This was the chief of staff, von Xylander, who appeared uncharacteristically downcast. He informed his superior that news of Guderian's audience had just arrived:

'The Führer has rejected everything—Kurland, reinforcements from the West, and Schlittenfahrt. The front line stays where it is, and the situation remains the same. The Führer does not believe that the Russians will attack.' (Thorwald, 1950, 39)

PART II

From the Vistula to the Oder

CHAPTER 5

Breakthrough on the Vistula

Konev and the 1st Ukrainian Front

ON THE NIGHT OF 11–12 JANUARY 1945 the ten armies of the 1st Ukrainian Front made ready to deal the first blow of the Soviet offensive on the Vistula. It was physically impossible to observe silence in the Sandomierz bridgehead because the tanks, assault guns and towed artillery pieces were moving into position by the thousand, but loudspeakers blared music into the night, overcoming the growl of the diesel motors. Marshal Konev placed his observation post in a small house near the edge of a wood. One of the windows faced west and should have given him a fine view over the nearby German main line, but now the fog, low clouds and blizzards reduced the visibility at times to literally zero. Air support would not be at hand, though the artillery would be firing against pre-registered targets, and the bad weather gave the infantry and tanks an extra element of surprise.

The Russian heavy and medium artillery was ranged literally wheel to wheel in concentrations of up to three hundred pieces per kilometre of front, and the first bombardment fell on the Fourth Panzer Army and the right-flanking Seventeenth Army at 0435. The air incandesced with an unnatural light, and before long a 'sky of fire and smoke lowered over the country on the west side of the Vistula. The frozen soil was torn up hundreds of times over, houses flared up like torches, bunkers collapsed, roads were broken up and men were ripped apart' (Haupt, 1968, 283–84).

The first Russian troops moved forward at 0500. They came not as a great wave, but in swarms of 'forward battalions'— miniature combat teams which overwhelmed the outermost German trenches and explored to a depth of some six hundred metres to the rear, which was far enough to enable the Soviets to pinpoint the major strongpoints which still survived between the first and second trench systems.

The weight and ferocity of the first attack shook the Germans so badly that they thought they were dealing with the main assault, and not just a reconnaissance in force. They were unprepared for the principal attack, which had unsuspected horrors in store. At 1000 the Russian artillery received the order to open fire once more:

> The recent silence gave way to a general thundering, booming, crackling and whistling. Shells and mortar bombs fell on an area tens of kilometres wide and deep, from where there arose plumes of smoke, fire and dust compounded with snow. The ground quivered, and the very earth of the battlefield was blackened. (Lelyushenko, 1970, 275)

For the next 107 minutes the bombardment worked up and down the full depth of the defences, and 'the detonations of drum fire threw up mighty clouds of black explosive smoke and brown dust. They blended with the enemy [Soviet] smoke-screen to form a layer which extended to a depth of ten kilometres over the battlefield' (Ahlfen, 1977, 47). Under the weight of these terrible blows the headquarters of the Fourth Panzer Army was destroyed, and the Germans lost about two-thirds of their artillery and one-quarter of their personnel. The surviving troops were ashen-faced and trembling, and for almost the first and last time in that war the Soviets saw Germans running from their positions in panic.

The main force of Russian infantry attacked late in the morning, exploiting along 150-metre-wide lanes of ground which had been left deliberately untouched by the shellfire. Specially assigned tanks and assault guns acted in immediate cooperation with the foot soldiers, but the Russians still had to commit their two tank armies and three separate tank corps, which formed an armoured fleet of more than two thousand tanks and motorised guns. On the right centre the snow-plastered tanks of the Fourth Army were scarcely visible against the landscape when they moved off at 1400. They were in action an hour later, and by 1700 they had advanced up to twenty kilometres and were beginning to swing north-west behind the defended urban area of Kielce. The matching formation on the left centre was Rybalko's Third Guards Tank Army, which accomplished another breakthrough and joined the action which was developing against the armoured reserves of the Fourth Panzer Army.

The reserves in question were the two armoured formations of General Walther Nehring's XXIV Panzer Corps, standing side by side in the path of the Russian tank armies, namely the 16th Panzer Division in the north and the 17th Panzer Division in the south. Forces of this kind are supposed to hold themselves out of reach of an initial enemy attack, so as to preserve the freedom to deliver counterstrokes, preferably into the flanks of the advancing hostile forces. In the event, the restraining orders imposed by Hitler kept the Panzers immobilised closely behind the 'tactical zone of defence,' where many of their units were caught by the second Russian bombardment. The damage to command posts and radio communications was particularly disruptive, and General Nehring had to wait impatiently while the appalling noise of the Soviet attack crept around his southern flank.

Nehring gained clearance to commit the XXIV Panzer Corps only in the late afternoon, and then only in the form of an order to close up to the 'cornerstone of Kielce' on his northern flank. By the time radio communication was established with the headquarters of both Panzer divisions, the Soviet armoured columns were cruising almost unchecked through or past the assembly areas of the German tank forces. One fine battalion of Tiger tanks was caught in the open while refuelling, and it was completely annihilated. The remaining German forces straggled north-west towards the appointed rallying area of Kielce in disconnected fragments. The 17th Panzer Division had the furthest to go, and in the course of the night and the following day, its headquarters was destroyed and the divisional commander, Colonel Brux, was wounded and captured.

Colonel-General Josef Harpe lost contact altogether with the right flank of the Fourth Panzer Army, where the LXVIII Panzer Corps was disintegrating in the face of the forces which erupted from the southern sector of the Sandomierz bridgehead. This corps, in spite of its designation, did not have any full Panzer divisions under its command, and lacked even the theoretical counterpunch that was available to Nehring in the north.

On 13 January, the second day of the offensive, the Russians burst right through the German rearward positions and advanced to depths of between twenty-five and forty kilometres along a total frontage of sixty kilometres. On the fourteenth the Russians made passages across the Nida River for most of its length, and they girded their loins for the pursuit.

The Fourth Panzer Army meanwhile passed out of existence as a recognisable entity. On the southern flank the LXVIII Panzer Corps disappeared from the maps (its cadre was eventually assigned to the Seventeenth Army). In the centre the remnants of the infantry divisions of the XXIV Panzer Corps fell back in the general direction of Kielce, screened by the survivors of the 16th and 17th Panzer divisions, which were engaged in bitter battles with the Soviet armour. Nehring was unable to re-establish radio contact with his superiors, though his upbringing (he was a West Prussian) and his instincts told him to take his men along the roads which led north. He delayed his departure out of a sense of obligation to his left-hand neighbour, General Hermann Recknagel's LXII Corps, which had been standing on the north flank of the Russian bridgehead and was now in

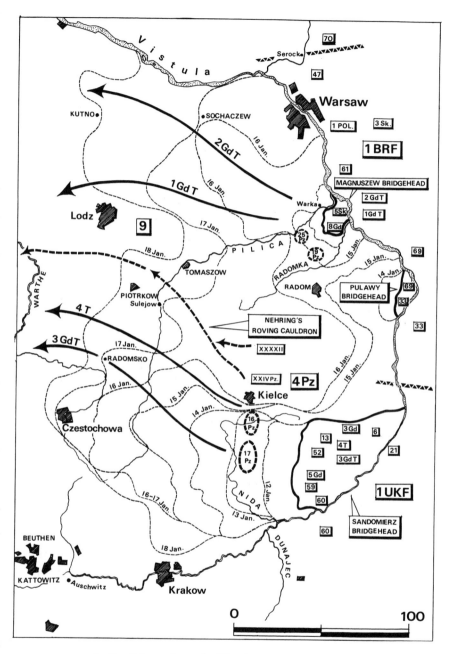

3. **Breakthrough on the Vistula, 12–18 January 1945**

danger of being pressed against the Vistula. Recknagel's troops abandoned their heavy equipment and reached Nehring's forces on foot in the course of 18 January. The mixed command is known in history as Nehring's 'roving cauldron,' and its odyssey now began (see p. 81).

Zhukov and the 1st Belorussian Front

What had already happened to the Germans was assuming the dimensions of a catastrophe, for Army Group A had lost one of its three component armies (the Fourth Panzer) and the Soviets had blasted a clear breach through the line in Poland. On 14 January, two days after the beginning of the offensive in the south, Marshal Zhukov's 1st Belorussian Front opened its great assault from the Pulawy and Magnuszew bridgeheads.

Ready to meet the Russians was the Ninth Army. This was one of the most proud and battleworthy formations of the Wehrmacht. Its commander, General Freiherr Smilo von Lüttwitz stood in line of succession with the celebrated generals Walter Model and Fedor von Bock, and he cultivated a reputation of leading his troops from the front. The Germans were on a high state of alert after what had happened to the Fourth Panzer Army, and their two Panzer divisions (the 19th and the 25th) were ready to be committed from operational reserve at short notice. None of this was going to prove of much avail against the weight of the Russian onslaught.

Zhukov had deployed two rifle armies and two tank corps in the little Pulawy bridgehead on his left flank. The German defences on this sector were shallow but very tough, and the Russians designed an appropriate response—a single and concentrated bombardment of two hours' duration, followed by attacks of the armoured and rifle forces in rapid succession.

The Russian troops in the Pulawy bridgehead spent a cold, sleepless night, then at 0830 on 14 January the artillery opened its bombardment and 'for kilometres on end the earth groaned and trembled under a veil of smoke. The discharges and the bursting of the shells merged in a continuous thunder' (Yushchuk, 1962, 107). As soon as the cannonade had ceased, the Russians attacked on a frontage of thirteen kilometres. Already on the first day the Thirty-Third and Sixty-Ninth Armies fought their way to a depth of twenty kilometres, and the two tank corps began to exploit very briskly indeed in the direction of Radom, which was an important road and rail junction and the main supply base of the German Ninth Army.

The attack from the Pulawy bridgehead had been timed to the second with the opening of the larger offensive on the right from the Magnuszew bridgehead, which involved three all-arms armies and two full tank armies. General Bezarin's Fifth Shock Army was poised to strike from the centre of the bridgehead, and the staff had been unable to sleep:

> Those final hours before the attack were wearisome and anxious. Everything seemed to have been prepared, calculated and checked, and yet we were uneasy in ourselves. Our eyes were drawn involuntarily to the map, which was streaked with arrows, and crossed by the dark blue markings which indicated the enemy defensive positions—and there were seven of them between the Vistula and the Oder. . . . It is easy to imagine the feelings of General Nikolai Erastovich Bezarin, and in fact he kept consulting the time and smoking cigarettes. . . . The dawn was approaching, but the dense fog had not dispersed. (Bokov, 1979, 52)

Bezarin had been counting on heavy air support, and he knew now that it would not be forthcoming. The tension was broken when Zhukov arrived at the observation post to learn the state of the army. He was pleased by what he heard, and he remarked that he had a 200 per cent guarantee of success.

Many of the Russian aircraft were indeed grounded by the fog, but the targets for the artillery had already been registered, and at 0825 the gunners received the order to load. The 'Ready' followed four minutes later, and at 0830 the bombardment began. The artillery strike was short (twenty-five minutes on most sectors) but very intense, and it ranged up to seven kilometres deep. Assault engineers and mine-clearing tanks worked in close cooperation to clear eight hundred passages through the enemy minefields. This systematic and dangerous work permitted 'forward battalions' to pass through to attack the first German trenches, which in turn opened the way for the assault of the main rifle forces. No second bombardment proved necessary.

In general terms, therefore, Zhukov had adopted the same tactics as Konev, but once the attack had fairly begun he was content to let his rifle forces and close-support tanks gnaw their way through the depth of the German defences before he committed his two tank armies. The commanders of the tank forces were straining at the leash. General M. E. Katukov of the First Guards Tank Army was waiting in enforced idleness at the tactical headquarters of Colonel-General Chuikov, whose Eighth Guards Army was clearing the way for him: 'Chuikov was hurling short phrases down the telephone, though I could not distinguish what he was saying on account of the din. Outside, a scattering of infantry showed black against the white landscape. Otherwise Chuikov could scarcely bear to put down his binoculars, for he knew that his most decisive minutes were approaching' (Katukov, 1976, 346).

Just to the north the Fifth Shock Army was performing the same service for the Second Guards Tank Army. The rifle forces were crossing the Pilica River at a number of places—it was a perilous business, for the thin covering of ice was pockmarked with German shell holes, and broken in places by stretches of fast-flowing and murky water. Artillery fire was still raining down on the passages when one of the divisional commanders, Colonel Antonov, reached the river during the night:

> We deployed in a chain and began to cross the ice. We had almost reached the opposite bank when shell fire burst

near us. The ice split and a large lump struck me on the head. I fell into the water, but the cold brought me to my senses. Captain Konozobko hastened up, and with his help I was retrieved from the water and brought to the bank. (Antonov, 1975, 218)

The German mobile reserves fared just as badly as their counterparts which had confronted Konev two days before. On the face of it the Germans should have done much better, for the relevant formations, the 19th and 25th Panzer Divisions (see p. 72) received clearance for the counterattack as early as 0745 on the fourteenth, and they crossed their start lines at 1030. The Germans were undeniably quick on their feet, but they squandered this single advantage by launching separate counterstrokes on divergent axes—the 19th Panzer Division against the Sixty-Ninth Army (from the Pulawy bridgehead) and the Eighth Guards Army, and the 25th against the Fifth Shock Army.

On 15 January Zhukov's all-arms armies broke through the rearward positions of the 'tactical zone of defence' against heavy local counterattacks. Keeping up the impetus of the very rapid advance from the Pulawy bridgehead, the Sixty-Ninth Army covered fifty kilometres and burst into the city of Radom. The nearest formation from the Magnuszew bridgehead was Chuikov's Eighth Guards Army, which opened a formal attack at 0900 in the direction of the railway leading north from Radom to Warka on the lower Pilica. Chuikov was present in person when the Russians smashed across the tracks at sunset with the support of a full brigade of thirty-six Katyusha multiple rocket launchers.

Northwards again the Fifth Shock Army had to contend with German counterattacks against its bridgeheads across the lower Pilica. Colonel Antonov had recovered from his ducking, and he was up with his division south-west of Warka:

The morning was grey and misty. Under its white snowy mantle the valley stretched below the hill where we stood

. . . very close to its foot companies of riflemen were digging trenches and preparing pits and foxholes. The artillerymen and the detachments of the assault guns were setting out their pieces. On all sides we were making ready for action. Colonel Kazantzev led me to the binocular mount. Looking through the lenses, you could see that enemy columns were moving through the little woods which were scattered between the heights and the valley. They were in the process of deploying into lines, and their tanks were moving at full speed and outstripping the infantry.

Antonov alerted his regiments by radio and field telephone, and for a little while yet the silence was undisturbed:

A first thunder-like sound carried through the morning air—this was a salvo from the divisional artillery group. Almost simultaneously the German heavy artillery opened fire from the direction of Warka against our positions. The ground shivered from the exploding shells and the tracks of the approaching tanks as they rumbled forward. The air was filled with a curious tinkling noise. Disregarding the losses from our artillery barrage, the German tanks, carriers and dismounted infantry pressed on at speed and opened a combined armoured and infantry attack which lasted for several minutes. At that juncture there crashed out the salvoes from Kovalevskii's artillery division, the self-propelled divisional artillery and all the pieces which were deployed in the direct fire role. The rifle battalions simultaneously opened fire with all the weapons at their disposal. Plumes of black smoke now arose from knocked-out German tanks, and their infantry hugged the ground as protection against our shells and mortar bombs.

By noon no less than five counterattacks had been beaten off and 'the cannonade thundered on without pause. In the morning, the valleys, hills and clearings had been covered with pure white snow, but now everything was blackened' (Antonov, 1975, 219–21, 223). A sixth and final counterattack was repulsed early in the afternoon.

Finally, even the demanding Zhukov was satisfied with the progress of the rifle formations—they had broken through the tactical zone of defence and beaten off all the counterattacks against their gains on the far side. On his left centre the First Guards Tank Army had been condemned to hours of frustrating inaction. At last a field telephone shrilled, and General Katukov received from Zhukov the simple message: 'Get the ball rolling!' This was the agreed signal to commit his armoured fleet to the breakthrough.

The First Guards Tank Army now roared through the sector of Chuikov's Eighth Guards Army to deliver its blow in the direction of Lodz and Posen. In the lead was the 44th Guards Tank Brigade under the dashing Colonel I. I. Gusakovskii, who had the task of gaining a bridgehead on the far side of the Pilica before the Germans could turn it into a defensive line. He reached the river on the night of 15–16 January, and sent his mechanised infantry over the ice on foot. It was imperative to get tanks and assault guns across to lend immediate support, but the cover proved to be too thin to bear these heavy machines. The engineers found a solution by discovering a ford, and they blew a lane through the ice for the vehicles. Twenty tanks and six assault guns drove into the black water, which surged up to (and sometimes over) the exhausts, and piled fragments of ice high against the turrets of the tanks. Six of the tanks and two of the assault guns were abandoned in the river (to be fished out later), but the rest struggled across and gave Gusakovskii some desperately needed firepower.

The remainder of the parent XI Guards Tank Corps arrived on the scene, together with a sixty-ton tank-bearing bridge, and with the help of the companion 45th Tank Brigade, Gusakovskii was able to beat off every counterattack delivered by the 25th Panzer Division as it came on in line after line of tanks, assault guns, personnel carriers and dismounted infantry.

The exploitation force on Zhukov's right-central axis was the Second Guards Tank Army, a massive formation whose deployment covered an area about fifteen kilometres wide and fifty to sixty deep. Its path across the lower Pilica had been cleared by the Fifth Shock Army, as we have seen, and it was able to cut north-west and begin rapid progress in the direction of Sochaczew, which was an important road and rail junction behind Warsaw. The Polish capital was threatened simultaneously from the north, where the Forty-Seventh Army had sprung into life and forced the Vistula downstream of the city.

Meanwhile on the left hand axis of the Soviet breakthrough in Poland, the Third Guards Tank Army of Konev's 1st Ukrainian Front was exploiting in the German rear, while the Fourth Tank Army was fighting through and around the city of Kielce.

By the end of 15 January the two Soviet Fronts had made a clean breach through the German tactical zone of defence. They were linking up their Vistula bridgeheads along a frontage of five hundred kilometres, and on most sectors their tank armies, tank corps and mechanised forces were advancing through open country up to a hundred kilometres beyond the start lines of the offensive. German Army Group A had lost all cohesion. Units and formations were engulfed without trace, and the remnants were split into disconnected fragments and were fighting for their lives.

CHAPTER 6

The First German Response

The Moves of Grossdeutschland
and the Sixth SS Panzer Army

BY 15 JANUARY not even Hitler could pretend any more that the Eastern Front could 'make do with what it's got.' That day was the last of his sojourn at Ziegenberg in the Hessian woods. Guderian was far distant, and without asking for his advice, the Führer ordered two divisions of the Grossdeutschland Panzer Corps down from East Prussia to the scene of the fighting at Kielce.

The formations concerned were first-class—the Hermann Göring Parachute Division ('Parachute' being an honorific) and the Brandenburg Panzer-Grenadier Division—and in a conventionally paced campaign there might have been something to be said for such a redeployment. Guderian was aghast, for in the present circumstances the transfer weakened the German forces in East Prussia just when they were coming under heavy Soviet pressure (see p. 169), and yet Grossdeutschland would probably arrive too late to plug the gap in south-central Poland, where things were already out of control.

Guderian expressed himself with as much vehemence as the roundabout communications between Ziegenberg and Zossen would allow, and the relations between Hitler and his chief of staff were already strained by the time the Führer returned to Berlin on the sixteenth and installed himself in the Chancellery bunker. 'Berlin is very convenient as a headquarters,' commented one of Hitler's SS adjutants. 'You just have to take the

79

suburban train for the little journey from the Eastern Front to the Western' (Paul, 1978, 55).

Hitler's order to entrain had gone out early on the fifteenth. The intention was for Grossdeutschland to close the breach on the sector of the Fourth Panzer Army facing Konev's Front, but the corps came nowhere near its destination. The railway communications between East Prussia and Poland were poor. Worse still, the staggered start of the Soviet offensive (with Konev attacking on the 12th, and Zhukov further north on the 14th) meant that Grossdeutschland was still moving south when it was hit in its left flank by the 1st Belorussian Front. The stations along the way were already crowded with ethnic German refugees, and the waggonloads of troops and vehicles were in the nightmarish situation of having to detrain by dribs and drabs in the neighbourhood of Lodz in the path of Zhukov's Front, which immediately brought them under fire:

> Their leader was General von Saucken, a lanky individual of medium size, who was an old East Prussian cavalryman. The eighteenth of January found him in front of a textile factory on the outskirts of Lodz. He was scanning the snow-covered terrain with his binoculars. Behind him the flight [of the ethnic German civilians] from the city had begun. Here and there Soviet tanks were pushing forward, and little white clouds of snow showed where their shells were landing. (Thorwald, 1950, 80)

Dietrich von Saucken could see that he was unable to carry out his mission in southern central Poland, for the First Guards Tank Army was sweeping down from the north and about to cut his most direct path of retreat. He accordingly threw out his forces in a screen east and south of Lodz, and hung on as long as he could so as to cover the shattered forces of the Ninth Army. When his time finally ran out he broke through to the south-west and made his way to the Warthe River, where he received Nehring's 'roving cauldron' on 22 January (see p. 86).

The combined force then made good its escape to the Oder and joined the formations defending the heartland of the Reich.

Grossdeutschland was just a corps, though a very fine one. Guderian was still more concerned about the destination of the Sixth SS Panzer Army, which had become disposable after the end of the Ardennes offensive. This was a reserve on the grand operational scale, and Guderian wanted to retrieve it for the main Eastern Front, utilising the several railway tracks which led to Berlin.

Guderian went to Hitler in the Chancellery on 16 January and found that the Führer was determined to send the Sixth SS Panzer Army all the way to Hungary to safeguard the oil wells and refineries. The railway routes in this direction were roundabout and limited, but Hitler insisted on having his way. The discussion was stormy, and not just on this account but because Hitler was furious at what had already happened in Poland. He announced that he was going to dismiss Colonel-General Harpe and replace him as commander of Army Group A with Colonel-General Ferdinand Schörner, a fanatical, brutal and energetic individual who was utterly devoted to the Führer.

The Saga of Nehring's 'Roving Cauldron'

There is something unreal and abstruse about discussing war at the purely operational level. The day-to-day reality for the Germans in Poland was that of a fight for survival by harried or cut-off units and formations which had lost all communication with the High Command. Most of the isolated German forces were eventually wiped out by the Soviet rifle troops, who came up in the Russian second echelon, but others coalesced into battle groups which tried to escape through the gaps between the Soviet armoured spearheads. These became known as 'roving cauldrons' and they were called after the senior officer present. The German talent for improvisation showed to the best advantage at this level of command.

The most famous of the 'roving cauldrons' was the group of General Walther Nehring, whom we left facing the 1st Ukrainian Front in the neighbourhood of Kielce. We shall therefore follow his story in a little detail. Nehring commanded the XXIV Panzer Corps, which was built around the 16th and 17th Panzer Divisions. On 15 January very little was clear to him except that he was cut off or would shortly be so. He fought on in the area of Kielce until the snowy night of 16–17 January, when he broke out to the north-west. He wrote later:

It was obvious to everyone that only by holding together would we all reach our destination. To split into individual groups would have spelt death or captivity. Comradeship, discipline and self-sacrifice were still in evidence, but the physical demands were extreme, and many of our fellows died under the ordeal. (Ahlfen, 1977, 56–57)

Nehring was lucky enough to encounter a fuel convoy at the outset of his journey, and he filled the tanks of his vehicles to overflowing. As a matter of principle, he now avoided all unnecessary contact with the Soviet forces and moved by night, following paths and woodland tracks. In the daytime the troops bivouacked, while the tanks were hidden, as far as possible, among houses and barns.

Early on 18 January Nehring arrived about forty kilometres north of Kielce and found that a strong Russian force was advancing from the Pulawy bridgehead and barred his intended path of escape to the north (see p. 72). He broke contact and made westwards—a direction which fortunately coincided with the approximate boundary between the Fronts of Konev and Zhukov. During the course of the day the path of the XXIV Panzer Corps converged with that of the disorganised and hard-pressed infantry of the LXII Army Corps, which was escaping from the pocket between the Sandomierz and Pulawy bridgeheads. Nehring was at last repaid for his wait at Kielce, but out of the five divisions of that corps only the 342nd (Major-General

Heinrich Nickel) retained any fighting capacity. Together with the 16th Panzer Division it formed Nehring's main striking force. The commander of LXII Corps, General Hermann Recknagel, came under Nehring's direction, but was killed five days later.

On the night of 18–19 January the roving cauldron established its first contact of any kind with the outside world. Using a Luftwaffe radio, Nehring's staff was able to hold a brief conversation with Luftwaffe General Seidemann at Posen. Seidemann himself had no idea where the Russian forces or the German positions were, but he in turn notified Guderian, who alerted the newly arrived Grossdeutschland Corps to be on the lookout for Nehring.

The twentieth brought the lost command to the fifty-metre-wide barrier of the Pilica. The details of the accounts are contradictory, but in essence the Germans beat off an armoured thrust and arrived at a small bridge which Nehring had detected on his map between Sulechow and Tomaszow. The Germans reinforced this flimsy structure with tree trunks, which permitted trucks and light armour to cross. The last force to make the passage was the rearguard, which drove two tanks into the water to prop up the disintegrating bridge, then sent its Panzer IVs racing across before the timbers finally collapsed.

On the far side the German vehicles made their way in single file through the banks and ditches of a strong position—the *a-1 Stellung* (see p. 377). There was nobody holding the line, which was evidence of some kind of failure on the part of the High Command, but a dense fog spared the column from further attentions by the Soviet tanks and planes.

On 21 January Nehring's force came unawares very close to the left flank of Chuikov's Eighth Guards Army, which was driving through Lodz. Without knowing exactly why, Nehring disregarded his staff officers, who advised him to take the good road which led west through Lodz, and instead led his group on a left-hand circuit through the woods and heaths to the south. The Germans had to abandon and blow up vehicle after

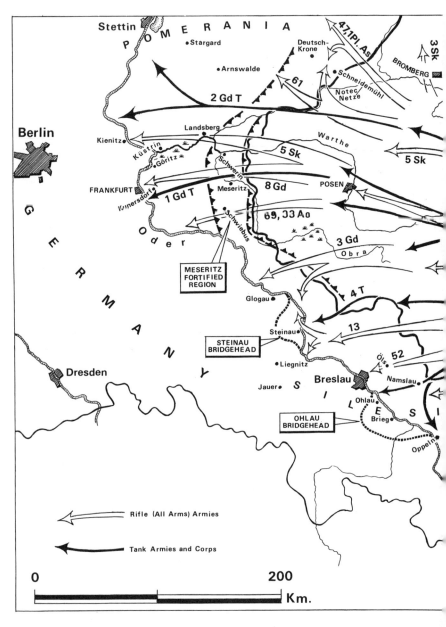

4. The Vistula–Oder Operation, 12 January–2 February 1945

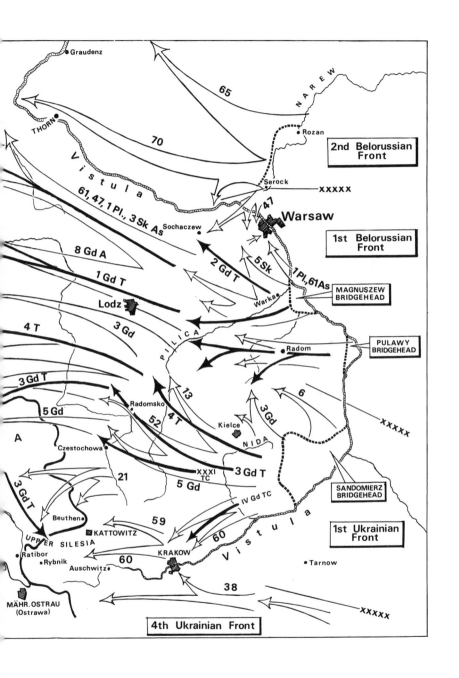

vehicle when they ran out of fuel, but units of the 16th Panzer Division came across road signs which bore the insignia of Grossdeutschland, and finally encountered an armoured reconnaissance troop which told them that the corps was waiting on the far side of the Warthe at Sieradz and that a small force was in position on the right bank to receive them.

Still under the protection of the fog, Nehring's advance guard reached the Warthe on the morning of 22 January, having covered 250 kilometres in eleven days, though the rest of the roving cauldron was still so strung out that it took several days yet for the last of the exhausted troops to complete the crossing. All the tanks had been lost.

Nehring was told by von Saucken, the commander of Grossdeutschland, that the rescuers were themselves cut off, for the Russians had already seized a number of road junctions on the direct way to the Oder. The joint force threaded its way for one hundred kilometres to the river, and on the twenty-seventh, on the final leg from Guhrau, Nehring's command came across a stretch of road several kilometres in length where a column of refugees had been shot up or crushed by the rampaging Russian tanks. The troops crossed the Oder at Glogau in an appalled silence, but (so desperate was the situation of the Reich) they were at once thrown into a counterattack against a Russian bridgehead just to the south (see p. 96).

CHAPTER 7

Konev's Exploitation

The Liberation of Czestochowa and Krakow

It is evident that the Russian armoured spearheads must have driven very fast and far indeed after they had broken through on the Vistula. As early as 16 January the Soviet armoured and mechanised forces had reached objectives which had originally been set for much later in the operation. STAVKA therefore exploited the breakthrough by ordering Konev and Zhukov to push on west and north-west in the direction of Breslau and Posen. By pressing on without a halt, the armoured and mechanised troops were to meet and overthrow any German reserves and prevent the enemy from consolidating on the river lines. Konev (who had less far to go) was going to be the first to reach German territory and arrive at the natural barrier of the Oder.

The rates of advance during the pursuit were the highest achieved by the Soviets in the war so far. The rifle forces moved at up to thirty kilometres every twenty-four hours, and the tank and mechanised forces at between forty-five and seventy. The Russians crossed the Nida, the Pilica and the Warthe in their stride. At many places they seized the crossings intact, and at others the bridges and ice passages were constructed by the engineers, who arrived close behind the leading combat units. On occasion, the engineers took a direct part in the fighting.

On the night of 16–17 January the Nehring battle group had escaped from Kielce, which removed the last German area of resistance in the neighbourhood of the old Sandomierz bridgehead. The far right flank of Marshal Konev's 1st Ukrainian Front was now secure, and the entire Fourth Tank Army was free to join in the general exploitation, which on some sectors already extended well to the west. The pilgrimage town of Czestochowa fell undamaged to the Russians on the evening of 17 January, and soon the

> caterpillar tracks of the tanks were screeching and heavy guns rattling along snow-covered back streets and down the main thoroughfare of the town, the Avenue of the Virgin Mary. . . . A dead, bloodstained silence settled over the western bank of the Vistula; just freshly ploughed land, fallen trees, dead horses, and mutilated bodies remained where the German lines had been. (Koriakov, 1948, 49)

On the same 17 January STAVKA assigned the ambitious new objectives. Konev was given two main tasks:

- To send his leading forces (spearheaded by the Third Guards Tank Army) racing for the German city of Breslau on the Oder.
- To bring the two all-arms armies on his left flank (the Sixtieth and the Fifty-Ninth) up from the second echelon and open a southerly axis of advance by way of Krakow to the Upper Silesian Industrial Region.

Konev in person directed the operation to clear Krakow. While the Sixtieth Army exerted frontal pressure, the Fifty-Ninth Army and the IV Guards Tank Corps closed in from the north and west. The Germans pulled out at speed on 19 January, without being given time to set off their demolition charges under the buildings. Konev remarked: 'It is said that in the course of a long war soldiers get used to the sight of ruins. But, however accustomed to ruins they become, they can never reconcile themselves to them, and we were enormously happy that we had been able to liberate such a city as

Krakow intact' (Konev, 1969, 31–32). This was an important prize, both for its associations as the ancient capital of Poland, and because it opened the way to the Upper Silesian Industrial Region.

On that day and the next, units of the Third Guards Tank Army crossed the German border to the east of Breslau, which was an event of still greater symbolic magnitude. There was little to check the progress of the Russians except a few scratch units which were thrown in their way. Major Tenschert and his six-hundred-strong battalion of the Training Army took up positions near Gross Wartenburg, and

> at the estate of Grunwitz we discovered that the proprietor, a singularly resolute lady, was about to escape. She had her essentials loaded on a two-horse cart with rubber tyres, but she found the time to guide us through the house, and took special care to show us the eatables in the dining room and the bottles in the cellar, advising us to select the oldest vintages first and leave nothing to the Russians. Last of all she gave us the keys to the house and the courtyard. I sometimes wonder what happened to that lady and her things. She was one of the last to leave, long after the individuals who preached last-ditch stands had made themselves scarce. (Ahlfen, 1977, 87)

The Third Guards Tank Army and the Fall of the Upper Silesian Industrial Region

On the southern flank of the great breakthrough, the Upper Silesian Industrial Region was still working with unabated energy for the Reich. It now became the object of some intricate economic and military calculations. The region had a productive capacity of 95 million tons of coal per annum (from 104 mines), and 2.4 million tons of steel (from fifteen plants), and its output of finished goods included the celebrated 88-mm gun, the main factory for which was at Kattowitz (Katowice). These efforts were vital to the Reich, as was pointed out by the armaments minister Albert Speer, and the region became still more precious after the Saar was lost, and the mines, factories and transport systems of the Ruhr had been heavily damaged by Allied bombing.

Speer did what he could to persuade the Wehrmacht to turn a blind eye to Hitler's orders to destroy the region in the path of the Soviet advance, and in the event, the Russians moved so rapidly, and the Germans were so short of pioneers and demolition experts, that the Führer's scorched-earth policy became a simple impossibility. The Seventeenth Army (General Friedrich Schulz) was responsible for defending the region, and it held a line which extended along the northern edge of the conurbation from the Oder at Oppeln to Dabrowa, and then south to Auschwitz (Oswiecim) near the Carpathians. The German positions were 120 kilometres long, and the region was so heavily cluttered with mines, plants and settlements that Schulz worked out that he needed twelve full-strength divisions to defend it instead of the seven wrecks he had at his disposal.

On the Russian side Konev was taking stock of the situation on his southern flank. Stalin had left him in no doubt as to the importance he attached to the region as an economic prize (see p. 17), which seemed to argue against smashing the place up in a set-piece battle. Fighting in an urbanised area like this, which measured 70 kilometres by 110, and which contained many buildings of solid masonry and ferroconcrete, was in any case a very expensive business, which left Konev further disinclined to stage a second Stalingrad. At the same time, Konev was convinced that he must move rapidly to forestall a German buildup there, for he overestimated the enemy strength in the region at eleven divisions, and he knew that reinforcements were on the way.

As a solution, Konev launched a wide envelopment that was intended to bring the region under attack from three sides and force the Germans into the open, in other words applying on a grander scale the technique by which he had cleared Krakow:

- Konev ordered the Sixtieth and Fifty-Ninth Armies on his far left to continue their westward advance and approach the region frontally.
- The Twenty-First Army was to swing down from the northeast and embrace the northern flank.
- The final element in the design, and the boldest of all, concerned Rybalko's Third Guards Tank Army, which had been heading due west towards Breslau in central Silesia. It was now instructed to turn sharply to its left, or south, and take the Region in the deep rear.

The Third Guards Tank Army executed its change of direction on 20 January and began to exploit up the right bank of the upper Oder. This sharp turn was carried out on the move, and it was a considerable technical achievement in its own right. Driving south-south-east, Rybalko at once proceeded to unseat the German forces which were still fighting to the east of the upper Oder, and so helped the rest of the centre and left-flanking forces of the 1st Ukrainian Front to approach the river on a wide sector. More significantly, he threatened the Upper Silesian Industrial Region with a deep envelopment, as was clear to the headquarters of German Army Group A by 23 January. The three Russian all-arms armies were pressing simultaneously from the east and north, and General Schulz, as commander on the spot, asked the Army Group headquarters on 25 January and again on the next day for permission to withdraw from the developing cauldron. Both requests were refused.

On 26 January the Third Guards Tank Army was approaching Rybnik and was poised to close off the German path of retreat. Konev was aware that he had it in his power to eliminate the estimated 100,000 Germans in the cauldron, but he remained true to his aim of winning the Upper Silesian powerhouse of the Reich in a rapid and economical operation—applying the ancient principle of the 'Golden Bridge' in the age of Total War.

Konev drove to the front line (he does not state the actual date in his memoirs) and ordered the Twenty-First Army to attack frontally rather than carry out a turning movement to the north-north-west, as had only just been arranged. The marshal continued on to the Third Guards Tank Army, and through the radio of Rybalko's command car the two leading corps were ordered to halt, while an undeployed corps from the second echelon was diverted in the direction of Ratibor on the upper Oder. Konev and Rybalko then waited on a hilltop for the orders to take effect. The field of view was excellent, and Konev noticed that many of the tanks had been festooned with white silk netting from a warehouse as camouflage against the snow:

> Ahead of us was the battlefield spread before our eyes, and we could see the movement of Rybalko's tanks. His brigades were manoeuvring before us as if they were on a good reviewing ground, moving under enemy fire toward the Silesian industrial area. In the distance we saw the industrial area with its smoking factory chimneys. On our left, where Gusev's Twenty-First Army was fighting, we heard incessant artillery fire and spotted the advancing infantry. From the depth of our rear new masses of tanks were coming into the foreground: that was the corps which Rybalko was now turning towards Ratibor by radio. . . . And that is how I see in my mind's eye that picture with all its contrasts: the smoking chimneys of Silesia, the gunflashes, the grinding caterpillar tracks, the tulle-covered tanks, and the tank-borne infantrymen. (Konev, 1969, 38–39)

On the night of 27–28 January the Germans began to pour out of the Kattowitz salient like liquid through the neck of a bottle. Konev ascribes the movement to the frontal pressure which was being exerted by his all-arms armies, but it was in fact the result of an order from German Army Group A. What was surprising about the clearance was that it came from Colonel-General Schörner, who had arrived as commander on 20 January with the express commission from Hitler to stiffen the resolution of the Germans in southern Poland.

Ferdinand Schörner, the Bavarian ex-schoolteacher, the devotee of Hitler, had enough military sense to be aware that the Kattowitz salient had become totally untenable. Not until the extrication of the Seventeenth Army was well under way did he telephone Hitler:

> 'My Führer! I have just ordered the Upper Silesian Industrial Region to be evacuated. The troops have put up a hard fight there for seventeen days, and they can do no more. If we don't pull out, we'll lose the whole army. . . . We're going back to the Oder. That's where we will make a stand.'

Schörner had expected an outburst, but the Führer replied in a weary and broken voice: 'Yes, Schörner, if that's what you think. You are doing well' (Thorwald, 1950, 116). Schörner was probably the only general who could have gotten away with it.

The Soviets gained the grimy wealth of the Upper Silesian Industrial Region on 29 January, and only the south-western extension into Moravia (see p. 143) remained in the hands of the Germans. Also in the possession of the Russians was probably the most terrible place there has ever been on earth—the death camp at Auschwitz, which had been uncovered by the Sixtieth Army a couple of days before. If the Soviet soldiers needed any justification for why they were fighting, they found it in the skeletal corpses, the bones and the grey mud which were all that remained of the victims, and in the mountains of clothing, suitcases, false teeth, spectacles and shorn hair. Konev passed close by but did not permit himself to make a detour:

> I had already received the first reports of what that camp was actually like. It was not that I did not want to see that

death camp with my own eyes; I simply made up my mind not to see it. The combat operations were in full swing, and to command them was such a strain that I could find neither time nor justification for abandoning myself to my own emotions. During the war I did not belong to myself. (Konev, 1969, 35)

Konev's Advance to the Oder

From a saddle in the southern hills the Oder wound for more than seven hundred kilometres through some of the fattest lands of the Reich to the lagoon of Stettin and the Baltic. On the middle reach between Oppeln and Küstrin, the river measured between one hundred and two hundred metres wide and two metres or more deep, and where the ice cover was continuous, it was still too thin to bear tanks or artillery. This was one of the natural barriers which helped to limit and define the shape of the Vistula-Oder Operation.

By 20 January the Soviet forces were already crossing the old German border into the province of Silesia, as has just been noted. 'After one week's fighting, the German defensive system had been staved in, overrun or bypassed, Fourth Panzer and Ninth Armies reduced to a drifting mass of men and mangled machines, left far to the rear and oozing in a glutinous mass in the direction of the Oder and hopefully home' (Erickson, 1975–83, II, 460).

Only the right-angled turn by the Third Guards Tank Army had prevented it from spearheading the advance of Konev's Front to the Oder, and now the push to the river was led by the right-hand tank army—Lelyushenko's Fourth—and the neighbouring all-arms armies. From 22 January the Russians forced a number of crossings which gradually coalesced into two main bridgeheads:

- A southern bridgehead began to take shape late on the twenty-second, when units of the Fifth Guards Army reached and crossed the Oder near Brieg, above Breslau. This holding gradually expanded into an area measuring eighty kilometres wide and about twenty-five deep. It became known as the Ohlau bridgehead.
- More significant was the northern, or Steinau, bridgehead downstream from Breslau. This was opened by Colonel Churilov's mechanised group of the Fourth Tank Army, which crossed at Göben on the night of 22–23 January. The Germans were completely unaware that the Russians had crossed the river at this point, and the next day

> a steamer appeared from the direction of Breslau, evidently laden with military supplies. Colonel Tkachuk, as commander of the relevant tank regiment, concealed his vehicles in ambush. The steamer approached unsuspecting. Upon a signal which had been agreed by Colonel Churilov, two of the tanks opened fire. After three minutes the vessel sank in flames in the fareway. Another craft appeared a couple of hours later and shared the same fate. (Lelyushenko, 1970, 286)

The Steinau bridgehead was widened with the help of the Thirteenth Army, which arrived on the left. However, the Germans were now on the alert, and the Russians also had to cope with a variety of natural and mechanical hazards. Lelyushenko himself was nearly lost to view on 26 January, when the motor boat which was towing his ferry broke down and he was carried some distance downstream.

At first the Germans defending this part of Silesia could put up just an improvised defence, for the only forces available to them were troops falling back under pressure from the Vistula, or units which were being rushed up from the rear. Among the latter was Major Tenschert's battalion (see p. 89), which was isolated when the Russians reached Oels, near Breslau. He and his men broke out early on 23 January, cutting across the Oels airfield and through the town:

> The aircraft were out of fuel, and they had been parked close together. We dashed wildly among them under machine-gun and mortar fire, and ran through the town . . . and out through the Breslau Gate. The interior of the town was deserted and unnaturally quiet. A number of isolated fires were burning, but otherwise the black night lay over everything like a pall. (Ahlfen, 1977, 90)

Breslau itself stood in immediate danger until the 169th Infantry Division arrived from the Western Front to stiffen the resistance, and the city (sprawling over both banks of the Oder) remained as a German bastion between the Ohlau and Steinau bridgeheads. The name Steinau is something of a misnomer in this context, for the personnel of the NCO training school at Jauer were still putting up an extraordinarily obstinate fight in the town of Steinau itself. The old sweats were finally eliminated only on the evening of 3 February.

Scarcely less heroic was the undertaking of von Saucken's Grossdeutschland Panzer Corps and the remnants of Nehring's roving cauldron, which had only just completed their harrowing retreat from central Poland. They were short of tanks, ammunition and fuel, and without being given the time to recover, they were flung against the north flank and rear of the Steinau bridgehead. Advancing from Glogau along the western, or 'near,' bank of the Oder, Nehring's 16th Panzer Division was stopped short by the Russians at Gaffron. Grossdeutschland was in a still worse situation. Not only was it committed on the exposed eastern side of the Oder, but it was ordered by Hitler to swing away from its communications and come at the Russians from the east. Von Saucken's progress was halted by the Soviets on the natural barrier of the Bautsch Niederung (Hollow) south of Guhrau, and the history of Grossdeutschland might have terminated there and then if Nehring had not thrown a pontoon bridge across the Oder and opened a new path of retreat. The last of Grossdeutschland crossed to safety on 2 February, but the blameless von Saucken was relieved of command.

By conventional standards of reckoning, Marshal Konev had achieved a victory of a major order. His 1st Ukrainian Front had destroyed a major force of the German Fourth Panzer Army, dealt a body blow to the Reich by capturing the Upper Silesian Industrial Region, and rounded off its triumphal progress by gaining bridgeheads across the Oder for the final push into the heart of Germany. Konev's offensive, however, was just the southern axis of the Vistula-Oder Operation. We still have to take into account the advance along the northern axis, which extended from the middle Vistula to the immediate approaches to Berlin.

CHAPTER 8

Zhukov's Exploitation

WE LEFT Zhukov's 1st Belorussian Front at the close of 15 January, by when the Russians had erupted from the Pulawy and Magnuszew bridgeheads, and begun to force crossings over the Pilica in the rear of the German tactical zone of defence.

On 17 January STAVKA assigned new and ambitious objectives for the continuation of the offensive (see p. 88), and by the eighteenth and nineteenth the leading elements of the Front were engaged in a full-blooded pursuit in the general direction of Posen. As on Konev's Front the going was made by the tank armies, the tank corps and the faster-moving elements of the first-echelon all-arms armies. Everything told in favour of a rapid exploitation, for the German Ninth Army was incapable of offering an organised resistance, and the frost, though not paralysingly cold, was sufficient to freeze the rivers and the ground under its light covering of snow. Two main axes of advance emerged during these exciting days.

The Southern Axis—Lodz and Posen

The First Guards Tank Army forged ahead along a southerly route which lay by way of Lodz (Litzmannstadt) and Posen, with General Chuikov's Eighth Guards Army not far behind. Chuikov himself kept close up with his leading troops, and he relished the freedom which came from the fact that the High Command was so frequently out of touch with events. Already on 16 January he reached Borki in the wake of his XXVIII Guards

Rifle Corps, and he came across a crowd of Polish peasants. They were shouting and wailing, and in their midst Chuikov discovered the bodies of a miller and his son, who had been shot by the Germans. At that juncture a column of German prisoners appeared from the west:

> They were a miserable lot, trudging along and shivering with the cold in their ersatz-wool greatcoats. Only the two officers at the head of the column preserved a soldierly bearing. We were afraid the crowd would fall on the Germans and were ready to act to prevent a lynching. But the Poles kept their distance, only shaking their fists and shouting curses: '*Psia krew! Psia krew!* Dog's blood!' (Chuikov, 1978, 92)

On 18 January Chuikov was surveying the scene around Lodz. This was the second largest city in Poland, and was thought to contain 'a large enemy garrison,' and rather than leave this potential trouble spot in his rear, Chuikov decided on his own authority to put in a swift assault from the north and west. On a sunny 19 January the Russians cleared Lodz without any significant resistance. Teutonic signs were everywhere—on street corners, over shop fronts, and at the entrances of cafés and restaurants—all testifying to the Germanisation of 'Litzmannstadt,' but when the Eighth Guards Army entered the city, Soviet and Polish flags appeared in profusion on roofs, balconies and windows. 'Polish women had sewn these flags in the long winter months at peril to their lives. Now, rejoicing over their liberation, they adorned the victorious path of the liberators' (Chuikov, 1978, 99).

The next city on the southern axis of Zhukov's army group was Posen (Poznan), a place of some military and symbolic moment. Posen stood guard over the junction of six railways and seven roads, including the main avenues to Berlin from the east, and unlike the open city of Lodz or the mock 'fortress' of Warsaw, it was a genuine strongpoint, defended by an inner citadel and a ring of eight massively built forts, which were relics of Prussian rule in the nineteenth century.

The Germans had repossessed Posen after Poland was divided between the Soviets and the Reich in 1939, and the city became the capital of the new German province of the Warthegau, which evolved into a test-bed for the German colonisation of Eastern Europe. The countryside was opened up by roads, railways and new agricultural settlements, and ethnic Poles were deported with the intention of making way for displaced Germans from Russia and heroes returning from the war. All of these processes were overseen by the gauleiter and commissar for defence (*Reichsverteidigungskommissar*) SS General Arthur Greiser, who was a native of the province.

In the event, the happenings at Posen foreshadow those in many German territories which lay under Soviet threat in 1945. Greiser trusted completely in Hitler, and he refused to do anything to evacuate German civilians until 20 January, the day he received orders to report to Berlin. The three phases of the relevant contingency plan were now compressed into one, and the refugees of the eastern Warthegau were left at the mercy of vengeful Poles and ferocious Russians.

Greiser made good his own escape after he had assembled his staff for the last time on the evening of the twentieth. He was pale and exhausted, and there was nothing of the old dynamism in his words:

'Gentlemen, the Russians will be in Posen within one or at the most two days.' His eyes were fixed somewhere above the crowd—there was something mournful and unfocussed about them, and he could look nobody in the face. A number of people in the audience assumed that Greiser was now going to launch into an address on 'Fortress Posen' and a 'fight to the finish.' Instead he merely explained: 'Here I lay down my life's work, uncompleted. My connection with this land could not be stronger, and my son rests in its earth.'

100

He was still looking above the audience, as if so many questioning faces caused him pain. 'Tonight I leave Posen. An order from the Führer has summoned me to Berlin to fulfil a task under the direction of the *Reichsführer SS*, and my deputy will take over the direction of the Warthegau.' He added a few words of thanks, then left—or rather fled—from the room. (Thorwald, 1950, 88)

The Soviet First Guards Tank Army was already nearing Posen, and on 21 January units of the XI Guards Tank Corps forced a passage of the Warthe below the city and hurried around the northern outskirts. However, the Russians found it difficult to establish adequate bridgeheads in this direction for their follow-on forces, and on 24 and 25 January the army put its main effort into effecting passages above Posen and so bypassing the city to the south. In the process the Russians overran a series of airfields where no less than seven hundred planes fell into their hands. At first the army commander, Katukov, refused to credit these figures, and STAVKA was so sceptical that it sent a special commission, which reported in due course that the number was correct.

It was no business of tank armies to become involved in fighting for cities, and Posen was left to the attention of the all-arms armies coming up behind. The first on the scene was Chuikov's Eighth Guards Army, which outpaced the Sixty-Ninth Army to its left and carried out a series of probing attacks on the suburbs. By 25 January Chuikov had established that Posen was heavily fortified and resolutely held. There was still no sign of the Sixty-Ninth: 'We enquired at Front headquarters, but our question evoked surprise and they began to assure us that the Sixty-Ninth Army was fighting in the centre of Posen. Well, we had no time to sort that out' (Chuikov, 1978, 130).

On 26 January, with the Sixty-Ninth Army still absent, Chuikov threw two divisions into an assault on Posen and captured two forts on the southern perimeter, but it was now clear that the Germans had no intention of being manoeuvred out of the city in the way which had happened at Lodz, and Chuikov knew that he was in for a long fight.

Posen was in fact held by a large but essentially weak garrison of 60,000 men, comprising cut-off or straggling units of the Wehrmacht, together with Volkssturm, police and ground personnel of the Luftwaffe. The one truly effective force was a body of 2,000 bellicose officer cadets. The military commandant, Major-General Ernst Mattern, a massively built former officer of the police, was too sensible and too philosophical to have any illusion about the outcome of the siege, but, true to his obligations, he issued an appropriate order of the day to the garrison. It ended with the resounding sentences:

> We have brought the enemy to a halt, just when they thought they had nearly reached their objective. We will continue to hold them in the same style. This critical hour calls us to do our duty. It will find us ready and willing!

His adjutant noticed that his hand trembled as he wrote (Thorwald, 1950, 93).

Meanwhile the spearheads of the First Guards Tank Army neared the old German border on the Obra River, where the Second World War had begun on 1 September 1939. We have therefore followed the advance on Zhukov's southern axis from the bridgehead zones on the Vistula to the immediate proximity of the old Reich. It is time to take up the story of the events on Zhukov's right flank over the same span of time.

Warsaw and the Northern Axis

The hideous wreck of Warsaw lay on the immediate north flank of Zhukov's break-out from the Magnuszew bridgehead. Flight, deportations, bombings, combat, massacre and hunger had reduced the population of the Polish capital from its original

1,310,000 citizens in 1939 to a mere 162,000 survivors. After suppressing the uprising of the Polish Home Army in October 1944, the Germans had carried out a vandalistic programme of demolitions, destroying St. John's Cathedral, the Royal Palace, the Opera and Ballet House and the Library. The Germans could not even plead military necessity for what they had done, for no attempt was made to turn the ruins to tactical advantage, and in the middle of January 1945 the city was held by a token force consisting of a few engineer and artillery units and four battalions of fortress infantry. The quality of the garrison may be judged by the fact that one of the units was an 'ear battalion,' which was recruited in its entirety from a military hospital— all of the men were deaf to some degree, and nearly half of them needed daily treatment.

The threat to the 'fortress' of Warsaw took shape very rapidly indeed. On 16 January the Second Guards Tank Army was fed into the breakthrough on the northern sector of the Magnuszew bridgehead, and by the end of the seventeenth its leading units had entered Sochaczew. This was an important centre of communications eighty kilometres to the west of Warsaw (see p. 78), and the Russians thereby cut off the garrison from the main body of the Ninth Army. Warsaw was more closely enveloped by the Forty-Seventh Army, which made crossings of the Vistula below the city, and by the First Polish Army and the Sixty-First Army which cut in from the south. By the morning of 17 January, forces of all three armies were fighting in the streets.

The Germans in and around Warsaw were already extricating themselves as best they could. The XXXVI Panzer Corps, which had been positioned behind Warsaw, was squeezed out of its deployment area by the converging attacks, and was forced to seek refuge with the German Second Army on the far side of the Vistula. Warsaw itself was patently untenable, and late on the evening of 16 January the headquarters of Army Group A (using a freedom which it had been allowed by the OKH) ordered the city to be evacuated. The resistance on the seventeenth was in the nature of a rearguard action, and by 1400 Warsaw was completely free of the Germans.

A small group of officers of the Second Guards Army now entered the capital to investigate the state of the streets for the passage of forces: 'The city lay in silence. We were thunderstruck by the scale of the devastation. . . . Every building had been reduced to ruins, and the streets were blocked by piles of smashed masonry' (Semenov, 1970, 191). A division of the Third Shock Army came up close behind: 'The further we penetrated into the city, the more we were possessed by feelings of shock and outrage. We had seen many towns and villages which had been turned to ruins, but I truly believe we had encountered nothing to compare with the barbarity and the dimensions of the destruction about us' (Shatilov, 1970, 162).

The news of the events at Warsaw came to Hitler in a way he found peculiarly infuriating. Because of a muddle in communications he was told first that his 'fortress' had already fallen, and then that Warsaw was still in German hands, though its evacuation was imminent. Hitler renewed his orders to hold the place to the last man, but the situation had deteriorated beyond hope of repair and Warsaw was abandoned anyway.

To Hitler the Warsaw episode was further proof that the Wehrmacht lacked loyalty and resolution, and on the night of the eighteenth he ordered Colonel Bogislaw von Bonin (as chief of the Operations Branch of the OKH) and two of his lieutenant-colonels to be arrested at gunpoint. In a gesture of solidarity Guderian insisted that he too should be subjected to questioning, and the result in the OKH was that 'hours of long interrogation by SS personnel considerably strained our working power and nerves during these fateful days when the battle of life and death for our homeland was being waged on the Eastern Front' (Humboldt, 1986, 90). Von Bonin was passed from one concentration camp to another until he was finally discovered by the American forces, who put him in prison once again.

The Second Guards Tank Army, having turned Warsaw, sped on west-north-west, supported by the Forty-Seventh and

Sixty-First armies. Soviet commanders now showed that they were capable of acting with skill and daring, even when they had lost touch with their parent formations.

The experience of Lieutenant-Colonel Dolbanosov's motorised 1,181st Rifle Regiment was typical of this phase of the campaign. He spearheaded the advance of the northern flank of the Forty-Seventh Army down the left bank of the Vistula, and he set a cracking pace. During the first night he progressed an initial sixty kilometres without incident, though a deep rumble of artillery from beyond the Vistula indicated that heavy fighting was taking place on the sector of the 2nd Belorussian Front. The regiment's path lay through the village of Pyaski, and Dolbanosov and his chief of staff, Borodin, drove towards the place in full confidence that the way had been cleared by the Third Battalion, which was acting as 'point':

> All of a sudden the column came to a halt, and from ahead we heard heavy small-arms fire and the explosion of shells. . . . Our reconnaissance reported that our leading platoon had opened fire on German armoured personnel carriers which were deployed in ambush.
>
> 'But where is the Third Battalion?' enquired our regimental commander.
>
> 'We don't know. There is nobody at all on our route of advance.'
>
> 'Comrade Borodin,' ordered Dolbanosov, 'take the staff over to that wood on the left and organise an all-round defence. Get on the radio, call up the artillery, and make contact with the Third Battalion and find out where it is. Platoon commander! [now speaking to the reconnaissance party] Spread the word to contain the ambush.'
>
> The regimental headquarters and the supporting sub-units turned off the road and concealed themselves in the wood. The reconnaissance troops kept the Germans bottled up in their ambush positions, but being armed only with sub-machine-guns, they were unable to eliminate the enemy. Noth-

ing was heard from the Third Battalion, and the minutes ticked anxiously by. (Gurevich, et al., 1979, 186)

About one hour later the regimental battery of 57-mm guns arrived on the scene and broke the German resistance. First light revealed five burnt-out infantry carriers along the edge of the wood, together with thirty-two survivors who gave themselves up. Shortly afterwards the Third Battalion rejoined the main force, and its commander explained that he had lost his bearings in this featureless countryside. The advance was resumed, and in the course of ten days the regiment covered a total of 250 kilometres in its role as advance guard.

In general terms, the further progress of the formations on Zhukov's northern flank may be described as a push westwards to the Oder, while forces peeled off to the north to guard the long and increasingly vulnerable northern flank facing the German province of Pomerania, where the Russians were forced to attack or isolate a series of towns—Bromberg, Deutsch Krone, Pyritz, Arnswalde, Bahn, but especially the 'cornerstone' of the defence of East Pomerania at Schneidemühl.

The garrison of Schneidemühl was commanded by the able Colonel Remlinger, and some particularly heavy fighting developed against the troops of the Forty-Seventh Army in the extensive railway marshalling yards. A German armoured train operated to very good effect, and it managed to retrieve a whole train loaded with ammunition and supplies from under the noses of the Russians. In another incident Germans and Russians were plundering the same train simultaneously from opposite ends. Schneidemühl fell on 14 February when the garrison broke out—only a thousand men got through, and all the rest were killed or captured over the next few days.

* * *

Zhukov's Advance to the Oder

In the last week of January Zhukov's armies had a glimpse of the end of the war. On the twenty-sixth a number of his units crossed the old German border. They described the landscape in terms which differed little in kind from the language used by the Russian soldiers who arrived in German lands in 1757, 1813 and 1914:

> Our troops were curious and alert as they gazed from their trucks and tanks over the newly cultivated fields, the clipped plantations along the roadsides, the pointed roofs of the farms, and the grey sandy soil of the ploughland. It was difficult to believe on that serene January evening that this was where the war had been engendered. (Bokov, 1979, 77)

On 27 January Zhukov reported to STAVKA that the Germans no longer held a continuous defensive front or major reserves. He therefore proposed to continue his advance to the Oder, replenish his supplies, and push on straight for Berlin. STAVKA approved, and on the next day Zhukov received orders to move to the Oder, restore his supply levels to two 'fills' of fuel and two 'units of fire' (see p. 329), and open the offensive on Berlin at the beginning of February, with the intention of rushing the city by the fifteenth or sixteenth. Konev was instructed in similar terms on 29 January. The one source of concern was that the right, or northern, flank of the 1st Belorussian Front was becoming very long. Zhukov had by now far surpassed his original phase lines, and a large gap was opening between his army group and its right-hand neighbour, the slow-moving 2nd Belorussian Front under Marshal Rokossovskii. However, there was no hint of doubt in the order of the day which Zhukov issued after he received STAVKA's clearance:

107

There is ample evidence to indicate that the enemy is bringing up forces to take up defensive positions on the approaches to the Oder. But if we manage to establish ourselves on the west [i.e. far] bank of the Oder, the success of the operation to capture Berlin will be guaranteed.

This was the first time that the word 'Berlin' had been mentioned in such an order, and the impact on the soldiers was considerable.

A great blizzard was blowing when the borders of the heartland of Brandenburg were attacked by the 1st Belorussian Front on 28 January. By now Zhukov's western frontage had been squeezed to about one hundred kilometres, between the boundary with Konev's command in the south, and the increasing German resistance in Pomerania to the north.

Zhukov's left-flanking armies ran almost at once into a sequence of defensive lines which extended backwards from the old Polish-German border along the marshy Obra River. The Russians called this defensive system the Meseritz Fortified Region, while the Germans termed it the Tirschtiegel Barrier (*Tirschtiegel Riegel*). The region had been constructed before the war in order to defend the shortest routes to Berlin from Poland, and the positions were inherently strong, even though the works had been stripped of most of their equipment and the guard was abandoned to the Volkssturm. The result was some very confused fighting which escaped from the control of the respective high commands.

On some sectors the Volkssturm were left undisturbed or were able to beat off the Russians with a show of resistance. Friedrich Helmigk and his company were holding a bunker about ten kilometres south-west of the town of Meseritz, and they caught their first sight of the enemy in the shape of a force of thirteen tanks which rolled towards the outlying anti-tank obstacle:

The first tank now emerged from the sunken road, followed by a second and a third. They halted in front of the barrier. In addition to my hunting binoculars I had my rifle with the telescopic sight, which had been accurately zeroed in. The hatch of the leading tank opened, and a number of Russians climbed out. A stout officer with a crooked stick walked with two men to the barrier and inspected the obstructions. . . . They were behaving as if it were peacetime. After I had spoken a couple of words to my sergeant-major, I laid my graticules on the officer, aimed at the navel and fired. The range was only 150 metres, and he folded like a jackknife. The Russians sped off in all directions at the sound of my shot, and our machine gun hammered away at the running men. We had already settled on a shot as a signal for the six turrets to fire at will, and at the same time our mortar peppered the Russians with a sequence of ten or a dozen bombs. The sergeant-major and I slid into our shelter like greased lightning. We had scarcely got inside before five or six 152-mm rounds blocked our door with rubble. The machine gun fell silent—it had been wrecked by the fire, and one of our men had been lightly wounded. We did not know what, if any, casualties the Russians had sustained. They had disappeared, and only the tanks stood where they were.

Not long afterwards Helmigk and his men drove off an attack by Russian infantry, and at 1500 the enemy tanks retired by the way they had come (Kissel, 1962, 165).

In contrast, a deep and damaging penetration of the Meseritz Fortified Region was made by Babadzhanyan's XI Guards Tank Corps, which spearheaded the advance of the First Guards Tank Army. Babadzhanyan forced the Obra on the night of 28–29 January, then formed his forward detachment into two brigade columns. The left-hand column comprised the 44th Guards Tank Brigade under Colonel I. I. Gusakovskii, whom we last encountered in the middle of January when he was

wading the Pilica (see p. 77). Gusakovskii sent out a party of
sappers to investigate the chosen route in the direction of Kochwald, and the commander duly returned:

'Comrade Colonel,' he reported in some haste, 'Our troops
have discovered that the main road is obstructed by a bar-
ricade. It's made of rails.'
'But can you pull them out of the way?' asked Gusakovskii.
'I think so, Comrade Brigade Commander!'
'Well then, clear the road as quickly as you can.'

Gusakovskii decided to press on without waiting for the main
body of the corps. In the evening the sappers levered the obstacle out of the way, and they established that the road beyond
had not been mined. This was good news in itself, but it indicated that a German armoured counterattack was on the way.
The going deteriorated by the minute:

The sky was hidden by low, fast-moving clouds—a sure
sign of the gusty and humid weather blowing from the Baltic.
The icy crust on the roads was contracting, and water now
shone from puddles. The sound of bursts of machine-gun
fire carried from the heights at Kochwald—this was the enemy firing at the brigade's patrols. (Katukov, 1976, 362)

Gusakovskii deployed his brigade into combat formation and
by 0300 on 30 January he had slipped through the main zone
of the fortified region in the neighbourhood of Calau without
losing a single tank. By now the Russians had a German map
of the defences (see p. 179), and probably Gusakovskii was one
of the Russian commanders who were able to take advantage
of this great asset. At any rate, he pressed on in the course of
the day to Schwiebus, where units of the Sixty-Ninth and
Thirty-Third armies and the VIII Guards Mechanised Corps
were in the process of dealing the *coup de grace* to a German roving cauldron which had attempted to break through

110

to the west. Barrages from German tanks and divisional artillery were falling on both sides of the town, and the sky was lit in an incongruous style by flares of rose red and a delicate salad green.

Gusakovskii continued his advance well into the rear of the fortified region, and he lost all contact with his parent formation when the Germans closed the road behind him. The cut-off force now had to go into an all-round defence while the rest of Babadzhanyan's corps and the First Guards Tank Army battled forward to the Oder. On 1 February the leading brigade of the VIII Guards Mechanised Corps on the left flank was itself cut off at Kunersdorf, where the V SS Gebirgsjäger Corps seemed to be bent on revenging the defeat which Frederick the Great had suffered in the same location at the hands of Russians and Austrians on 12 August 1759. The Germans were repulsed with the help of a battery of Katyusha multiple rocket launchers, and the 'fields around Kunersdorf were littered with the scorched corpses of the Hitlerites. Our tank crews, when they had run out of ammunition, opened their hatches and beat off the attacks of the SS with grenades' (Katukov, 1976, 370).

The First Guards Tank Army, the Sixty-Ninth Army and the Thirty-Third Army all broke through to the Oder in the course of the same day, and established small lodgments on the far bank.

On the whole of Zhukov's frontage the nearest thing to a clear run to the river was enjoyed by his right flank, where the Second Guards Tank Army and the Fifth Shock Army raced across the rolling country north of the marshy depression of the Warthe. On 30 January the Russians crossed the field of Zorndorf (the scene of a bloody and indecisive battle between the Russians and the Prussians in 1758), and on the morning of the thirty-first Colonel Khariton F. Esipenko with his forward detachment of the Fifth Shock Army passed the ice of the Oder on foot and took unopposed possession of the little town of Kienitz.

The episode appeared totally unreal. Berlin radio was broadcasting that the Germans were putting up a brilliant defence in prepared positions on the Bzura, not far from Warsaw, and yet here were the Russians only sixty-eight kilometres from Berlin. German soldiers were strolling through the streets of Kienitz, and officers were sitting in a restaurant. It seemed natural for the station master to approach Esipenko:

'Are you going to allow the Berlin train to leave?'
To this Khariton Fedorovich replied with due solemnity and elaborate courtesy: 'I am sorry, Station Master, but that is impossible, the passenger service to Berlin will undergo a short interruption—let's say until the end of the war.' (Bokov, 1979, 80)

The Russians clung to their foothold at Kienitz, but the follow-on forces of the Fifth Shock Army were faced with all the difficulties of an opposed crossing when they arrived at the edge of the high river bank to support and expand the bridgehead. Below they could see how the white level of the frozen river extended to the western side, where a dark strip signified the embankment where the Germans were waiting.

The army's 301st Rifle Division was ordered to execute an assault crossing on the night of 2–3 February. Secrecy was so important that the Russians did without their artillery bombardment, and a group of officers was standing in some anxiety at their observation post when the attack began:

Suddenly, a rocket rose from the opposite bank. It burst, and a series of flares was suspended over the river. The white surface of the ice stood out clearly, and across it were moving the dark lines of our regiments.

At that instant the enemy machine-guns opened up from the far bank, and a fiery stream of white tracer coursed through the darkness of the night. In turn, our artillery pieces struck back at the German machine-guns. The rifle companies raced across the ice with an impetuous urgency, but even

now they refrained from their customary battle cry of *Ura!*
The mighty wave rolled over the embankment and the night
battle on the western side of the Oder now began. (Antonov,
1975, 325)

Lastly, in the centre of Zhukov's Front, Colonel-General
Chuikov came up with the two disposable corps of his Eighth
Guards Tank Army from the direction of Posen, and on 2 February he ordered his troops to cross the river barrier with whatever materials were at hand: 'I looked at the Oder through a
telescope. A wide river it was, lined with dykes' (Chuikov,
1978, 155). The infantry made their way gingerly across the
frozen surface, bearing planks and bales of brushwood which
they arranged into ice bridges. A few anti-aircraft guns were
mounted on improvised skis and pushed onto the far side, but
all activity for the day was terminated when Focke-Wulf 190s
arrived in waves of seven or nine at a time, bombing and straf-
ing. The Russians renewed the crossing under still more difficult circumstances on the following day.

On the 'Russian' bank of the river the Germans still held
significant bridgeheads of their own at Frankfurt, and downstream at Küstrin, where Russian tanks were driven out by a
scratch force of Volkssturm and Hitlerjugend armed with Panzerfausts. Elsewhere the defence of the Oder was thin or non-
existent.

By 2 February, therefore, the army groups of Konev and
Zhukov had reached the middle Oder at points along almost
all its length and had established a multitude of greater or
smaller bridgeheads on its left bank. On that day STAVKA
declared that the Vistula-Oder Operation was at a formal end.

CHAPTER 9

Stay of Execution

Stalin at the Gates!

STALIN ANTE PORTAS! This was the tenor of the panic-stricken cry which sped through the capital of the Reich, when news arrived this morning that the Russians had succeeded in crossing the Oder. They have established a bridgehead west of the Oder at Kienitz, and they are advancing with one hundred tanks on Wriezen, which is only sixty or seventy kilometres from the municipal boundary of Berlin. There is nothing between Wriezen and Berlin—no anti-tank gun, no anti-tank obstacles, not a single soldier.

So runs the entry which Goebbels' secretary Wilfred von Oven penned in his diary on 31 January 1945 (Oven, 1974, 564).

Four days later General A. I. Antonov, chief of the Soviet General Staff, outlined for the benefit of the Allied leaders at Yalta what the Russians had achieved since 12 January, when they had begun the series of offensives which had extended in breadth from the Carpathians to the Baltic. The centrepiece was the Vistula-Oder Operation, which had taken the Upper Silesian Industrial Region, isolated East Prussia, liberated Poland and carried the Russians as far as the Oder. The Soviets had advanced at an unprecedented average rate of thirty kilometres a day. They had destroyed Army Group A, and inflicted losses which STAVKA put at 400,000 men and at least forty-five divisions [the Russian casualties were very light, at around 15,000 killed and 60,000 wounded, which is about the same order as the British losses on the first day of the battle of the Somme, on 1 July 1916].

At first the Germans almost despaired of containing the Russian bridgeheads across the Oder, or of holding the stretches of the river in between. Lieutenant-Colonel Hans Ulrich Rudel had arrived from Hungary with his flight of tank-killing Ju-87G Stukas, and the 1st Flieger Division now put all its aircraft at his disposal. However, the celebrated *Panzerknacker* could see little profit in strikes against the ice passages, for it appeared simple for the enemy to cross the ice between the isolated holes which were made by the bombs. On other stretches of the river, where the Russians had not yet arrived, the Germans tried to break the ice with explosive charges. These had little effect. Battalions of air-defence personnel were then sent out on the river with power saws to cut the ice into sections, but the blocks obstinately froze together again before they could be hauled out.

For the Germans twenty-two nightmarish days had transported the theatre of war from somewhere in central Poland to within earshot of the capital of the Reich. The loss of the Upper Silesian Industrial Region was a death blow in itself. Armaments Minister Albert Speer had emphasised repeatedly how important the region's mines and factories were, and at the end of January he composed a new memorandum which

> began unambiguously enough with the simple statement: 'The war is lost.' He gave it to me [Guderian] to read before submitting it to Hitler. Unfortunately there was no contradicting it. He [Hitler] read the first sentence and then locked it away in his safe along with all the other warnings he had received. (Guderian, 1952, 407)

It requires only a passing acquaintance with the chronology of the Second World War for us to be aware of something very odd—we have accompanied the Russians to within a few hours' drive of Berlin, and yet we know that the war in Europe lasted a good three months more. The reasons are complicated, and it would be insulting to the reader to pretend otherwise, but it is possible to present them in some kind of order. Very briefly:

- The Vistula-Oder Operation, although it was the focus of the Russian offensives early in 1945, could not be consolidated or exploited unless the supporting attacks on either flank kept pace. In the event, the Soviet forces on both the highland and the Baltic flanks ran into unexpected difficulties, and Konev was forced to turn his attention south, just as Zhukov had to look north. These developments will be followed in later parts of the book.
- An early push across the Oder became unappealing to the Soviet High Command for more immediate reasons. The armies were distant from their bases of supply, the troops were exhausted and increasingly undisciplined, air support failed and the Germans on the Oder were beginning to fight very hard. The relevant details now claim our attention.

'Avalanche of Fire and Metal'—The German Frontal Defence of the Oder

The Russians lost the momentum of their victory very suddenly, you might almost say instantaneously. The fourth of February, the first day of the meeting of the Allied leaders at Yalta, was devoted to introductions and briefings. Churchill and Stalin met early in the crowded schedule, when the Soviet leader was still buoyed up by the unprecedented success of his forces in Poland and eastern Germany. Only hours later Stalin went to Roosevelt in a state of some despair and talked about the tremendous opposition which was building up on the Oder. In the evening General Antonov outlined what the Russians had achieved so far (above), but he confirmed that the Germans were determined to defend Berlin with all the resources at their command and that reinforcements were pouring in from the west.

We return to von Oven's diary for a first clue as to the processes at work:

1 February: The formerly threatening situation before Berlin has changed in our favour literally overnight. The splashing in the gutters sounds to our ears like choirs of angels. The Oder and the Warthe, and the marshes of those two rivers and the Netze, together with a multitude of little watercourses, have become obstacles which enable us to consolidate our defence on the threatened sectors. . . .

3 February: The thaw continues. Mild spring air wafts through the streets of Berlin, and everywhere we are working energetically to build anti-tank obstacles and emplacements for the anti-tank guns.

The thaw rendered the grass airstrips in Poland unusable and contributed to depriving the Russians of air support at a crucial moment. More important still, the thaw melted the dirt roads across Poland and disrupted the flow of supplies to the Russian armies, which had approached the Oder at their last logistic gasp. The usable railways extended only as far as central Poland, and trucks were faced with round trips of one thousand kilometres or more.

The Oder ice now began to melt at a gratifying rate, and the Germans speeded the process by explosives and ice-breakers. The river embankments and other defensive positions were lined with high-velocity guns from more than three hundred anti-aircraft batteries which had been removed from their static installations in the interior of the Reich and rushed to the Oder theatre on the direct orders of Hitler. These guns made excellent tank-killers. Substantial ground forces were disengaged from the Western Front, and with the help of the railways and hard-topped roads of the Reich they were redeployed at speed against the Russians. Thirteen or fourteen divisions now barred the direct way to Berlin, and about thirty-three began to pile up threateningly in Pomerania on Zhukov's right flank.

The Luftwaffe attacks against the first Russian ice passages had been more effective than Rudel had supposed, and the Germans now regained air superiority with the help of aircraft which were switched from air defence against the British and Americans to close ground support on the Eastern Front. Hitler had been responsible for providing most German fighters with bomb racks, and this precaution now paid dividends. Operating from the many concrete airfields around Berlin, the Luftwaffe was able to keep up a very high rate of sorties against the nearby bridgeheads, the Oder passages, and the Russian forces which were strung out along the flank with Pomerania.

Rudel's own flying career came to an end early on 9 February, when he took off with a number of planes of his flight of Stukas and went looking for tanks in a new Russian bridgehead north of Frankfurt near Lebus. This had become particularly dangerous work, because the Russian anti-aircraft gunners were experienced and skilful, whereas Rudel had several new crews who were at special risk. He told his other Ju-87s to hold off, and he carried out repeated attacks in his usual style—diving at a steep angle, straightening out for an instant to get in a few rounds of wolfram-core shot from his twin 37-mm cannon, weaving away at low altitude, then climbing as rapidly as possible to regain a height of 2,400 feet, out of reach of the small-arms fire. He would not have accepted this risk even on his own account if the Russians had not been so close to Berlin.

One of Rudel's cannon jammed, after he had accounted for a succession of tanks, but he went on to attack a thirteenth machine:

> And already I zoom down from 2,400 feet. Keep your mind on your flying, twist and turn; again a score of guns spit at me. Now I straighten up . . . fire . . . the tank bursts into a blaze! With jubilation in my heart, I streak away low above

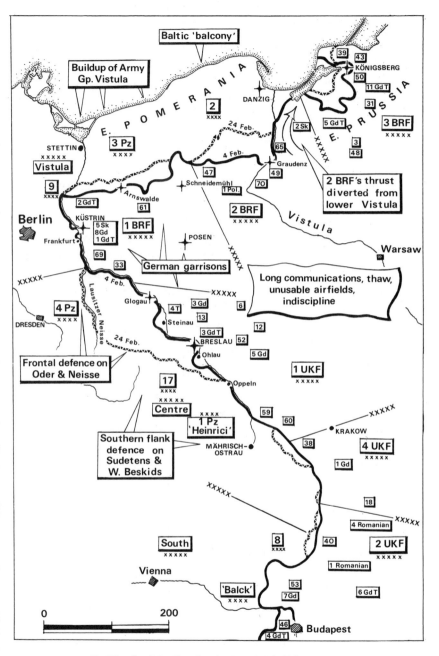

5. The Soviet offensive is contained, February 1945

the burning tank. I go into a climbing spiral . . . a crack in the engine and something sears through my leg like a strip of red hot steel. Everything goes black before my eyes. I gasp for breath. But I must keep flying . . . flying . . . I must not pass out. Grit your teeth, you have to master your weakness. A spasm of pain shoots through my whole body. (Rudel, 1952, 223)

A bumpy landing brought him to the ground semi-conscious but alive.

The counterattacks against the Oder bridgeheads were unrelenting from both air and ground, and the ferocity of the combat was shown by the records of the IX Rifle Corps of the Fifth Shock Army, which had suffered only 961 casualties during its advance from the Vistula to the Oder between 14 and 31 January, but sustained 3,154 between 1 and 10 February. This army was the target of 5,008 Luftwaffe sorties on 2 and 3 February alone:

> The roar of the tank and aircraft engines, the rumble of the bursting shells and bombs, the dry rattle of the automatic weapons—none of this ceased for an instant. It seemed scarcely possible that the earth, let alone human beings, could endure such an avalanche of fire and metal. (Bokov, 1979, 101)

Zhukov knew that he was asking a great deal when on 4 February he ordered the Fifth Shock Army to expand its bridgehead north of Küstrin. He told the army to attack only at night, and for clearly defined objectives. During the daytime the Russians were to concentrate on beating off the counterattacks by the German ground forces and on surviving air attack by digging deep and putting up a massive barrage of anti-aircraft fire.

Such were the conditions under which the Russians pushed the Germans slowly back in the course of the fighting in February and March. By the end of March the Fifth Shock Army had enlarged its bridgehead to twenty-seven kilometres in length and between three and five in depth. In the Russian rear the German defenders of Posen tied down four divisions of Chuikov's Eighth Guards Army and two divisions of the Sixty-Ninth Army. The citadel did not fall until 22 February (see p. 250), but the energetic Chuikov retrieved his forces, and by the end of March he had expanded his bridgehead south of Küstrin to a breadth of fourteen kilometres and an average depth of four.

The Changing Psychological and Moral Balance

It is not easy to establish Zhukov's viewpoint at this time of important decisions. The German historian Erich Murawski, in his detailed account of events on the Pomeranian flank (*Die Eroberung Pommerns durch die Rote Armee*, 1969), emphasises the importance of General Vasilii Danilovich Sokolovskii, a brilliant but political-minded Ukrainian whom Stalin had sent to the front as an informer and a kind of super chief of staff. It was Sokolovskii, according to this analysis, rather than Zhukov who drew the attention of STAVKA to the vulnerability of the Pomeranian flank, and advised that the 1st Belorussian Front should halt on the Oder and turn north to clear at least the neighbourhood of Stettin before it could continue the advance on Berlin. Zhukov is said to have shared the desire of Chuikov and other generals to press on straight to Berlin, arguing that delay would give the Germans time to build up an impregnable redoubt in Bohemia to the south as well as to strengthen the defence on the Oder and perhaps even allow the Western Allies to reach Berlin before the Soviets. After violent arguments between the two of them, Stalin pronounced in favour of Sokolovskii on 4 February.

Murawski cites no sources, and against this interpretation we have the evidence of an urgent message which Zhukov sent to STAVKA on 31 January, 'stressing that the frontage of the

1st Belorussian Front had now reached 500 kilometres, that Rokossovskii's left flank [i.e. of the 2nd Belorussian Front] was lagging appreciably behind the right flank of the 1st Belorussian Front—Rokossovskii *must* push his Seventieth Army forward —and Marshal Konev should gain the Oder line as speedily as possible' (Erickson, 1975–83, II, 453–54). He was aware that he was running short of supplies, and that the Luftwaffe had gained the temporary command of the air. No clear guidance came from STAVKA; which was not entirely in contact with the situation on the ground, and was still trying to make sense of a directive from Stalin that both Zhukov and Konev were to participate directly in the ultimate drive on Berlin. In the event, Stalin was now guided by his cautious instincts and decided that Zhukov and Konev must stop on the Oder and clear their respective flanks in Pomerania and Silesia.

Whatever Zhukov's views may have been at the turn of January and February 1945, he felt under an obligation after the war to defend the decision to halt the push on Berlin. Colonel-General Chuikov was the most persistent of his critics, and Zhukov replied in the *Military Historical Journal* for June 1965 ('Na berlinskom Napravlenii,' *VIZh*, 1965, VI). He explained himself further to a live audience at a study day held by the Group of Soviet Forces in Germany, agreeing with his questioner, Major-General S. M. Yenyukov, that it would have been physically possible for the First and Second Guards Tank armies to have reached Berlin, and perhaps to have taken the city. In fact, both he and Chuikov desired it at the time:

But, Comrade Yenyukov, it would have been impossible to turn back, as the enemy could easily have closed off the escape routes. The enemy, by attacking from the north, could have easily broken through our infantry, reached the Oder crossings, and put the troops at the front in an embarrassing situation. Let me emphasise that one must be able to control oneself, resist temptation, and avoid throwing oneself into rash adventures. When a commander is making decisions, he must never relax his grip on common sense. (Golovnin, 1988, 25)

The danger of pushing good fortune too far is raised again in Zhukov's memoirs, which refer to an old war against the Poles: 'Very instructive in this respect is the lesson learned by the Red Army during the Warsaw offensive back in 1920, when its headlong, unprotected advance led to bitter defeat, instead of success, of our Western Front' (Zhukov, 1971, 574). Another precedent which weighed with him heavily was that of the reckless pursuit after the battle of Stalingrad in 1943, which left the Soviets vulnerable to Manstein's counteroffensive at Kharkov.

All the time, the advantages which had been gained by the Soviet armies were being vitiated by the encouragement which had been given to the soldiers to revenge themselves on the German population. Zhukov and Konev could do little to stay the plunder, rape and incendiarism (see p. 275) which ensued. An officer who defected to the West explained after the war:

> In general terms, the explosion of these low and cruel instincts tore apart the fibres of the otherwise notoriously strict discipline which bound the Red Army. This process interfered with the functioning of the signals and supply systems and with the issue and execution of orders. To put it in a nutshell, the effectiveness of the Red Army was crippled in front of the gates of Berlin and in Silesia (quoted in Ahlfen, 1977, 153).

While the Soviets were bogging down in the physical and moral sense, it became easier for Hitler to present himself as the only possible savior of the German people. The Russian atrocities played into his hands, as did the outcome of the enemy summit meeting at Yalta. The Allies had failed to settle the political complexion of the new government of liberated Poland, but they had agreed that the Poles were to receive a 'considerable accession of territory in the north and west' at the expense of Germany, and that the rest of Germany was to be carved up into Allied zones of occupation. Hitler was delighted when page after teleprinter page of the final Yalta communiqué was brought to him on 13 February:

> So much for the drivel talked by our coffeehouse diplomats and foreign ministry politicos! Here they have it in black and white—if we lose the war, Germany will cease to exist. What matters now is to keep our nerve and not give in. (Irving, 1977, 769)

PART III

The Southern Flank:
Konev and
the Continuing
Contest for Silesia

CHAPTER 10

The Actions on the Oder

Soviet Plans

THE NOMINAL close of the so-called Vistula-Oder Operation meant little in real terms. Zhukov had certainly come to a halt against the lower-middle Oder, but further south in Silesia Konev and his 1st Belorussian Front were merely drawing breath before they launched themselves into the intended two-Front offensive on Berlin. The plans as they affected the 1st Ukrainian Front had been sent by Konev to STAVKA on 28 January. Konev was going to approach the German capital from the south, while Zhukov attacked head-on fron the east. However, Konev's immediate objective was to encircle the city of Breslau in Silesia by a pincer movement. He could then push west and align himself with Zhukov's army group, thereby setting himself up for the grand offensive on Berlin.

The Silesian provincial capital of Breslau extended over both banks of the Oder, and it posed the one major obstacle to Konev's progress across the open country of Lower Silesia. STAVKA therefore approved Konev's plan for a double envelopment from his two main bridgeheads on the 'German' bank of the Oder on either side of Breslau:

- The left-hand force consisted of two all-arms armies and two tank corps in the Ohlau bridgehead.
- The main attack was to come from the right-hand Steinau

127

bridgehead, where two all-arms armies and the Fourth Tank Army were reinforced by Rybalko's much-travelled Third Guards Tank Army, which was retrieved from Upper Silesia. This 'Lower Silesian Operation' was due to begin on 8 February. Meanwhile the Russians reshuffled their forces, enlarged their bridgeheads and made an isolated push by way of Grottkau deeper into Silesia.

The German Forces on the Eve of the Lower Silesian Operation

Since 20 January German Army Group A (soon to be redesignated Army Group Centre) had been in the keeping of Colonel-General Ferdinand Schörner, who was renowned as probably the leading exponent of the National Socialist style of leadership in the Wehrmacht. Hitler had boundless trust in him, and Goebbels testified that Schörner was

> no chairborne or map general; most of the day he spends with the fighting troops, with whom he is on terms of confidence, though he is very strict. In particular he has taken a grip on the so-called 'professional stragglers,' by which he means men who continually manage to absent themselves in critical situations and vanish to the rear on some pretext or other. His procedure with such types is fairly brutal; he hangs them on the nearest tree with a placard announcing: 'I am a deserter and have declined to defend German women and children.' (Goebbels, 1977, 80)

While a stability of sorts was achieved on Army Group A's sector which faced Zhukov, the state of affairs further south in Lower Silesia was dangerously fluid. Here the Germans (General Fritz Gräser's Fourth Panzer Army) had a scratch garrison and two infantry divisions in or near Breslau, but otherwise only about as many field divisions as Konev had full armies.

The units which had been cut off beyond the Oder were lost beyond recall, and the German High Command feared that the Soviets might seize a further prize—the containers of liquid poison gas that were held near the village of Dyhernfurth, on the enemy bank of the Oder below Breslau.

It was one of the oddities of the Second World War that none of the belligerents went so far as to employ poison gas in warfare. However, they continued the necessary research and development, and at Dyhernfurth the Germans had large stocks of some of their latest and deadliest toxins. The Fourth Panzer Army was told that it was not enough to raid the factory and blow up the tanks, for sufficient residue would be left to be analysed by the Russians. The Germans must therefore seize the factory and hold it long enough to permit the liquid to be pumped into the Oder. Gräser entrusted this delicate operation to Major-General Max Sachsenheimer.

At first Fourth Panzer Army envisaged a conventional attack, complete with an artillery bombardment, and a set-piece assault delivered by two companies of 'dismounted' parachutists who were summoned from neighbouring army groups. Sachsenheimer analysed his task more closely and grasped that the essence must be to secure enough time to enable the pumping-out to go ahead undisturbed. This could best be achieved by a swift and silent strike with the forces immediately at hand, formed into a little battle group of several hundred infantry, two batteries of dual-purpose 88-mm guns, and a light pioneer assault boat company with eighty-one craft. Two scientists and eighty technicians provided the expert help.

On a personal reconnaissance Sachsenheimer saw that the railway bridge to Dyhernfurth was intact, apart from the two spans nearest the 'German' bank, and that it was guarded only by two machine-guns, one on each side of the railway embankment on the far bank. Beyond the Oder the railway curved left past Dyhernfurth, and a spur line led directly into the wooded compound of the chemical factory, which meant that the Germans could not go far astray if they simply followed the line of the tracks. Russian soldiers could be heard singing in Dyhernfurth Castle: 'But perhaps "singing" was not the right word for the noises which were carried to our ears. It was a bawling which grew in volume, and from which we concluded that the Russians were in a state of increasing drunkenness' (Ahlfen, 1977, 129). Sachsenheimer gained Gräser's approval for the plan, and the motley force approached the river on the morning of 5 February.

The main body made directly for the bridge along the axis of the railway, Major Josse and a small team disposed of the Russian machine-gunners with hardly a sound, while 88-mm guns were deployed behind the river embankment on the near side, and twenty-six assault boats were assigned to transport a diversionary crossing which began two-and-a-half kilometres downstream half an hour later.

On the far side of the Oder the technicians and their escort penetrated the deserted compound of the factory, while the rest of the main force of infantry threw out a screen of Panzerfaust detachments on all the approaches to the plant. The pumps were found to be in full working order, and the engines were started only sixty-five minutes after the operation had begun.

The Soviets reacted only after 1300. They made their first attack with a force of eighteen tanks from the direction of Seifersdorf to the north, but the thrust was checked by the screen of Panzerfausts. Just before nightfall a much more dangerous push developed from Kranz, a short distance to the east, when a body of eight tanks moved towards the railway by the bridge, threatening to cut off all the Germans who were on the right bank of the river. Now the 88-mm guns came into their own:

> The barrels were cranked up until they projected just above the top of the Oder dyke, they were laid rapidly on their targets, and they spouted their familiar long tongues of reddish-yellow fire with a sharp crack. The range was just 750

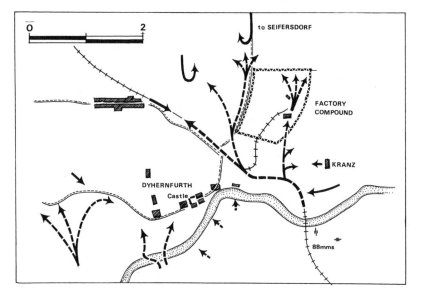

6. The Dyhernfurth raid, 5 February 1945

metres, and the sounds of the impacts followed the discharges with scarcely an interval. (Ahlfen, 1977, 132)

Six of the Russian tanks were hit, and most of them burst instantly into flames. The Germans had won a few more hours of darkness to complete their work in the compound. When the containers had finally been drained, the scientists delivered a written attestation to Sachsenheimer, who in turn radioed army headquarters with the news that his mission had been accomplished. In the course of the night the raiding force withdrew to the left bank of the Oder without any further incident. Almost certainly the Russians never noticed the significance of what had taken place under their noses.

The operation at Dyhernfurth on 5 February does not figure largely in the annals of war, but it was a classic of its kind, notable for the accurate selection of the aim, simplicity of con-

131

ception, and speed and economy in the execution. The two companies of parachutists, by the way, never made an appearance.

Cheering news also came from beyond Gräser's right flank, where the Seventeenth Army sent in a two-divisional counterattack which pushed back the Russian force that had penetrated through Grottkau. On 7 February the populations of Ottmachau and Neisse were delighted to see German tanks rolling eastwards once more: 'The sun has come out again. So the German Wehrmacht really does exist! The whole population, both natives and refugees, has turned out on the streets to cheer the troops' (Ahlfen, 1977, 121).

The Lower Silesian Operation, 8–24 February 1945

The little triumphs at Dyhernfurth and Grottkau were entirely eclipsed by the Soviet offensive which burst from the Oder bridgeheads on 8 February. The Lower Silesian Operation was opened by a single fifty-minute bombardment, and at 0600 the troops and tanks crossed the start lines. The ground had been softened by the thaw, and on some sectors the Russians moved with apparent slowness. Near Herzogswalde on the sector of the 40th Infantry Division (Fourth Panzer Army) a newly formed company beat off an initial attack by a battalion and two tanks. Reserve Captain Heinze writes:

> An illuminating round from a Russian artillery piece had set fire to a haystack next to the cattle shed. We salvaged a stock of ammunition and drove the animals out. Meanwhile the two tanks had advanced from Rädlitz to Ischerey—one of the machines halted next to our farmstead and the other to the west. I called for a Panzerfaust and wriggled towards the tank. This Panzerfaust was a new and unfamiliar model,

132

and I had to experiment before I could release the safety device. There was a crack and a shower of sparks. It was a hit! Three infantrymen who had been riding the tank now slid off. The tank burnt, and the ammunition blew up. My comrades fired a Panzerschreck [heavier version of the Panzerfaust] at the other tank, but they missed, and the vehicle drove into cover behind our barn—which I unfortunately discovered too late. The back doors were blocked. I hastened across the burning floor of the stalls so as to take it under fire from the window, but it had not found the situation to its liking, and it made back to the wood, from where it rained shells on us.

Lieutenant Jung, the adjutant, was severely wounded (a shot through the lung). I received a splinter in my left heel. A shell blew a cow into bloody tatters. . . . I was left alone shooting from the window in the roof . . . my assault rifle jammed, and I snatched up an ordinary rifle. Further tanks were rolling from Rädlitz. It was madness to offer further resistance in this location. (Ahlfen, 1977, 112–13)

Madness indeed—Schörner had deployed the Fourth Panzer Army against the Steinau bridgehead, and the Seventeenth Army against the Ohlau bridgehead, but by the end of the day the cohesion of the Germans was collapsing and the Russian armour had penetrated up to sixty kilometres.

The city of Breslau was now almost isolated by the Russian tide, but it stood like a rock against the centre of Konev's offensive, effectively checking the progress of two of the all-arms armies. Konev therefore ordered Rybalko's Third Guards Tank Army to execute a left about-turn and link up behind Breslau with the forces which were advancing from the Ohlau bridgehead. It was a reproduction on a smaller scale of the Third Guard Tank Army's move behind the flank and rear of the Upper Silesian Industrial Region a couple of weeks earlier.

On 10 and 11 February the main force of the army roared eastwards along the autobahn between Liegnitz and Breslau, announcing that the Soviets intended to encircle the Silesian capital. The Germans extricated what they could of their 269th Infantry Division through the narrowing gap, but on 15 February the ring around Breslau was closed when all-arms armies from the two bridgeheads joined hands just outside the city and the Third Guards Tank Army positioned itself to the west. Some 35,000 German regular troops and 80,000 civilians were cut off:

> Meanwhile the whole area inside the encirclement was seething. The encircled garrison units rushed hither and thither in search of an exit. Sometimes they fought desperately, but more commonly surrendered. An enormous number of cars and horse-drawn carriages packed with people jammed the roads south-west of Breslau; having lost all hope of finding even the smallest gap, they were now rolling back to the city. (Konev, 1969, 57)

Now that Breslau had been encircled, the run of uncontrollable German disasters in Silesia came to an end, and by the middle of February the fighting on this theatre began to stabilise and cohere in a distinctive way, forming a pattern that endured for the next two months. In essence, Konev's 1st Ukrainian Front was now contained inside a right angle of German forces:

- The Fourth Panzer Army which faced east, and tried to hold the lines of the little rivers which flowed north to the middle Oder. This deployment barred Konev's further progress westwards into the German heartland.
- The Seventeenth Army which occupied the axis of the Sudeten hills and faced north, thereby threatening Konev's very long left or southern flank. It was a mirror image of the buildup of German forces in Pomerania which hovered over Zhukov's right flank.

By diverting Rybalko against Breslau, Konev had weakened the westward push of his right wing from the old Steinau bridgehead. Lelyushenko's Fourth Tank Army advanced without support, but although it was not counted as one of the more dashing of the tank forces, it reached the Lausitzer Neisse as early as 14 February. This unaccustomed daring was punished when on the same day the Fourth Panzer Army carried out a pincer movement against the Russian communications immediately to the west of the Bober stream—with the Grossdeutschland Panzer Corps thrusting north, and the XXIV Panzer Corps pushing south. The two German formations had been through a great deal together in recent weeks. On this occasion they were unable to effect a junction, but for a time the Russian army was cut off and fighting for its life. 'A bitter two-day battle developed. Everyone was caught up in the combat, from private soldiers to generals' (Lelyushenko, 1970, 400).

The Germans broke off their attack on 19 February, by which time Lelyushenko had cleared his communications and the Third Guards Tank Army and the Fifty-Second Army had come up to support him respectively to left and right. The Russians closed up to the Lausitzer Neisse on a frontage of one hundred kilometres. Here they were checked by six German divisions, which were fighting very bitterly. German reinforcements were arriving on this sector, and Konev also had to take stock of the increasing danger to his left flank and rear, and on 24 February he declared the Lower Silesian Operation closed. The Soviets abandoned most of their bridgeheads beyond the Lausitzer Neisse, retaining only a hotly contested lodgment between Forst and Guben. Thus the Russians finally lost the impetus of the attack which had begun on the Vistula on 12 January.

The German Counterattacks from the South— Lauban 2–5 March, and Striegau 9–14 March 1945

The Central European highland chain, which was here called the Sudetens, extended along Konev's left flank. Together with the fringes of the plain at their foot, they were held by the

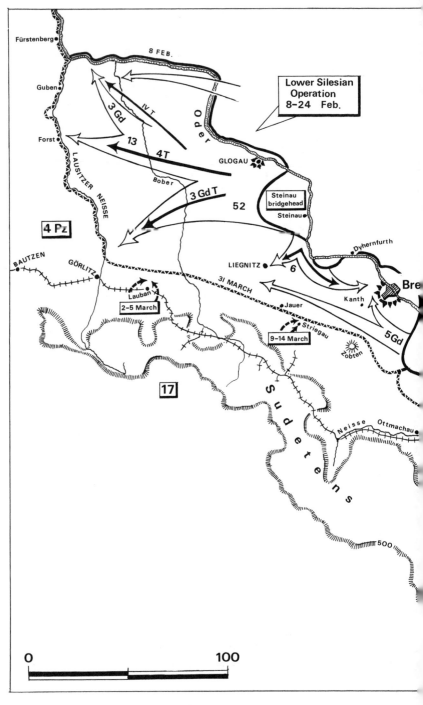

Fürstenberg

Guben

Forst

8 FEB.

**Lower Silesian
Operation
8–24 Feb.**

O d e r

3 Gd

IV T

13

4 T

Bober

GLOGAU

3 Gd T

52

**Steinau
bridgehead**

Steinau

Dyhernfurth

4 Pz

BAUTZEN

GÖRLITZ

LAUSITZER NEISSE

Lauban

2–5 March

LIEGNITZ

31 MARCH

Jauer

6

Kanth

Bre

9–14 March

Striegau

Zobten

5 Gd

17

S u d e t e n s

Neisse

Ottmachau

500

0   100

7. **Silesia, February–March 1945**

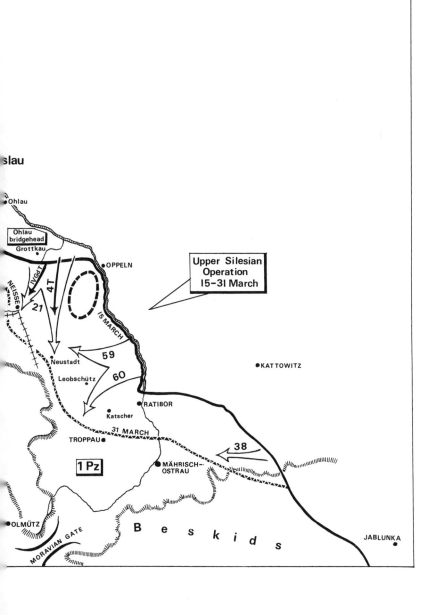

Seventeenth Army under General Friedrich Schulz. He was the son of a Silesian farmer, and he had served as chief of staff to Field-Marshal Model. 'As a native Silesian, the fulfilment of his task was not just a matter of intelligence, obedience and will. He felt it sprang from his heart—a vocation to do everything that was possible or conceivable to protect his homeland and save his countrymen' (Ahlfen, 1977, 151).

Along one sector the frontage of the Seventeenth Army ran within twenty kilometres of the outskirts of beleaguered Breslau, and this circumstance tempted the Germans into launching a three-divisional counterattack against the ring of Russian forces. On 14 February the 19th Panzer Division established brief contact with some of the fortress troops, but on the next day the enemy closed the gap once more and the Germans recoiled to their start lines.

The fighting south of Breslau, together with the difficulties which the Russians experienced beyond the Bober to the west, nevertheless showed that the 1st Ukrainian Front needed to consolidate and replenish. Konev concluded 'as early as the eighth day of the operation, that we should not be able to achieve the aims envisaged by our military plan in the near future, and that an offensive against Berlin was as yet impossible' (Konev, 1969, 61).

By early March German morale and effectiveness recovered so far that Schörner was able to organise a rather elaborate counterblow from the far left wing of the Seventeenth Army in the neighbourhood of Lauban, a little town where the battered 6th Volksgrenadier Division had been forced to give ground to the Russians. By retaking Lauban the Germans would regain free use of the important railway which ran from the heart of Germany to Silesia just north of the hills. In a wider context, a successful blow might disrupt the regrouping of the Third Guards Tank Army and encourage Konev to draw off forces from his far eastern flank in Upper Silesia.

Schörner delegated the command to the headquarters of Nehring's XXIV Panzer Corps. Rather than feed more forces into the street fighting in Lauban, Nehring devised a converging movement by elements of two Panzer corps against the Bunzlau road well to the rear of Lauban. The Germans crossed their start lines on the night of 1–2 March. The Third Guards Tank Army was taken completely by surprise, but after the first shock had passed, the Russians began to put up a heavy resistance against the outer jaws of the German pincer movement. The German progress fell behind schedule, and to avoid the possibility of the Russians escaping scot free down the Queis valley, Nehring embraced a suggestion from one of his subordinates for a 'small solution' to cut in just to the north of Lauban. On 5 March the Führer-Grenadier Division linked up with the 8th Panzer Division on the Lindenberg, while the German artillery hammered the path of the retreating enemy down the Queis. The prisoners amounted to only 176 men, but Lauban was free of the Soviets, and the wreckage of 162 of their tanks littered the country behind. The German tank losses amounted to ten.

The victory at Lauban came as a tonic to Goebbels, who greeted it as a vindication of Colonel-General Schörner's philosophy of the mailed fist for the Russians and the hangman's noose for shirking and defeatist Germans. Goebbels drove out on 8 March to visit the scene of events. 'The weather is clear and frosty; the whole countryside is bathed in wonderful sunshine. On leaving the ruins of Berlin one enters a region apparently quite untouched by the war. One feels really happy to see open country and breathe fresh air again' (Goebbels, 1977, 79).

Schörner met the minister at Görlitz, and on the drive to Lauban he briefed him on the situation of his army group and on his plans to unbalance the enemy by a series of counterblows. Goebbels continues:

Paratroops, who had made a great name for themselves in the Lauban operation, were on parade in the totally ruined market-place of Lauban. Schörner addressed the troops and his speech included the most complimentary remarks about me and my work. In particular he eulogised my permanent and indefatigable struggle for total war and he wished me good fortune in my efforts. He said that I was one of the few men who had the ear of the front-line troops to the full. I replied with a very strong appeal to the morale of the troops, referring particularly to the historic duty they now had to perform. A little bit of local colour provided an excellent background. In this area there is hardly a town or village in which Frederick the Great did not win one of his victories or suffer one of his defeats. (Goebbels, 1977, 81)

According to Goebbels' secretary, the minister spoke with fiery eloquence, and he was repaid with an equally burning enthusiasm on the part of the officers and men when he went on to tour the battlefield with its shattered hulks (Oven, 1974, 601). Students of historical documentation will perhaps be interested in the perspectives of the genuine front-line heroes of the Führer-Grenadier Division, who were ordered to put together a contingent for the honour of being harangued by the minister:

After much coming and going, about one hundred men were assembled and sent to Lauban by truck. On 8 March Goebbels duly delivered his address to the soldiers and Volkssturm who had gathered on the market square of Lauban. Praises were heaped on Schörner, praises were heaped on Goebbels, and the deeds of the troops were mentioned as a kind of afterthought. A few members of the Hitlerjugend were awarded the Iron Cross, but there were no decorations for the men of the units. (Ahlfen, 1977, 164)

Schörner's next blow was a two-divisional enterprise directed at Striegau, some seventy kilometres further east, where the battle opened on 9 March. It was in every respect a grim affair. Winter had returned for a brief visit, with freezing temperatures, fog and showers of snow. This time the Germans did

140

not have enough forces to carry out a double envelopment, and the battle settled down to a brutal struggle for Striegau and the heights to the north-east. On the night of 11–12 March the main force of the Russians broke out in a wild stampede—the *wilde Sau* in the parlance of the *Landser*, who proceeded to shoot down as many as they could in the beams of vehicle headlights. Fighting went on until the Russians were finally cleared from the area on 14 March. The Germans greeted the warm sunshine on the next day as the final conquest of winter by spring, but they could also see around them the full extent of the horrors the Russians had visited on the people of Striegau.

Schörner had been husbanding Nehring's command of four divisions for a grand attempt to relieve Breslau. Fresh from their triumph at Lauban this force was moved east by rail to the foothills of southern Silesia, within close reach of the city. The Germans had observation posts on the Zobtenberg, from where the fires at Breslau were visible day and night. Nearer still was the stretch of autobahn at Kanth, where the Russian vehicles drove with blazing headlights in perfect security. The German troops were not angry, for this was part of the way things were by this stage of the war. Before the Germans could strike across the plain, Schörner had the initiative snatched from him by something he had long feared: Konev opened a powerful offensive against the German forces on the far eastern flank in Upper Silesia.

CHAPTER 11

Heinrici's Command and the Southern Highlands

The Threat to Konev's Deep Left Flank

FLASHBACKS are as tedious in historical writing as they are in the cinema, but there was something to be said for following the events in Lower Silesia and Lusatia in an uninterrupted sequence until the middle of March, by when it is impossible to ignore developments further east in the highlands where south-west Poland met Slovakia.

Just as the barriers of the middle Oder and the Lausitzer Neisse had defined the western limit of the Russian progress, so the southern edge was limited by the chains of mountains and hills which traversed Central Europe from east to west. Country of this sort does not favour offensive operations, and the result was that the German positions in the highlands projected eastwards in a salient between the Russian armies attacking across the flatter landscapes of Hungary in the south, and Poland and Lower Silesia in the north.

When the Vistula-Oder Operation began, the southernmost major formation of German Army Group A, 'Army Group Heinrici,' was still in possession of the region of Zips, the fertile country of eastern Slovakia and the whole chain of the High Tatras with their highest summit, the Kaiser Franz Josef Spitze: 'Nobody will forget the sight of the snow-covered summit as it shone with silvery light in the morning sun. It seemed to be

142

suspended from the clouds above the plains far beneath' (Ahlfen, 1977, 77).

The Germans in the highlands were being attacked head-on
by the 4th Ukrainian Front, but it was the collapse of the German forces in Poland which made Heinrici's original positions
untenable. The nearby Seventeenth Army in Poland was nearing disintegration, despite being reinforced, and the loss of the
Upper Silesian Industrial Region forced Heinrici to fall back to
a new line in the western Beskids on 29 January. These positions
covered the Jablunka Pass (threatened by Slovakian partisans),
and the still more important communication of the Moravian
Gate, which formed the saddle between the Beskids and the
Sudetens, or Silesian hills.

Heinrici also protected the economically vital area of Mährisch-Ostrau. The heart of the Upper Silesian Industrial Region
had indeed fallen to the Russians in the last week of January,
but the south-western fringes and extensions remained in German hands and gave the Reich virtually its last intact facilities
for refining oil and for producing iron, steel, chemical and tex-
tiles. The neighbourhood of Mährisch-Ostrau was a particularly
valuable resource, and although it had only recently been annexed by the Reich, its population (mainly ethnic Poles, Czechs
and Slovaks) worked peaceably under German direction. 'Instead of the beautiful folk costumes of the country folk, which
we had encountered in the valleys of the Carpathians and the
Slovakian mountains, we found the dress of the modern industrial worker. We were transported to a grey workaday en-
vironment, and a Babel-like confusion of the most contrasting
languages' (Ahlfen, 1977, 142). It made excellent defensive terrain, however disappointing the surroundings were in the aes-
thetic sense.

Heinrici's command settled into its positions under its old
name of the 'First Panzer Army.' Desperately over-extended
though it was, it survived a first battering from the 1st Ukrainian
Front from 30 January to 22 February. The Germans gave up

scarcely twenty kilometres of ground on the main front of attack to the north of the heights, which amounted to only one-third of the way to Mährisch-Ostrau.

Not the least of the credit goes to the cool professionalism of Colonel-General Gotthard Heinrici, a short, grey-haired man with a mask-like face. As a pastor's son, he was neither a stylish aristocrat nor a Nazi vulgarian, and he remained virtually unknown to the public. More relevant to his present task was the fact that he had been an officer of the General Staff in the Great War, and had observed with keen interest the cunning way the French had learned to thin out their troops before they were hit by the German bombardments.

On 23 February Heinrici received a distinguished guest, Armaments Minister Speer, who discussed the state of affairs in an open and realistic manner. Speer promised on the spot to send a reinforcement of Jagdpanzers, and seventy of these tank-killing vehicles duly arrived a few days later. We are a world removed from the hothouse hysteria of Goebbels' visit to Lauban.

The Upper Silesian Operation, 15–31 March 1945

By early March Heinrici's lone battle in the south-eastern hills had begun to exercise a major influence on the calculations of the rival high commands. On the Russian side STAVKA planned a new Upper Silesian Operation to clear the threat to the deep left flank of the forces on the Berlin axis. To this end the Fourth Tank Army was diverted from the area of the Lausitzer Neisse, where it had been standing only 120 kilometres from the German capital, and moved 180 kilometres east to regroup alongside Colonel-General Gusev's Twenty-First Army, ready to thrust against Heinrici from the region of Oppeln in the north. The other blows were going to be delivered from the east by Konev's two left-flanking armies (the Fifty-Ninth and the Sixtieth), and by the long-suffering Thirty-Eighth Army of the 4th Ukrainian Front.

Now that the Russians were clearly planning a move on a major scale in Upper Silesia, the German command postponed the intended relief of Breslau and assigned Nehring's XXIV Panzer Corps instead to Heinrici's sector. Both sides had given up something precious—the German garrison in Breslau was left to fend for itself, but the Russians had sacrificed still more when they withdrew one of their four tank armies from the Berlin axis and committed it instead to what was, for all its economic importance, a secondary theatre.

The first of Nehring's divisions to come into action was the 16th Panzer, which raced ahead of the parent corps and arrived east of Sohrau on 11 March, in time to beat off the tank forces of the 4th Ukrainian Front. On the fifteenth the Upper Silesian Operation proper opened in the form of a pincer movement converging on the area of Neustadt on the Silesian Neisse. The Russians achieved clear breakthroughs on the first two days, and on the night of 16–17 March the leading forces of the Fourth Tank Army, advancing from the north, forced the Neisse under heavy fire and began to feed their tanks across a pontoon bridge. At this point Lelyushenko had the privilege of a visit from his chief during a lull in the bombardment:

> I explained the situation to him, and Ivan Stepanovich Konev stopped to view the forces as they passed over. All of a sudden an artillery round came whistling from the enemy bank and hit the jeep containing the Front commander's escort. The vehicle jumped, but the missile did not explode and everyone escaped intact—it was evidently an armour-piercing shot. (Lelyushenko, 1970, 304)

The imperturbable Konev wished Lelyushenko good luck and continued on his tour of the front.

On 18 March the Russian forces advancing from the west

linked up at Neustadt with armour of the Fifty-Ninth Army coming from the east, which isolated considerable German forces in a cauldron extending in the direction of Oppeln. The German front, however, was saved from collapse by the 16th Panzer Division, which had completed its business in front of Mährisch-Ostrau and come back west. German forces were still being hunted down in the Oppeln cauldron, but by 19 March there were signs that the crisis was passing: 'In Upper Silesia our forces have in general terms escaped from the Soviet encirclement. The front has just held. The enemy is regrouping owing to his severe losses; some regrouping is also in progress on our side' (Goebbels, 1977, 185). It was with a good conscience that Heinrici could leave for an important new command in the north (see p. 242) on 22 March, relinquishing the First Panzer Army to the trusty care of Colonel-General Walther Nehring.

The Russians rounded off their Upper Silesian Operation with one last converging movement which began on 24 March. The clear sky favoured the initial bombardment from the ground and air, and

> a solid wall of clods of earth and indescribable debris, flames and smoke arose from the German positions after every Soviet barrage. The ground shook under the impact of the explosions, as if during an earthquake. German guns and their detachments which received direct hits flew into the air like rag toys, and heavy tanks were overturned by air blasts like empty tin cans. (Karpov, 1987, 200)

The Russians were rewarded by the prizes of Ratibor and Katscher on 31 March. Lelyushenko claims that the Upper Silesian Operation as a whole resulted in the destruction of about 40,000 enemy troops and the capture of 14,000 more, liquidating the powerful group of German forces which had hovered over the left flank of the 1st Ukrainian Front. He conceded that the ground gained was small, but this was 'determined by the intentions of the commanders, the nature of the terrain and the German system of defence' (Lelyushenko, 1970, 309).

In fact, the great penetrations reached no more than forty kilometres, or less than a single day's progress in the headiest period of the Vistula-Oder Operation. Over most of the frontage the Germans had ceded very much less ground, and before Mährisch-Ostrau and the Moravian Gate the front remained absolutely firm, except for a tract which Heinrici had relinquished by deliberate design just before the bombardment broke on 10 March. The Germans held Mährisch-Ostrau until 28 April, and the First Panzer Army remained a strong and cohesive formation which sustained a dogged fighting retreat in Czechoslovakia until the end of the war (see p. 295).

For good and ill, the tenacity and skill of the German forces on the southern flank of the central theatre contributed powerfully to securing a few weeks of extra life for the old order in Germany. Similar processes had taken place on a still larger scale on the northern flanks.

PART IV

The Baltic Flank

CHAPTER 12

The East Prussian Setting

The Germans

THE BALTIC SHORE swings north-east and north from the Gulf of Danzig in a sequence of sandy coastlands, river mouths and the long narrow sandspits which enclose the great lagoons called the *Haffs*. Pomerania in the west was ancient Germanic territory. West Prussia with Danzig and Gotenhafen formed a land bridge to East Prussia, which was the home of some of the proudest military families of the Reich. Further along the coast the Germans at the outset of 1945 still held the bridgehead of Memel at the outermost tip of East Prussia, and a much larger coastal enclave in Kurland (Western Latvia).

In the early months of 1945 the operations on the Baltic theatre interacted in complex ways, but viewed as a whole, the German military presence projected in a salient or 'balcony' along the right flank of the Russian forces which were committed to the Berlin axis. The German troops were in danger of being fragmented by Soviet thrusts to the coast, but they exercised a powerful diversionary effect which helped to prolong the existence of the Reich into the early summer.

Where Guderian and the OKH doubted the value of the diversion was in the Memel and Kurland bridgeheads, which were difficult to sustain and tied down a disproportionately large number of German forces. The two veteran divisions from Memel were withdrawn into the Samland region of East Prussia in the last week of January (see p. 164). However, the Führer agreed only to a partial scaling-down of the thirty or so divisions

151

of the Sixteenth and Seventeenth armies in Kurland, for 'territory' was sacred to him, and the Kriegsmarine needed the facilities of Kurland in order to keep a presence in the eastern Baltic, where it worked up U-boats on training cruises.

Guderian had no luck at all when in early February he tried to persuade Hitler that it was in the best interests of Germany to retrieve the forces from Kurland and build up reserves against the Russians moving on Berlin:

> Trembling all down the left side of his body, he [Hitler] jumped to his feet and shouted· 'How dare you speak to me like that? Don't you think I am fighting for Germany? My whole life has been one long struggle for Germany.' And he proceeded to treat me to an outburst of unusual frenzy until Göring finally took me by the arm and led me into another room, where we soothed our nerves by drinking a cup of coffee together.' (Guderian, 1952, 413)

The consent to evacuate the Kurland army group was given only on 3 May, after Hitler had committed suicide. Nearly 26,000 German troops were taken by sea to Holstein, but 190,000 more, together with 14,000 Lettish volunteers, were abandoned to the Russians.

German Army Group Centre (Colonel-General Georg-Hans Reinhardt) had the task of defending East Prussia and the adjacent areas of northern Poland. The German positions extended for 360 kilometres, and they were determined less by technical choice than by the way the fighting had ended in 1944. Reinhardt could ill afford to lose the armoured reserves which he was now ordered to dispatch to other theatres (four Panzer divisions were sent to Hungary in December alone). Moreover, the German forces were deployed in an irregular north-south alignment running well in front of the strongest natural and artificial defences, which had their cornerstone at the fortress of Lötzen amid the Masurian Lakes.

Hitler, as we might have expected, refused all the requests from Reinhardt to be allowed to withdraw to more advantageous positions. In detail, Reinhardt's army group comprised three individual armies:

- The Third Panzer Army on the left or north, guarding the northern and eastern access to the East Prussian capital of Königsberg.
- The Fourth Army in the centre, holding a wide salient which bulged into Polish territory north of the Masurian Lakes.
- The Second Army on the south or right. It faced the Russian bridgeheads across the Narew River, and its right flank extended as far as the boundary with Army Group A north of Warsaw.

The Soviets

The Russian plans for dealing with East Prussia formed one component of the grand offensive of January 1945. The attack was secondary to the assaults on the Berlin axis, but it was important for their success, for it was intended to hold and destroy the German forces hovering on the long Baltic flank.

In terms of numbers the opposing forces were very approximately equal, at around 1,650,000 to 1,800,000 troops each. However 3,800 tanks and assault guns, 25,000 towed artillery pieces and mortars, and ample fuel and ammunition gave the Russians the edge in mobility and firepower—advantages which they exploited by building up their main points of effort on either flank of East Prussia. The massing of strength corresponded with the two Soviet army groups:

- The 3rd Belorussian Front (Marshal I. D. Chernyakovskii) in the north, driving on Königsberg from the east.
- The 2nd Belorussian Front (Marshal Rokossovskii) in the

south, swinging west-north-west across the lower Vistula to the West Prussian and Pomeranian coast beyond, so as to cut off East Prussia as a whole from the rest of the Reich.

The joint effort was not intended to be a pincer movement against East Prussia, but a drive to the Baltic on nearly parallel axes. The whole weight of the attacks was therefore to fall on the Third Panzer Army and the German Second Army, which left the Fourth Army in the centre chiefly to the attentions of the very thinly spread Fiftieth Army of the 2nd Belorussian Front.

Chernyakovskii's army group attacked first, on 13 January, and since its operations form a coherent entity, we shall follow the campaign against Königsberg in an uninterrupted sequence into February.

CHAPTER 13

The 3rd Belorussian Front in Northern East Prussia

The Opening, 13–24 January 1945

ON THE FOGGY and frosty morning of 13 January, the 3rd Belorussian Front opened its offensive against northern East Prussia with a bombardment of nearly 120,000 rounds. Major Baumann was returning at this time to his battery with the Third Panzer Army:

> Already en route to the front, on the train travelling through the East Prussian countryside, one became aware of an almost unnoticeable vibration in the air. Leaving Königsberg railway station, one could hear a soft and deep rumbling—the sound of the continuous barrage between Gumbinnen and Schlossberg, at a distance of approximately 100 to 120 kilometres away. (Glantz, ed., 1986, 399)

In fact, the noise was more impressive than the reality. The Russian gunners were frustrated to find that the weather had worsened overnight:

> The moon grew dim in the freezing air, and the higher it rose in the sky the more the fog spread on the ground. By five in the morning the moon was finally engulfed. The visibility was now minimal, and this had a considerable effect on the opening of the offensive. (Krylov et al., 1970, 375–76)

The Russians did not see that the Germans had already abandoned their outermost positions on purpose, so as to absorb the weight of the bombardment, and so, after a brief unopposed advance, the Russians ran into dogged opposition and fulminating counterattacks. Moreover, the German defences on this sector were exceptionally strong, for they lay on the direct approaches to Königsberg and, for once, the Germans had reached an accurate estimate of the number of forces facing them.

A particularly hard fight developed for Kattenau in the centre, which was retaken by the Germans on 14 January, though at the price of committing the 5th Panzer Division, which was their sole operational reserve. The expenditure was probably worthwhile, for the Russian offensive threatened to stall after it had scarcely begun. The 3rd Belorussian Front sustained nearly 80 per cent of the total Russian casualties in the whole of the East Prussian Operation, and the delays and cost of its initial attack were going to have far-reaching consequences on the events on the whole Baltic flank, and indirectly on the planned offensive against Berlin.

It was in some ways too late when Marshal Chernyakovskii redeployed his forces and made his breakthrough. Displaying the kind of flexibility which is too rarely credited to the Russians, he shifted all his disposable forces (the Eleventh Guards Army and two tank corps) from behind his centre to his right, where the Thirty-Ninth Army was making some headway in the sector north of Schlossberg. On 20 January Chernyakovskii finally broke through the German defences. The powerful new striking force cruised through the gap between the Pregel and Niemen rivers, and the line of the Niemen itself was breached by the hitherto inactive Forty-Third Army, which sprang to life and crossed the ice near and below Tilsit, where, 'just as we had supposed, the Volksgrenadiers and the Volkssturm at once streamed away to the rear in disorganised mobs, the commanders having ceased to exercise any control over their forces' (Beloborodov, 1978, 356).

Late on 23 January a state of *wilde Sau* broke out in the German rear, and by the twenty-fourth the Russians were exploiting the passages they had made on the Deime, the Pregel and the Alle, which formed the last respectable river lines short of Königsberg. A Russian war correspondent reached a little town in the wake of the victorious armies:

> Under the low, gloomy and smoky sky . . . the streets were in the grip of the flames, and they looked like aisles extending between the pillars of some infernal cellar. Here and there long thick tongues of flame burst out of the windows, lashed over the walls, brought down the shop signs and reached out to the middle of the street as if to unite with the fires raging on the opposite side. . . . The oil paint on the walls of the rooms ignited, the waxed and meticulously carpentered parquet floorings crackled and burst into flames, and the hangings, panelling and household furniture took fire along with everything else which could burn. (Paul, 1978, 84)

The First Siege of Königsberg, 27 January to 26 February 1945

The German defence of northern East Prussia had been smashed, and now the city of Königsberg itself was at stake. The unspeakable East Prussian gauleiter, Erich Koch, had seized the chance of making good his escape while the railway to the south-west was still open, and his *Gauleiter Sonderzug* had drawn out of the city on the night of 21–22 January. It took some time yet for the reality of the situation to dawn on minor functionaries, and three days later a group of retreating German soldiers had a frustrating experience outside Königsberg at Waldau, just ahead of the Russians:

> There we found a mighty store of provisions in a gymnasium, which was stocked with things like coffee, chocolate

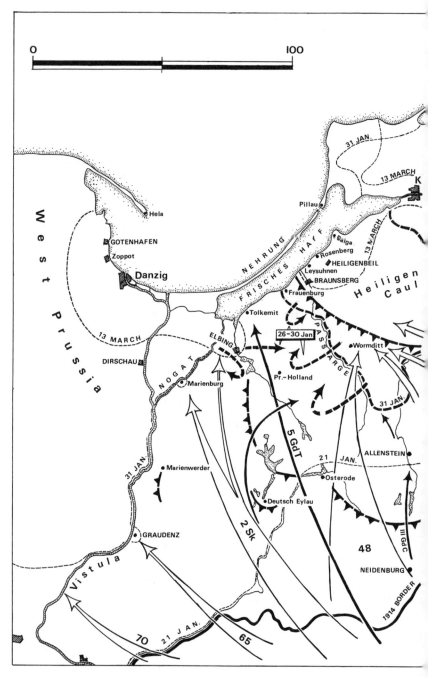

8. East Prussia, January–April 1945

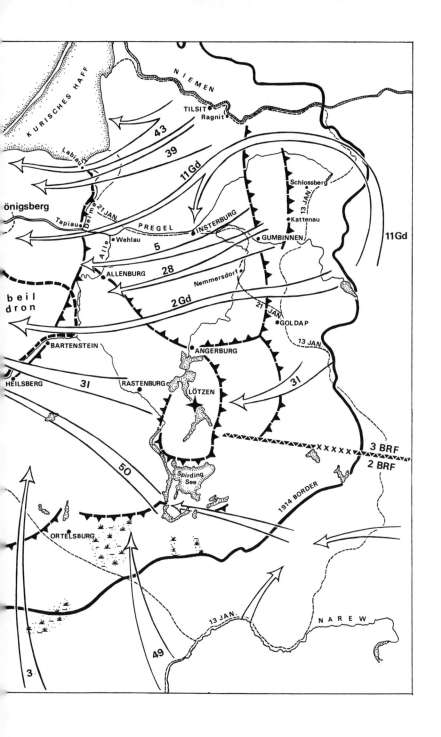

and spirits—great treasures which for a long time had existed for us only in rumours. We were infantrymen, and therefore the last troops to arrive before the Russians, and yet the resident quartermaster refused to yield up anything without the appropriate Forms A and E, which had to be signed by an officer. (Dieckert and Grossmann, 1960, 95)

On 27 January Königsberg was embraced by a semi-circle of Russian forces which very nearly touched the Frisches Haff on both sides of the Pregel estuary. Inside the city the hospitals were overflowing with 11,000 wounded, and the refugees streamed in from the countryside

mixed together with disbanded mobs of the Luftwaffe, the Organisation Todt and the army. Peasant carts were jammed along the gutters in long rows, and on the roads between there was an intermittent movement of prams, bicycles, sledges, trucks, grey-green artillery pieces, and snow-encrusted motor cycles, and all the time a mass of humanity trudging onwards. . . . The cold had become sharper still than a few days before, but these people knew the enemy were after them, and their numb faces were running with sweat, such was their exhaustion and terror. (Thorwald, 1950, 182)

Nearly all the members of the Nazi hierarchy had by now fled, but they left a standing instruction that, in the case of a Russian breakthrough, all the population must escape by way of the road which led around the northern end of the Frisches Haff to the seaport of Pillau. Using loudspeakers, the Party issued the appropriate order on 27 January. Nobody had thought of contacting the military command, and the result was indescribable confusion just east of the city when thousands of people took to the road only to find that the way to Pillau was already a combat zone.

On that day and the next it was almost literally true that the

Russians could have walked into Königsberg. The only prepared defences consisted of the ring of a dozen nineteenth-century forts which were held by 'stomach' and 'ear' battalions and other low-grade security garrisons. The mobile forces (the 5th Panzer Division, two Volkssturm divisions and one infantry division) were not enough to check the progress of the Russians, and on the evening of the twenty-eighth a Soviet force drove down the axis of the main road from the north against Fort Quednau. It was a race between the advancing Russians and the 367th Infantry Division, which had been rushed up by the tenuous railway communication from the south-west and was now deploying in the face of tanks and dense masses of infantry:

> At this juncture, like a gift from heaven, the assault guns arrived on the scene and rolled forward on the road to Kranz. Russian tanks were driving to meet them, but in the light of the illuminating rounds the Germans were able to recognise them in good time. With considerable skill our five or six assault guns took up position behind a swell in the ground, and they shot up between six and eight Russian tanks in short order, including some Stalins. The whole landscape was as bright as day with the light from the exploding and burning Russian tanks. (Lasch, 1977, 51)

Altogether thirty Russian tanks were destroyed in this engagement, and more than two months were to pass before the enemy once more came so close to the heart of Königsberg.

Königsberg lay near the mouth of the Pregel, just five kilometres from the outermost end of the Frisches Haff. The centre of the city was now secure against a *coup de main*, but the Germans had to keep open the routes which led around the sides of the lagoon if they were to ensure that the place could be defended over the long term.

The south-western communication from the Fourth Army in central East Prussia was narrow and vulnerable. It was inter-

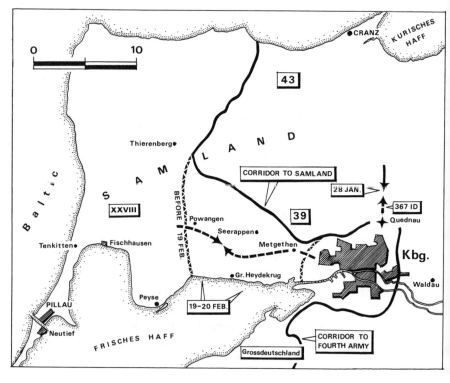

9. The first campaign for Königsberg, January–February 1945

rupted repeatedly by the Soviet Eleventh Guards Army, and it was kept open at all only through the combined efforts of the Königsberg garrison operating from the north-east, and the detached Panzer-Grenadier division (Major-General Karl Lorenz) of the Grossdeutschland Panzer Corps, which was attacking from the direction of the Fourth Army. During one of the snowstorms an NCO of Grossdeutschland became aware of forms stumbling towards him:

> Were they Russians? I couldn't be sure. I raised the barrel of the Schmeisser, released the safety catch and stared through the blizzard at the snow-covered shapes which were

moving slowly towards me. When they came within ten metres, I recognised women and children, and I jumped up and shouted: 'Over here!' Weeping girls with pale, anxious faces fell around my neck: 'Help us! Help us!' Children cried 'Mutti! Mutti!' All the other men and women stood silently with white frozen faces, and their clothing all sodden from the snow. (Dieckert and Grossmann, 1960, 134)

Still more important for Königsberg was the other lifeline, which ran due west along the northern shore of the lagoon to the Samland peninsula and the port of Pillau. The Russians therefore dealt a potentially mortal blow when on the night of 29–30 January they thrust silently towards the *Haff* to the west of the city. The German command in Königsberg was unaware of what was going on, and on the same night Reserve Major Dieckert was ordered to make his way to the airfield at Seer-appen, where he was supposed to take command of an 'alarm battalion' of Luftwaffe ground personnel. When Dieckert drove west, he could see nothing but refugees and small groups of soldiers, and abandoning his car in the deep snow, he made his way cross-country in the direction of the airfield. Still some way short of his objective he came across a farm building:

I had scarcely reached the barn before I saw that two shapes were approaching. They carried weapons. I made ready to open fire, since it was not a good idea to call out to them. When they came nearer, they turned out to be two German *Landser*. The older man in particular made an outstanding impression. They explained that they had come from the airfield, which was already abandoned, and that they were under orders to take up a new position here. They formed the main line of defence, and behind them there was nobody else. (Lasch, 1977, 43)

Another German probe towards the west was attended with far more tragic consequences. On the morning of 30 January a refugee train left the garden town of Metgethen for Pillau. Short of Seerappen the track was blocked by a Russian tank which fired into the train, forcing it to come to a halt, whereupon the passengers were hauled out by Russian soldiers who gave themselves up to an orgy of plunder and rape.

This was the beginning of the first blockade of Königsberg, for it was clear that the way to the west was now completely blocked. A new commandant, General Otto Lasch, brought some order among the refugees, though the interior of the city was extremely crowded and he could provide no adequate shelter against artillery and aerial bombardment. He remustered the unformed troops who had arrived with the refugees, and he incorporated the Hitlerjugend (who were probably more highly motivated) into the battalions of infantry:

> These lads threw themselves into the training with extraordinary enthusiasm. Most of them were not issued with steel helmets, for these were too big for them and fell over their eyes when they fired. There was not much we could do about that. On account of their tender years they were issued with special luxuries in the form of chocolate and sweets, instead of alcohol or cigarettes. (Dieckert and Grossmann, 1960, 158)

All the time, the core of the defence remained the 5th Panzer Division and the veteran East Prussian 1st Infantry Division.

A pair of Russian armies (the Thirty-Ninth and the Forty-Third) and a stretch of ground between twelve and twenty-eight kilometres wide now separated the defenders of Königsberg from the positions which the Germans still held around the western end of the Samland peninsula, where the two divisions of General Hans Gollnick's XXVIII Corps had arrived from Memel (see p. 151). Between 3 and 7 February the Samland force battled its way forward to the commanding Thierenberg (110 metres), and on 17 February the overall command in East Prussia (Army Group North) ordered the two German forces to open simultaneous attacks and join up.

General Lasch was willing to stake everything on the gamble. He had been instructed to attack from the Königsberg side only with designated units of the 5th Panzer Division and the 1st Infantry Division. With considerable moral courage he now resolved that he must throw in the full force of those divisions, with the 561st Volksgrenadier Division on top. He radioed the Samland forces to tell them what he had decided. General Gollnick rejoined that Lasch must accept full responsibility: 'To this I replied that only a full-blooded commitment would help, and that I was willing to answer for it, for I knew that the life and death of the whole garrison and civilian population hung on the success or failure of this attack' (Lasch, 1977, 70).

Lasch and Gollnick attacked from their respective sides on 19 February, concentrating their efforts against the Thirty-Ninth Army on the southern sector of the Russian blocking force.

The thrust westwards from Königsberg was spearheaded by the 1st Infantry Division, for in spite of the frost the ground for the first few kilometres was too soft to permit the 5th Panzer Division to deploy away from the road and railway embankments. The Germans moved forward at 0400. At the point of the advance was a captured T-34 tank, which was crewed by Germans dressed in Soviet uniforms and commanded by a sergeant-major who spoke perfect Russian. A column of five Tigers followed immediately behind:

> At the appointed hour the T-34 rolled forward, and continued down the road without firing a shot. At the enemy observation post the tank commander told the Ivans in Russian that they must go back, for the Germans were on his heels. The Tigers meanwhile came up from the rear. The Russians ran—some of them springing from bed in their underclothes. (Plato, 1978, 262)

The 1st Infantry Division captured Metgethen after a hard fight for the Girls School, which the Russians had turned into a strongpoint:

On the streets lay the bodies of old people, women and children. They were totally despoiled and some of them were frozen together in grisly heaps. Others were found as charred corpses in the smoke-blackened ruins. In the station there still stood carriages of the train which had been surprised by the Russians at Metgethen a couple of weeks earlier. On the carriage floors the Germans found the bodies of women of every age, lying with their clothes ripped open. (Thorwald, 1950, 194)

The 5th Panzer Division could now go into full action, and by the end of the day it had carried the German penetration to a depth of ten kilometres.

The XXVIII Corps meanwhile attacked from Samland. On this side the Russians stood their ground still more firmly than at Metgethen, but Gollnick too attacked with three divisions (the two from Memel, and one already in Samland), and he was supported by shellfire from the heavy cruiser *Admiral Scheer*. The two German forces joined hands to the north-west of Gross Heydekrug on 20 February, and over the following days they secured a corridor between five and ten kilometres wide, through which the refugees from Königsberg could at last make their way to Pillau. This averted a human catastrophe of the first order, and relieved much of the pressure on the defenders. The Russian Supreme Command decided that the German concentration in the area of Samland and Königsberg was too hard a nut to crack, and on 26 February both the Thirty-Ninth and Forty-Third armies were put on an indefinite defensive.

CHAPTER 14

The 2nd Belorussian Front in Southern East Prussia

Rokossovskii's Change of Direction

THE OTHER two German armies in East Prussia were the Fourth (in the centre) and the Second (in the south), and their fate was associated directly with the course of the war on the Eastern Front as a whole.

The Soviet attacking force was the 2nd Belorussian Front (Marshal Rokossovskii). Its task as originally envisaged (see p. 154) was to push west-north-west to the lower Vistula on a wide frontage, and exploit across the river into West Prussia and East Pomerania, in other words well away from central East Prussia. The main attack was to be delivered from the right, by three all-arms armies (Second Shock, Forty-Eighth and Third), with the Fifth Guards Tank Army moving up fast from deep reserve as the exploitation force. Two all-arms armies and one tank corps were assigned to the secondary attack on the left from the Pultusk and Serosk bridgeheads over the Narew. It was reasonable to hope that the German Second Army would be crushed by superior forces, and that the Fourth Army, being isolated in East Prussia, would collapse of its own accord.

The planning and preparation were just as meticulous as they were for the offensives of Konev and Zhukov in central Poland:

> At headquarters we discussed all the plans before taking final decisions, exchanged views on the utilisation and co-

ordination of the various arms and services, and heard and considered reports by officers from various formations. In this way all of the Front's commanders were kept constantly informed of events and could react quickly. We were thus able to avoid wasting time summoning department, arm and service chiefs, and listening to long, tiresome reports. Procedures that had seemed suitable in peacetime did not justify themselves in war (Rokossovskii, 1985, 274).

Fog and snow were almost certain to limit the effectiveness of the first artillery and air strikes, but the targets were carefully surveyed, and the commanders of the aviation groups, regiments and squadrons went to the forward positions to establish liaison with the ground forces:

> We felt out of our element when we made our way on foot to the trenches and observed the German defences from the outposts. Mortar bombs whistled unpleasantly over our heads, we felt as if we were being torn apart by the flying shells, and the bullet streaked past with a horrific whistle. The ground was erupting with arbitrary explosions. We ducked involuntarily at every bullet, shell and bomb, and yet the infantrymen paid not the slightest heed. They proceeded calmly with their various occupations. (Koryander, 1978, 240)

The Russian attack opened in a familiar style:

> At 1000 on 14 January the cold air shivered and was torn apart by the salvoes of the many thousands of guns arrayed along the whole length of the front line. The frozen ground trembled. From the bank of the river [the Narew] to our forward positions, a multitude of yellow puffs of smoke arose from the white spread of the fields, the little woods and the hillocks. An instant later a black shroud veiled the area of the German deployments. (Skorobogatov, 1976, 160)

On 15 January the expanding Russian bridgeheads coalesced on broad frontages, and on the next day the bright weather enabled the Russians to bring into play the full weight of their air forces and ordnance:

The enemy crushed all resistance with their artillery and multiple rocket launchers. In the localities where any Germans were left alive, the tanks rattled forward, shot up any weapon position, and rolled over the foxholes. The soil was frozen and as hard as stone, and so the shells detonated instantaneously, which sent splinters flying just over the surface. (Dieckert and Grossmann, 1960, 100)

For the German theatre command in East Prussia (Army Group Centre, renamed Army Group North on 25 January) events were taking a horrifying shape. As early as the evening of the fourteenth, Reinhardt could see that the direction of the Russian attack presented the danger of a deep envelopment, and he telephoned Hitler with the first of many vain requests to be allowed to draw in his forces to shorter and more defensible positions. At 0300 on 15 January the chief of staff, Lieutenant-General Otto Heidkämper, received an order from the OKH to send the greater part of the Grossdeutschland Panzer Corps, the last major operational reserve on the Baltic, south to Army Group A in central Poland (see p. 79). While the German Second Army was falling apart, the Fourth Army to its left remained immobile in a salient which appeared every day more 'grotesque,' extending as it did in an irregular blob 170 or more kilometres inland from the coast.

Early on 21 January Guderian informed Reinhardt by telephone that Hitler still refused to allow the Fourth Army to be pulled back. 'The commander declared: "But that's quite impossible. It means everything is going to collapse." After a short pause Guderian's answer came in tortured words from the other end: "Yes, my dear Reinhardt." ' (Heidkämper, in Thorwald, 1950, 151). Only at noon, after a prolonged telephone argument with Reinhardt, did Hitler at last agree that the Fourth Army could retreat a little way.

It was already too late. STAVKA was worried about the slow and very costly progress which Chernyakovskii was making in northern East Prussia (see p. 156), and on 20 January it had ordered Rokossovskii to turn the axis of the four armies of his centre right northwards against the Fourth Army and the connection with West Prussia. Effectively, the direction of Rokossovskii's main force was switched from half-left to half-right. STAVKA's intention was to take off some of the pressure on the 3rd Belorussian Front, which had been having such a hard time in the north. This proved redundant, for 20 January was the same day that Chernyakovskii made his breakthrough in front of Königsberg. However, STAVKA's decision set off two chains of events:

- Most immediately, the main body of the 2nd Belorussian Front hit the long western flank of the German Fourth Army, bringing disaster to that formation and the civilian population of East Prussia.
- Zhukov was deprived of effective support on his northern, or Pomeranian, flank during his advance westwards on the Berlin axis. STAVKA did not relieve Rokossovskii of his responsibility of helping Zhukov, but the 2nd Belorussian Front now had only two armies (the Seventieth and the Sixty-Fifth) available for this purpose. They were not enough, and they made slow progress. The grand Soviet design of destroying Germany in the first weeks of 1945 was already falling apart.

The German Fourth Army Is Isolated in Central East Prussia

When the main effort of the 2nd Belorussian Front inclined northwards from 20 January, it became the left-hand jaw of a pincer movement against East Prussia, converging with the offensive of the 3rd Belorussian Front from the east.

The Russian exploitation forces raced ahead of the all-arms armies, taking the German civil and military authorities in East Prussia totally by surprise. On the right flank the III Guards Cavalry Corps moved rapidly over the snow, burst into Allenstein at 0300 on 22 January and caught the Germans while they were unloading tanks and artillery from railway cars: 'Attacking daringly (not on horseback, of course!) and stunning the enemy with a hurricane of artillery and machine-gun fire, the cavalrymen captured the trains, which turned out to be full of enemy units transferred from the east to close the breach made by our troops' (Rokossovskii, 1985, 283). On the central axis a lone Russian tank had reached the railway station of Elbing on the day before and shot into the crowds of refugees who were waiting to leave for the west. A heavily laden train was able to get away under fire, but all the rest of the people had to run for their lives.

The main Russian striking force was the Fifth Guards Tank Army, rushing up at speed from the deep rear, where its presence had been completely unknown to the Germans. On 23 January one of its corps bore down on Elbing at a time when the *Oberbürgermeister* was still assuring the civilians that the front had stabilised. Captain Dyachenko was ordered to come at the town from the east with his seven tanks and his battalion of infantry, and by inserting his force among the refugees and the civilian vehicles streaming in from Preussisch-Holland he was able to approach Elbing undetected. From 1700 onwards the tanks cruised among the trams and shoppers, halting occasionally to fire into the buildings and becoming targets themselves for the Panzerfausts of the scratch garrison. The departing intruders left four of their tanks smoking inside the town, and the Russians did not enter Elbing again until 10 February.

On 24 January the main body of the Fifth Guards Tank Army broke through to the shore of the Frisches Haff to the east of

Elbing, which signified that the great pincer movement had succeeded. East Prussia was now severed from the rest of the Reich, and eight divisions of the Second Army were cut off in the province, together with the whole of the Fourth Army and the remains of the Third Panzer Army.

The defenders of Königsberg were pinned down and irretrievable, but the Fourth Army in central East Prussia so far had not been heavily engaged, and its commander, General Friedrich Hossbach, was now contemplating desperate measures. Hossbach was an abrasive Prussian officer who had been brought up in the proud and independent traditions of the General Staff, and as early as the night of 21–22 January he began to take troops from the south-eastern front of his salient and send them west to build up a striking force against the 2nd Belorussian Front. On the next day he informed Colonel-General Reinhardt, as army group commander, of what he was doing, and he gained the retrospective approval he had expected. Reinhardt had been thinking on almost identical lines, for he too believed that his responsibilities to his 400,000 troops and the countless refugees in central East Prussia overrode an obligation to the Führer and the High Command.

The OKH was left in ignorance of what was happening, while the forces disengaged from the enemy in the south-east and struggled through snowstorms to reach their new deployment areas facing west. In the process the fortified complex of Lötzen amid the Masurian Lakes was abandoned on 24 January. The secret finally broke, and Guderian writes that 'the first we heard was that the fortress of Lötzen, the strongest of the bulwarks covering East Prussia, had been lost without a fight. It is little wonder that this news of the loss of our best armed, best built and best garrisoned fortress was like a bombshell to us and that Hitler completely lost all self-control' (Guderian, 1952, 400).

On Hossbach's instructions the attack was due to open at 1900 on 26 January. 'It was a night of full moon, and in front of the divisions stretched a bare and snowy landscape. The only relief was provided by the silhouettes of trees, little woods and gardens' (Dieckert and Grossmann, 1960, 116). Hossbach aimed to break through the overstretched Russian columns, and carry his troops (with the refugees sheltering in their midst) to the positions of the Second Army on the lower Vistula. The attack began on time on a frontage of about thirty-five kilometres, and over the next three days the Germans carved through the flank of the Russian Forty-Eighth Army, surrounded one of its divisions and made contact through their leading battalions with units of the German Second Army at Elbing and Preussisch-Holland.

Hossbach must have known that he was living on borrowed time. On 29 January the progress of his three under-strength corps was halted by the Russians. More fatal still were the changes in command ordained by the Führer. As a direct result of his disobedience, Reinhardt was told to make way as army group commander for Colonel-General Dr. Lothar Rendulić, 'an Austrian clever and subtle, who knew how to handle Hitler' (Guderian, 1952, 401). Rendulić flew from Kurland on 27 January, and the exhausted Reinhardt delivered up his command with the words: 'There is nothing more to say' (Thorwald, 1950, 164–65).

Hossbach had been a conspirator with his chief, and his remaining credit was undermined by East Prussian Gauleiter Erich Koch, who was storming Hitler with complaints: 'The Fourth Army is fleeing in the direction of the Reich. In its cowardly way it seeks to break through to the west. I shall continue to defend East Prussia with the Volkssturm' (Thorwald, 1950, 165).

On 30 January the Fourth Army, on higher orders, ceased its attack, and Hossbach was relieved by General Friedrich-Wilhelm Müller, a man who described his qualifications to army group headquarters in the following terms: 'I am a good NCO and I know how to carry out orders, but strategy and tactics are quite beyond me. Just tell me what I ought to do!' (Thorwald, 1950, 166–67).

On 31 January the Russians delivered their first attack against the western frontage of the Fourth Army, and over the following weeks they hammered at the contracting perimeter of the 'Heiligenbeil cauldron,' which was the last line of the Germans as they fought with their backs against the Frisches Haff (see p. 204).

CHAPTER 15

The Buildup of German Army Group Vistula

The New Army Group

By NOW we have left the troops of Lasch and Gollnick bottled up in Königsberg and Samland, and the German Fourth Army isolated and imprisoned against the shore of the Frisches Haff. The right-hand German formation in the Baltic theatre was the Second Army, which had caught almost the whole weight of the 2nd Belorussian Front when Marshal Rokossovskii opened his offensive on 14 January. On 20 January STAVKA swung the axis of Rokossovskii's effort from the north-north-west to the north (see p. 170). The thrust to Elbing fragmented the Second Army, whose left-hand formations were cut off with the Fourth Army to the east of the breakthrough. These happenings, which were so destructive to the Germans in one dimension, nevertheless weakened the westward momentum of the Russian January offensive and permitted the Germans, in however confused a way, to gather their forces and recover the initiative.

Most immediately, STAVKA, by intervening as it did on 20 January, reduced the Russian forces advancing against the lower Vistula from five armies to three. The main body of the German Second Army was able to make good its escape to the lower Vistula, and the Germans consolidated on that river behind the shelter of a chain of east-bank bridgeheads and outposts—the city of Thorn (lost on 2 March), the fortress of

Graudenz (6 March), the outlying town of Marienwerder (29 January), and the Nogat branch of the Vistula with the Marienburg castle (9 March) and the outpost of Elbing (10 February).

Furthermore, an ever-widening gap was opened between the 1st Belorussian Front of Marshal Zhukov, whose main effort was to the west on the Berlin axis, and the greater part of the 2nd Belorussian Front, which was now attacking north towards the Baltic. Only two of Rokossovskii's armies (see p. 170) were able to offer Zhukov any kind of close support. To begin with, the Germans themselves had very few forces facing the boundary between the two Russian army groups, and it was originally as a defensive measure that Guderian urged how important it was to form a new 'Army Group Vistula' as a complex of armies in the tract between the lower Vistula and the lower Oder.

The headquarters of Army Group Vistula took over command of the still battleworthy Second Army (Colonel-General Walter Weiss) on 24 January, and three days later it extended its area of responsibility south-west to embrace the remnants of the Ninth Army (General Theodor Busse). Finally, a new Eleventh SS Panzer Army (SS General Steiner) was put together from reinforcements by 10 February and formed a striking force between the two other armies.

Confusingly enough, the Eleventh SS Panzer Army was re-designated the Third Panzer Army on 24 February, after the headquarters of the original but now extinct Third Panzer Army arrived from East Prussia. The Soviet accounts fail to take cognizance of this event, and continue to describe the SS Panzer Army and the Third Panzer Army as separate entities, crediting the Germans with three instead of two armies in Army Group Vistula.

A reshuffling and redesignation of the army groups as a whole had already taken place on 25 January:

- Army Group A became Army Group Centre (Schörner).
- The new Army Group Vistula was inserted between that formation and the next to the north, namely

- Army Group Centre, which became Army Group North (Rendulić).
- Army Group North became Army Group Kurland (Vietinghoff).

At the end of the Ardennes offensive the invaluable resource of the Sixth SS Panzer Army was transferred straight to Hungary, much to the chagrin of Guderian, but other formations swelled Army Group Vistula to impressive dimensions in the first three weeks of February. German authorities have put the total size of the army group in the region of thirty-two to thirty-four divisions. A good Soviet source identifies 450,000 troops, with 5,000 artillery pieces and more than 1,000 tanks and assault guns (Babadzhanyan, 1981, 354–55), though such an estimate may be influenced by the supposition that the Germans deployed three armies and not two. What mattered at the time, however, was the impression that was made on the Russians of a great unengaged German force that was building up from the north-west against the uncovered angle between two of their army groups.

This was an administrative triumph on the part of the Germans, but Hitler had already jeopardised it by making a quite bizarre appointment of a commander. Guderian went to the Führer briefing on 22 January to propose Field-Marshal Freiherr Maximilian von Weichs as commander of the new army group:

At the time he was just the man for this situation. What happened? Hitler said von Weichs was too old. Jodl was present at the conference and I expected him to support me. But he made some remark about von Weichs' religious feelings. That ended the matter.

Then, whom did we get? Hitler appointed Himmler! Of all people—Himmler!

This was an 'appalling and preposterous appointment' (Ryan, 1980, 61).

Himmler at once travelled in his long personal train, the *Steiermark*, to Deutsch-Krone in Pomerania. Here he stayed for days on end without venturing into the snow. The train was luxuriously appointed but lacked the basic essentials of military command, which made Himmler's immobility all the less excusable. There was no radio with access to the military network, and all the planning had to be based on a single 1:300,000 map of Pomerania and the Warthegau which the operations officer, Colonel Eismann, brought with him to the *Steiermark* on 26 January. Eismann had taken his map as an afterthought, and when he reached the train, he found that there was no cartography of any description except for an out-of-date situation map in the commander's saloon. 'In no way did he correspond with the image which Eismann had previously formed of him. Himmler was not diabolical, not cruel—merely insignificant' (Thorwald, 1950, 275).

For a man who sent millions of defenceless beings to their deaths, Himmler was remarkably concerned about the state of his own health, and this obsession dictated his daily routine. He rose between eight and nine in the morning, and his first priority was to get himself worked over by his masseur. He got in a single hour's work before adjourning for lunch, which was followed by a siesta that lasted until 1500. This final working session terminated at about 1830, by when Himmler was exhausted and losing concentration.

No help was at hand from the chief of staff, the SS Brigadeführer (Major-General) Lammerding, who reached the *Steiermark* on the twenty-seventh. He was a powerfully built fighting soldier who was out of his depth in planning the work of large formations. Himmler's own military experience had been confined to rounding up stragglers and other broken troops on the Upper Rhine front at the end of 1944, and in this same spirit he ordered SS and police units to comb the rear areas of his new command for men for front-line duty. The thing was carried out with mindless brutality, and the trawl swept up essential civilian labourers like the dockers who had been unloading the ammunition ships at Gotenhafen.

Under the pressure of the Russian attacks the front line of Himmler's command had taken up the following configuration:

- On the east there was a short upright corresponding with the naturally strong positions of the Vistula and the Nogat branch.

- The main frontage ran from the lower Vistula westwards across the centre through West Prussia and East Pomerania, and it was supported by the principal 'breakwater' (*Wellenbrecher*) strong points of Schneidemühl (fell 14 February; see p. 106), Deutsch Krone (11 February) and Arnswalde (22 February). Here the fighting was on nearly equal terms between the weakened Russians and the reviving Germans, who enjoyed intermittent but very welcome support from the Luftwaffe.

- Finally, there was a downward-turning bar on the west, representing the Meseritz Fortified Region and the associated defence, which extended south across the Oder-Warta bend to the Oder near Grünberg. These were shortly assailed by Zhukov's 1st Belorussian Front. Himmler's first move of any operational significance was to send SS General Krüger with a mixed SS corps to bolster up the Volkssturm in that part of the world. The leading formation was the 21st SS Gebirgsjäger Division. By a terrible mischance its commander, SS Major-General Ballauf was surprised by Russian tanks near Zielenzich, and he was forced to flee from his car, leaving a map of the fortifications behind. This information helped the Soviet armour to drive through the Volkssturm positions on 30 January and press on to the Oder (see p. 110).

Things might have gone still worse for the new German army group if the thaw of early February had not supervened. As Himmler wrote to Guderian, 'In the present state of the war the thawing water is for us a gift of fate. God has not forgotten the courageous German people' (Ziemke, 1984, 427). By 4 February the Vistula was melting below the level of Marienwerder. On 6 February the lower Oder was unfreezing as well. On the evening of that day Colonel Antonov (Fifth Shock Army) was sitting in his shelter, absorbed in a map:

> Suddenly, a distinct report rang out. I could not understand what it could be and I went out into the street. There were no shells bursting and yet the ground was moving under my feet. My comrade-in-arms, the Kuban Cossack submachine-gunner Sergei Kurkov, was at his sentry post.
>
> 'And now, Comrade Sentry, what is going on here?' I asked him in a light-hearted way.
>
> 'Something's going on, all right,' he answered with a smile. 'It's cracking up, Comrade Colonel,' and then he turned to the Oder.
>
> 'What's cracking up, then, Comrade Sentry?'
>
> 'Why, the ice on the Oder!'
>
> There was a subdued tinkling and roaring noise as the hillocks of ice heaved themselves up on the sheet ice. Sergei Kurkov breathed an anxious sigh:
>
> 'You can't fight against Nature!' (Antonov, 1975, 250–51)

On 10 February the centre and the left wing of the 2nd Belorussian Front began a broken-backed clearing operation which only confirmed the impression that the initiative was slipping from the Russians. The Soviets cut off the fortress of Graudenz on the lower Vistula by a pincer movement, but in the course of five days of fighting they penetrated only about fifty kilometres, which was very disappointing compared with the rates of advance in the Vistula-Oder Operation. There was little prospect of further progress, for the terrain was broken and difficult, and the Russians were short of tanks and were losing more than they could afford to the Panzerfausts. Further to the Russian left, Marshal Zhukov was being forced to peel off armies from his right flank to face north against the German forces gathering in East Pomerania. Zhukov's troops managed to isolate the little town of Arnswalde, but they were thinly strung-out and vulnerable.

Operation Sonnenwende—the German Counteroffensive at Stargard, 15–21 February 1945

Guderian was afflicted by heart trouble and high blood pressure, and it was with his last resources of strength that he sought to gain permission for a bold stroke—a double pincer movement which was intended to pinch off Zhukov's 1st Belorussian Front on its two flanks. Army Group Vistula was to cut in from East Pomerania from the north, while another strong grouping was to drive north from the middle Oder between Guben and Glogau. The jaws would close behind Zhukov's spearheads, isolating and destroying them in the area of Küstrin. To create striking forces on such an ambitious scale it would be necessary to extricate the German formations from the Balkans, Italy, Norway and the Kurland bridgehead.

This proved too much for Hitler, as might have been expected, and he reduced the offensive to a single blow from the Stargard sector of Army Group Vistula. To work out the cutdown plan still represented a considerable effort on the part of Guderian, and he faced a further battle when he went to the Führer briefing on 13 February to propose Lieutenant-General Walther Wenck, his personal assistant at OKH, as the best man to command the attack. Hitler was outraged at the well-founded implication that Himmler was incapable of carrying out his duties:

> And so it went on two hours. His fists raised, his cheeks flushed with rage, his whole body trembling, the man stood there in front of me, beside himself with fury and having lost

all self-control. After each outburst of rage Hitler would stride up and down the carpet edge, then suddenly stop immediately in front of me and hurl his next accusation in my face. He was almost screaming, his eyes seemed about to pop out of his head and the veins stood out on his temples.

Having vented his spleen, Hitler walked calmly over to Wenck and told him to report to Army Group Vistula for duty, then returned to his usual chair and called Guderian to him:

'Now please continue with the conference. The General Staff has won a battle this day.' And as he said this he smiled his most charming smile. This was the last battle I was to win, and it came too late. (Guderian, 1952, 414–15)

Operation Sonnenwende (Solstice) was the name given to this enterprise, and it was entrusted to General Felix Steiner's Eleventh SS Panzer Army, which was not so much a settled formation as a command structure for the six divisions or divisional equivalents which were struggling along the roads and railways towards the region of Stargard. Guderian in person appeared in the deployment area on 14 February, and he spoke of the need to open the attack punctually on the next day, so as to exploit the element of surprise, which was the only asset available to the Germans. 'He left behind the impression of a man who was totally exhausted. Those who were present concluded that Guderian too had finally broken with Hitler' (Thorwald, 1950, 286).

The attacking forces assembled in three main groups on a frontage of fifty kilometres, facing south. Under the ferocious name of the Eleventh SS Panzer Army they formed a disparate mixture of genuine elite formations and bodies of foreign volunteers which were of variable quality:

- The main offensive was to be delivered by the central group, under orders to strike on a broad front from the area of

Jakobshagen and Zachan to relieve Arnswalde, then turn south-west against the Russian forces in the area of Küstrin. The central group was designated the III (Germanic) SS Panzer Corps (Lieutenant-General Decker) and comprised the Panzer-Grenadier Division Nordland (Scandinavian volunteers), Panzer-Grenadier Division Nederland (Dutch volunteers) and two German formations—the Führer-Begleit Division, and the Division Langemarck.

- A western group was to operate in the area between two lakes, the Madü See and the Plöne See. This was the XXIX Panzer Corps (Lieutenant-General Unrein), made up of the Panzer Division Holstein, the 10th SS Panzer Division, the 4th SS Police Division, and the Division Wallonien (Belgian volunteers).
- The weak eastern group was to protect the left flank, and then, if the offensive proved successful, advance to the area of Landsberg on the Warthe. It was composed of the Führer-Grenadier Division, the 281st and 163rd Infantry divisions and the tank-killing 104th Panzer-Jagd Brigade.

The movement of reinforcements for Army Group Vistula was funnelled by way of the bridges at Stettin, and it proved to be a crowded and slow business. Zhukov knew in general terms of the German buildup, and in the target sector he had two armies (Second Guards Tank Army in the west, Sixty-First Army in the east) as well as three more in deep reserve (First Guards Tank Army, Forty-Seventh, Third Shock). He was aware of the danger of a German attack, but the timing and objectives of such an offensive remained in doubt, and in the event, the Panzer-Grenadier Division Nordland achieved total tactical surprise on 15 February, when it thrust across the wet and heavy fields as far as the beleaguered German outpost of Arnswalde.

A general attack by all three German groupings opened on 16 February and won some ground in the face of Soviet counterattacks and the strong anti-tank defences. The most prom-

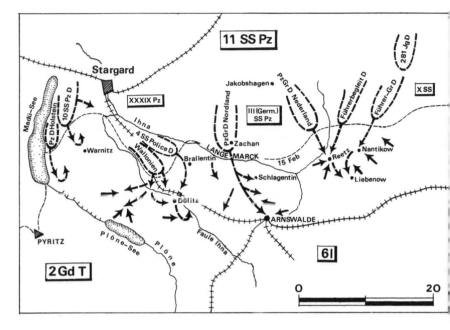

10. Operation Sonnenwende, 15–21 February 1945

ising progress was made by the western group, in the direction of Dölitz, and by the adjacent flanks of the central and eastern groups, which reached Reetz and Nantikow. The corridor in the centre to Arnswalde meanwhile held firm.

The culminating point of Operation Sonnenwende was reached on 17 February, when the Germans gained up to two kilometres on the most promising sectors, but sustained very heavy losses from the Russian anti-tank guns and mines. Earlier that day Wenck had been summoned to Berlin to report to Hitler. The briefing dragged on until 1400, and both Wenck and his driver were dog-tired when they began the return journey along the Berlin-Stettin autobahn. Wenck took over the wheel from the driver, who had been on duty for forty-eight hours, but he himself fell asleep and the car crashed into some obstruction by the roadside—a tree according to one account, a bridge parapet according to another. Wenck was badly hurt and he was incapable of serving for a number of weeks.

General Hans Krebs took over the direction of Sonnenwende, but the initiative was already being lost, and Krebs lacked the grip and the independence of mind which Guderian so admired in Weichs. Himmler was now completely useless, for he had now given himself up to his real or psychosomatic ills, and he was in the care of his doctor. On 18 February the Germans were everywhere thrown onto the defensive, and in the evening Army Group Vistula decided to abandon all attempts to renew the attack, 'so as to avert the needless attrition of our offensive formations' (Murawski, 1969, 167).

The German counteroffensive had been on a much smaller scale than the operation which Guderian intended, and it was cut short literally by accident. The numbers of forces involved on either side are impossible to establish, as are the respective losses. Sonnenwende nevertheless exercised a significant effect on the course of the war on the Eastern Front. Coinciding as it did with the termination of Konev's offensive on the Lausitzer Neisse, it further inhibited the Russian preparations for the offensive on the Berlin axis and helped to postpone the fall of the Reich for two and a half months.

From the Russian point of view Sonnenwende could not have struck at a more awkward time or place. It caught the right flank of the 1st Belorussian Front along a sector which Stalin and Zhukov had long known to be sensitive, and, together with the relative disappointment of the 2nd Belorussian Front's offensive between 10 and 14 February, it confirmed how weak the Russians were on their northern flank generally. This in turn was largely the consequence of the swing into East Prussia by Rokossovskii's centre right from 20 January.

CHAPTER 16

The East Pomeranian Operation

The Push North to the Baltic

BERLIN now ceased to figure on the list of immediate Soviet objectives, and STAVKA instead wove plans for an 'East Pomeranian Operation.' This was a set-piece offensive on a frontage of two hundred kilometres and was assigned to the adjacent flanks of two army groups—the right, or eastern, flank of Zhukov's 1st Belorussian Front, and the left or western flank of Rokossovskii's 2nd Belorussian Front.

The initial advance was to be on a common axis north to the coast between Kolberg and Köslin. In the second, or exploitation, phase the axes were to diverge, with the 2nd Belorussian Front wheeling right (eastwards) against the fortified region of Danzig and Gotenhafen, while the forces of the 1st Belorussian Front turned north-west towards Stettin and the mouth of the Oder.

As early as 13 February the 'Foreign Armies East' intelligence branch of the OKH assessed that the Russians were likely to postpone their attack on Berlin until they had cleared their flanks in Silesia and Pomerania. The German Second Army was already overextended, and a Russian thrust northwards through East Pomerania would sever it from the rest of Army Group Vistula. On the seventeenth the army group headquarters accordingly sought permission to retreat westwards and form a strong common front with the Eleventh SS Panzer Army.

The request was denied by Hitler, and a new German catastrophe was in the making.

The 2nd Belorussian Front opened the East Pomeranian Operation on 24 February. Rokossovskii had no support from the 1st Belorussian Front, for Zhukov was still reshuffling his forces to his right flank, but he pinned high hopes on the Nineteenth Army, commanded by Lieutenant-General D. T. Kozlov, which had just arrived from the near-static Finnish front. These fresh troops progressed twenty kilometres on the first day, but then slowed in a quite unexpected way in the face of lively German resistance, and it soon became clear that the Nineteenth Army had not been prepared for the scale and ferocity of the fighting in Pomerania.

On 26 February Rokossovskii inserted the III Guards Tank Corps on the narrow sector east of Neustettin and was immediately rewarded by a penetration of forty kilometres. He was disappointed to find that the rifle forces were still lagging well behind, and on the twenty-sixth he replaced Kozlov with Lieutenant-General Romanovskii. Senior Russian commanders were notoriously intolerant of failure.

The change of command could do nothing by itself to clear a threat that was developing to the right flank of the Nineteenth Army. Here, in the neighbourhood of Rummelsburg, the German Second Army was assembling the VII Panzer Corps (the remains of the 32nd Infantry Division, the depleted 7th Panzer Division [Rommel's old 'Ghost Division'] and the reliable 4th SS Police Division. Colonel-General Walter Weiss thereby weakened the southern sector of his own army (the Second), but he was striving to preserve his communication westwards with the rest of Army Group Vistula.

However, the real danger to the Germans in Pomerania came not from the slow-moving Nineteenth Army but from the Russian mobile formations. On 26 February the III Guards Tank Corps, exploiting its first breakthrough, breached the main German line (the *Pommernstellung*) at Baldenburg, and proceeded to fan out on the far side. Neustettin, the corner-stone of the

Pommernstellung, fell with surprising ease on 27 February to a joint attack by the adjacent III Guards Cavalry Corps, and by the II Guards Cavalry Corps from the extreme right of Zhukov's army group. On 2 March the last German links with the main force of Army Group Vistula were broken to the east of Köslin, and the Second Army was cut off.

The main force of the right wing of the 1st Belorussian Front had finally joined in the offensive on 1 March. The natural conditions were most unpromising—dense fog which interfered with artillery observation and air support, and wet snow and melt water which reduced the dirt roads to a condition which reminded the Russians of their *kasha* porridge. 'As for the hard-topped roads, they all ran from west to east, connecting central Germany with East Prussia, and virtually none ran from south to north, which was what was needed for the operation we had in mind' (Babadzhanyan, 1981, 261).

Zhukov's attack was delivered by an immensely strong grouping of three armies (Second Guards Tank, First Guards Tank, and Third Shock) which advanced northwards into Pomerania. The heaviest point of effort was in the area of Reetz, where the Russians hit the Third Panzer Army at the junction of the III (Germanic) SS Corps and the X SS Corps. On 2 March the breach in the line was total, and the Russians launched concentric attacks from the north-east, east, south and south-west against the German forces to the east of the breakthrough. These were the X SS Corps (Lieutenant-General Krappe) and the adjacent Corps Group Tettau, which made up the left or eastern wing of the Third Panzer Army. Colonel-General Erhard Raus, as commander of the Third Panzer Army, applied for permission to pull back Krappe and Tettau to safety. Both Himmler (now in Prenzlau) and Guderian were adamant in their refusal, and any hope of saving the left wing from encirclement vanished. In other words, two groups of German forces were now lost from sight—the whole of the Second Army, and the eastern flank of the Third Panzer Army.

By 3 March the fighting in Prussia had become fluid, and the Russian progress acquired a new tempo:

> If on the first two days of the offensive the rate of advance had not exceeded fifteen or twenty kilometres a day, it increased dramatically on the two days that followed. The impetus of the offensive became so great that, when the tanks burst into a town, we used to find the people going about their ordinary routine of life as if nothing had happened—policemen directed the traffic at the crossroads, strains of music wafted through the doors of the restaurants, businessmen were concluding deals at the exchanges, and every now and then Berlin radio transmitted the encouraging Goebbels version of the news.
>
> And suddenly, like a thunderstorm in a clear sky, there were tanks with red stars on their turrets! Just imagine what terror they struck into the hearts of the German burghers! And then the tanks streaked off to the north just as suddenly as they had arrived. Press on! That was our one priority. (Babadzhanyan, 1981, 270–71)

On 4 March, units of the First Guards Tank Army reached the Baltic near Kolberg on a frontage of eighty kilometres. First on the scene was Colonel M. A. Smirnov, a man of few words, who reported his arrival by sending bottles of seawater to his corps commander (Babadzhanyan), his army commander (Katukov) and to Marshal Zhukov.

Rokossovskii Exploits East to Danzig

By driving north to the Baltic the Soviets had broken the German forces in East Pomerania into fragments:

- The Second Army had been cut off in its entirety, and it was falling back east towards West Prussia and the fortress complex of Danzig and Gotenhafen.

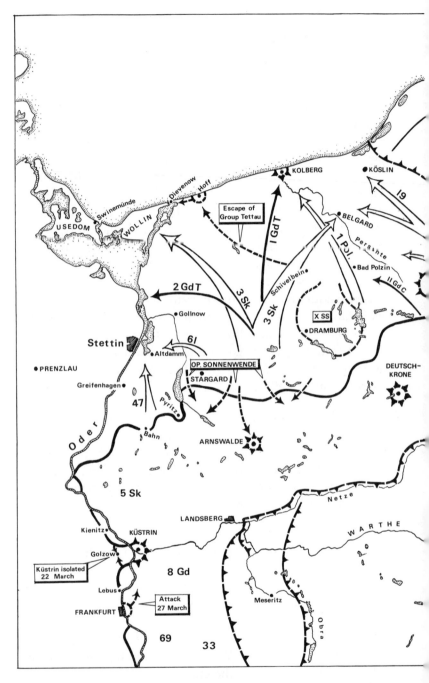

11. East Pomerania and the lower Oder, February–March 1945

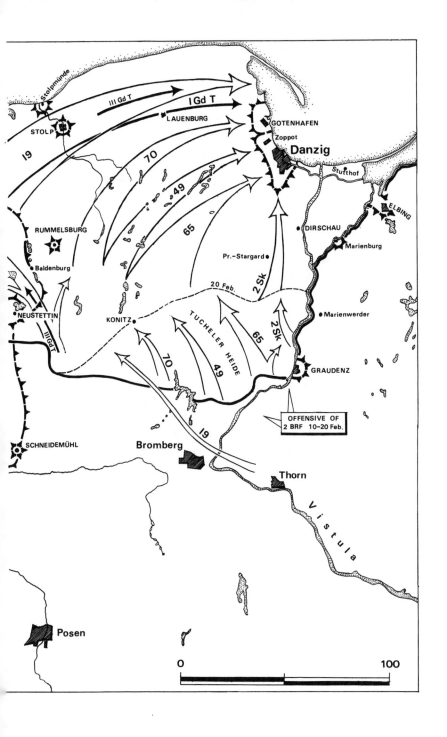

III Gd T

I Gd T

Stolpmünde

LAUENBURG

STOLP

19

70

49

65

GOTENHAFEN

Zoppot

Danzig

Stutthof

ELBING

RUMMELSBURG

• Baldenburg

• DIRSCHAU

Marienburg

Pr.-Stargard •

2 Sk

20 Feb.

• NEUSTETTIN

III Gd T

KONITZ

TUCHELER HEIDE

• Marienwerder

65

2 Sk

70

49

65

GRAUDENZ

SCHNEIDEMÜHL

19

**OFFENSIVE OF
2 BRF 10-20 Feb.**

Bromberg

Thorn

V i s t u l a

Posen

0   100

- In the direct path of the Russian breakthrough, the east wing of the Third Panzer Army was fighting for its life in a cauldron in the neighbourhood of Dramburg, while a mass of refugees was coalescing at the isolated port of Kolberg.
- To the west of the great breach the remainder of the Third Panzer Army was retreating towards the lower Oder and Stettin.

The Russian army groups now embarked on the second, or exploitation, phase of the East Pomeranian Operation. On 6 March Rokossovskii's command began a five-pronged converging movement against the coastal region of Danzig and Gotenhafen. The Second Shock Army, which had the shortest distance to go, drove due north across the Tucheler Heide (Heath) to the west of the lower Vistula, thereby outflanking the German positions on the Nogat branch and making the bridgehead of the Marienburg castle untenable. The defenders of the Marienburg held on a little time yet with the assistance of salvoes from the heavy cruiser *Prinz Eugen*, and 'the explosions threw up densely packed pillars which stood like a blackish grey wall. It began to the left on the bank of the upper Nogat and extended around the castle' (Paul, 1978, 188). The Marienburg was evacuated on the night of 8–9 March, and when the Germans lost Elbing on the tenth, it signified that the Russians had interposed an impregnable barrier between the two Prussias, East and West.

The three armies of Rokossovskii's centre wheeled north-east against the target area. On his left the Nineteenth Army and the III Guards Tank Corps traversed the Baltic coastlands from east to west in a 150-kilometre sweep. In an attempt to stay their progress the Germans moved the VII Panzer Corps (see p. 187) from the area of Rummelsburg to the Baltic flank. The entire corps had only thirty or forty operational tanks, and it was swept along with the other German forces in the direction of Danzig and Gotenhafen.

On 8 March the Russians took peaceful possession of Stolp,

which was the most important centre of communications and war industry in East Pomerania. On 10 March the XL Guards Rifle Corps of the same Nineteenth Army emerged from a zone of forest and advanced on Lauenburg. On the way to the town Russian tanks overhauled a column of refugees. A German signals officer describes the result:

> Towards 1400 we came under an unexpected flank attack by a strong Russian tank force, advancing from the direction of Striebelin, ahead and to our left. There was great confusion. Right in front of me the first shells from the Russian tanks tore apart refugee vehicles which were laden with women and children. . . . Not far in front of us there was the edge of a forest with dark trees. Everyone made for the trees, but in the attempt to extricate the vehicles from one another, they all became hopelessly stuck in the snow. The tanks reached the road in our rear, and drove up in the direction of Lauenburg, crushing everything under their tracks. (Husemann, 1971–73, II, 504)

Nobody had clean hands at that time. The Russians occupied Lauenburg without opposition (despite the tales in their histories), and they found nearby a concentration camp for Jewish females:

> A terrible scene was spread before our eyes—long barrack huts, bare plank beds, and human corpses everywhere. Our brigade doctors threw themselves into the work of rendering first aid to the survivors and transporting them to the town hospital. Wherever we looked, we observed startling contrasts—the death camp, and alongside it a number of sumptuous villas. We spent some time roving through one of them. The living rooms of the master of the house were positively palatial, and yet they were located a short distance from those terrible huts in their barbed wire compound. (Skorobogatov, 1976, 190)

The thrust to the coast was given additional power by the First Guards Tank Army, which on 8 March was switched from the 1st Belorussian Front to Rokossovskii's army group. The intention was to prevent the Germans from consolidating in the Danzig-Gotenhafen Fortified Region. In its effort to catch up, the First Guards Tank Army covered 120 kilometres on 9 March alone, and three days later its XI Guards Tank Corps arrived before the Gotenhafen fortifications. There were no German forces in the way except the relics of the VII Panzer Corps and a tumult of panic-stricken troops. The 4th Field Replacement Battalion of the 4th Police Division (VII Panzer Corps) was in danger of being swept away with the rest

> when all of a sudden our commander, SS-Sturmbannführer (Major) Auer, who bore the Knight's Iron Cross, appeared on the road in the midst of the chaos of fugitives. He had his pistol in his hand, and with the help of some of his subordinates he dragged the men of his battalion from the fleeing mass. We now combed the abandoned vehicles for weapons and ammunition, and the infantrymen were rearmed. The impossible had happened—within two hours the field replacement battalion was once more ready for action. (Dr. Pichler, in Husemann, 1971–73, II, 508)

On the eastern flank the exploitation phase of the East Pomeranian Operation was concluded, and Rokossovskii had to wait for the main bodies of his all-arms armies to arrive before he could think of assaulting Gotenhafen and Danzig.

Zhukov Exploits to the Lower Oder

In western East Pomerania the Russians occupied Stargard on 4 March, and by the evening of the next day the right flank of Zhukov's 1st Belorussian Front had shattered the frontage of the Third Panzer Army on a sector of two hundred kilometres.

Three of Zhukov's armies peeled off to the left and exploited westwards in the direction of the lower Oder, where the main formed body of the Third Panzer Army coalesced around Alt-damm, the bridgehead suburb of Stettin on the east bank of the Oder. The Russian Sixty-First Army took the Altdamm bridgehead under direct attack from the east while the Forty-Seventh came up from the south, driving down the right bank of the river. The fighting for Altdamm began on 6 March and lasted until the nineteenth (see p. 236).

To the north of Stettin and Altdamm the Oder gradually widened and then expanded into the lagoon of the Stettiner Haff, from where the waters oozed into the Baltic around the islands of Wollin and Usedom. To the east of this complex of obstacles we find Zhukov's two right-hand armies (the Second Guards Tank Army and the Third Shock Army), which now ran out of land. The 67th Regiment of the Third Shock Army reached the water early on 9 March:

> In the morning, when the mist had cleared, we stood on the low shore of the gulf and looked over the water. It was dove-grey, and intersected by sandy tongues of land. We breathed in the fresh air and were intoxicated by the tang of the sea. When the sun rose, we had to screw up our eyes against the unendurable blue glare of the sky. (Shatilov, 1970, 200)

The Destruction of the X SS Corps

By 5 March the X SS Corps was beset in the neighbourhood of Dramburg by Russian masses which converged from nearly every point of the compass—forces of the Third Shock Army from the west and south-west, the First Polish Army from the south-east and east, and by units of the First Guards Tank Army which turned aside from the Kolberg axis and were cutting in from the north.

The German corps could no longer be considered a battle-worthy formation, and in the evening Lieutenant-General Günther Krappe issued a final despairing order, for a general *sauve qui peut*. Krappe himself was badly wounded and taken prisoner, and most of the few survivors belonged to small knots of men of the 5th Jäger Division, who infiltrated through the Third Shock Army and reached the Oder. Major Keller describes how he and his troops would

> spend the day hiding up in dense woodlands, while at night we mostly marched across country with the help of map and compass. We did all we could to avoid clashes with enemy troops. All we had to eat were the few slices of bread and bacon we found in the wreckage of refugee columns which had been driven over by the enemy, or in abandoned forestry huts.

At 0200 on 14 March an inundation forced the troops onto a road which led directly to Fürstenflagge:

> Our tension grew by the minute, and we found ourselves marching with more and more haste. Then a sharp *Stoi!* rang out in front of us, followed immediately by a shower of grenades. All hell broke loose. Everyone started shouting and shooting in all directions. Completely unawares we had run into a Russian strongpoint from behind. Luckily, the Russians had thrown all their hand grenades, and their machine-guns seemed to have been emplaced to fire towards the west. All 150 of us raised a cheer and stormed resolutely forward. The Russians had no desire to make our acquaintance and disappeared into their foxholes. We ran hell for leather over the Russian positions and obstacles and reached the road to the west on the far side. A few hundred metres further on we were received by the garrison of a German strongpoint. (Murawski, 1969, 229)

The Escape of von Tettau's Roving Cauldron

Just to the north of the X SS Corps, five or more scratch divisions formed the command of Lieutenant-General Hans von Tettau in the area south of Belgard. The formations and the numbers cannot be stated with any precision, but the force was built around the Panzer Division Holstein and the Division Pommerland, and consisted of 10,000 to 15,700 troops. They were fighting not just for their own lives but for those of the up to 40,000 civilians who had sought safety among them.

Von Tettau had lost radio contact with the headquarters of the Third Panzer Army, and in near total ignorance of what was going on around him he and his group broke out of the encirclement early on the morning of 5 March. From the area north of Shivelbein, von Tettau had intended to make directly for a bridgehead which was reported to exist east of the Oder lagoon. Hearing that the bridgehead had been eliminated, he inclined north towards the coast. On 8 March the Panzer Division Holstein showed signs of panic, and the group nearly succumbed, but the Germans succeeded in infiltrating through the rear areas of the Third Shock Army, and on 9 March they reached the coastal resorts of Hoff and Horst, where they established a bridgehead. Von Tettau was disappointed in his hopes of being evacuated by sea, and he had to be content with winning a short breathing space before he made his do-or-die attempt to break through by land to Dievenow, from where the Kriegsmarine could ferry his people across the easternmost mouth of the Oder to the island of Wollin.

Von Tettau deployed his few passably battleworthy forces on a narrow frontage on the shore, and the break-out to the west began at 2200 on 10 March. Sergeant Borgelt arrived by air from the headquarters of the Third Panzer Army in time to witness the progress on the next day:

I was standing on the coastal cliffs with General von Tettau, whose vehicle had been abandoned. The Russian infantry came storming towards us with wild cries of *Ura!* but von Tettau called out with quiet confidence to one of his staff officers: 'Now then, gentlemen, let's give them something to remember!' We all proceeded to shoot at the attacking troops as calmly as if we had been on a rifle range. I picked up a rifle from one of the casualties and joined in—this was the first time in the war I had been so close to the enemy. The Russians then opened fire with mortars, but the bombs passed over us and landed on the beach. I looked in that direction and my stomach churned. Behind and beneath us, in the lee of the cliffs, the refugees were fleeing to the west, and the Russian shells were bursting among them. (Paul, 1978, 160)

At one stage a Russian counterattack from the south threatened to throw the whole mass of soldiers and civilians into the sea, but the troops finally broke through to Dievenow and the refugees completed the final twenty kilometres of their *via dolorosa* amid appalling scenes:

Never had I seen so many bodies—civilians, German and Russian soldiers—but especially the Russians in great heaps, lying this way and that on top of one another. Between the corpses were strewn dead horses, the overturned carts of the refugees, bogged-down military transport, burnt-out cars, weapons and equipment. . . . It was depressing enough to see the soldiers, who had had nothing to eat for days and were totally exhausted, but the faces of the women were indescribable. I saw mothers cast their infants into the sea because they could carry them no further. (Borgelt, in Paul, 1978, 160–61)

By the end of 11 March 6,000 soldiers and 26,000 refugees had been ferried from Dievenow to the island of Wollin. The passage of the rest was completed in the course of the twelfth.

PART V

The Siege of the Fortress Cities

THE IMPETUS which swept the Russian forces through northern Europe in the New Year of 1945 died away in the course of February. The ebbing tide revealed what an extraordinary collection of human debris had been thrown up on the isolated islands of German resistance—broken units of Wehrmacht and Volksgrenadiers, 'stomach,' 'ear,' and 'eye' battalions, men of the Luftwaffe without their aircraft, Fallschirmjäger without their parachutes, grimly determined SS, silver-haired Volkssturm, Hitlerjugend burning with enthusiasm, Baltic and Russian volunteers, Hiwi auxiliaries and, above all, thousands upon thousands of civilian refugees.

Large Russian forces were tied up with the task of eliminating the German strong points and asylums up to and even beyond the start of the Berlin Operation on 16 April. These episodes, which have scarcely entered the general literature of the Second World War, are the subject of the present part of this book. We shall begin at the East Prussian 'balcony,' then follow the Baltic coast by Danzig and Kolberg to the mouth of the Oder, and trace the course of the river and its hinterland as far upstream as Breslau, where the Germans held out almost until the end of the war.

CHAPTER 17

East Prussia

The Strategic Background

On 9 FEBRUARY General I. Kh. Bagramyan was summoned to the headquarters of the 3rd Belorussian Front, where General Chernyakovskii explained the state of affairs to him, 'smoothing his thick, dark hair' and speaking 'in a pleasant, sonorous baritone' (Bagramyan, in Erickson, ed., 1987, 221). The trouble was that the German forces in East Prussia, although they were fragmented in three parts, were still powerful and under effective control. Just how much fight the Germans had in them became evident in a few days' time.

On 20 February German troops, attacking simultaneously from Königsberg and Samland, drove through the Russian Thirty-Ninth Army and broke the first blockade of the city (see p. 166). Chernyakovskii himself had been killed on the eighteenth in central East Prussia, and the loss of this popular and respected commander would in any case have forced the Russians to review their priorities.

Marshal A. M. Vasilevskii took command of the orphaned 3rd Belorussian Front on 21 February, and on the following day he extended his area of responsibility north to take in the 1st Baltic Front, which was integrated in the main army group under the name of the Samland Front. Vasilevskii was now able to plan on the grand scale, and he decided to destroy the German Army Group North 'one chunk at a time,' concentrating his forces in turn against

- the Heiligenbeil Cauldron
- the fortress-city of Königsberg
- the Samland peninsula.

The Heiligenbeil Cauldron and the Destruction of the Fourth Army, 13–28 March 1945

The 'Heiligenbeil Cauldron' was the name given to the area defended by the German Fourth Army. After Hossbach had failed in his attempt to break out to the west at the end of January (see p. 173), this formation was isolated in the coastal region of central East Prussia, except for a narrow corridor extending to Königsberg. The army consisted of fifteen assorted divisions, of which the most effective were probably the 24th Panzer Division, the Hermann-Göring Parachute Division, and the detached Panzer-Grenadier Division of the Grossdeutschland Panzer Corps. The bridgehead was called after the town of Heiligenbeil, but until the middle of March the Germans held an area of ground which extended fifty kilometres as the crow flies along the shore from the neighbourhood of Frauenburg in the south-west to the approaches to Königsberg in the north-east. Inland the depth reached between ten and twenty kilometres.

Behind the bridgehead lay the Frisches Haff, where the ice remained firm enough to permit civilian refugees to escape to the Nehrung sandspit until the end of February. Travelling in the opposite direction, salvoes of 280-mm shells from the heavy cruisers *Lützow* and *Admiral Scheer* passed clear over the sandspit and the *Haff* and thundered into the Russian forces attacking the Frauenburg flank of the cauldron. Wormditt on the landward perimeter was abandoned on 11 February, and the planes on its airfield were blown up, but as a general rule when the Germans gave ground, it was dictated by the lack of fuel and ammunition rather than by pressure on the part of the Russians.

The Germans' term of grace expired on 13 March, by when Vasilevskii had built up a full seven armies against the cauldron. Some of the victims believed that the bombardment from artillery and the air was unprecedented:

Beneath this fire the German soldiers lay in their little foxholes—hungry, exhausted, hollow-cheeked and wearing sodden uniforms. The Russian armoured wedges drove forward, with the troops coming up behind roaring their *Uras!* But not all life was extinct. Covered with earth, the hardened *Landser* emerged from their holes. They threw their machine guns over the parapets of the trenches, shot into the grey-brown masses with their assault rifles and machine pistols, and dashed forward with their Panzerfausts against the enemy tanks. (Dieckert and Grossmann, 1960, 143)

It soon became clear that the Russians were concentrating along two axes—against the coastal corridor to Königsberg, and against the sector of the southern perimeter in front of Heiligenbeil. The Russians severed the communication with Königsberg on the first day, and when fine weather arrived on 18 March they were able to bring all their air forces into play.

On 21 March the obedient General Friedrich-Wilhelm Müller, as commander of the Fourth Army, sent an officer by air to Hitler to beg permission for the troops and heavy equipment to be evacuated from the port of Rosenberg while that operation was still a physical possibility. Hitler refused, even though Heiligenbeil, scarcely five kilometres inland, was already in the front lines. On the next day Russian aircraft deluged the German positions in Heiligenbeil with phosphorous bombs: 'The whole town was a sea of flames. The troops got through only with singed uniforms, and rubber capes which had shrivelled in the heat' (Dieckert and Grossmann, 1960, 147).

The Germans were cleared from the railway station of Heiligenbeil on the twenty-fourth, which deprived them of their last strongpoint in the town, and over the next three days the

Fourth Army disintegrated against the shores of the Frisches Haff. Three divisions were cut off at Leysuhnen and lost, while the rest of the forces crouched among the hundreds of vehicles at Rosenberg under heavy artillery and air attack, or, like the remnants of the 24th Panzer Division, hastened north along the *Haff* road to a final defensive line which was forming across the little Balga peninsula. A merciful fog grounded the Russian aircraft on 28 March and saved the Germans from final annihilation. On that day the last troops were embarked at Rosenberg, while the final craft to leave Balga evacuated 2,530 combatants, 2,830 wounded and 3,300 civilian refugees. On the landward side of Balga a small rearguard from the 562nd Division stood and fought under Colonel Hufenbach, who was ultimately killed along with his men.

According to Russian accounts, 93,000 German troops lost their lives in the battle for the Heiligenbeil Cauldron between 13 and 28 March. A further 46,448 men fell into Russian hands, along with 605 tanks and assault guns, 3,559 field guns, 1,441 mortars and 128 aircraft.

The Lull at Königsberg,
21 February to 1 April 1945

Even before Marshal Vasilevskii had finished off the Fourth Army, he was redeploying to attack the fortress-city of Königsberg. The wonder was that it had not fallen long since. In late January and early February it had been a kind of Rosenberg writ large, serving as a refuge for broken troops of another of those doomed German armies, in this case the Third Panzer.

For two days the Russians had it in their power to take Königsberg by a *coup de main*, but with the help of reinforcements the perimeter of the city was stabilised along the line of the ring road and the outer forts, and on 19 and 20 February the garrison of Königsberg attacked in concert with the German forces from Samland, and reopened the land corridor with the west (for these events, see pp. 157–166). When a corps of the Russian Forty-Third Army tried to break the connection, it found itself facing 'a wall of steel' (Bagramyan, in Erickson, ed., 1987, 226).

The German gamble paid off handsomely. Not only did it save Königsberg, but it forced the Russians to recast their whole scheme for the conquest of East Prussia, reducing it bit by bit instead of all in one rush (see p. 203).

Inside Königsberg the commandant, General Otto Lasch, did what he could to turn the reprieve to advantage. He established the main line of defence (*HKL*) along the perimeter of twelve outer forts which had been built between 1874 and 1882. Fox-holes were dug into the earth covering of these massive masonry structures, and wire and minefields were set out cunningly on the approaches, but the Germans did not have the artillery to strike at long range at the insolent Russians, who could be seen at their ease in their trenches, or driving in convoys at night with their headlights full on. The Germans prepared interior defences along the girdle of inner forts (1843–73), on the continuous ramparts of the city proper and finally in 'an old royal castle perched on the high bank of the Pregel River . . . serving as a hiding place for thousands of fanatical fascists' (Bagramyan, in Erickson, ed., 1987, 229).

The size of the garrison during the lull and the second siege stood at between 35,000 (Lasch) and 135,000 (the Russian accounts). The difference probably comes from the difficulty of defining which personnel were of combatant status. In terms of formations, the garrison consisted of four burnt-out divisions, including one of Volksgrenadiers, together with a further Volksgrenadier division (the 561st) which stood at the entrance to the Samland corridor.

During the first siege Lasch had put a great deal of effort into restoring the 5th Panzer Division and the 1st Infantry Division, and he was aggrieved that after the breakthrough on 20 February he had been compelled to yield up these two valuable formations to the Samland group, together with seventy-two of his high-velocity anti-aircraft and anti-tank guns. It was no compensation that General Müller had transported 10,000 lightly wounded men of the Fourth Army to the already crowded hospitals in Königsberg: 'It was contrary to any normal feelings of humanity to expect such battered troops to put up any kind of fight. Before the final battle, on the last day that communications were still open, I took it on myself to evacuate these men as speedily as possible to Pillau.' (Lasch, 1977, 80)

In the first three weeks after the siege had been lifted, about 100,000 citizens and refugees took the opportunity to leave Königsberg for the town of Pillau in Samland, from where boat-loads of civilians were being shipped westwards. Lasch had been hoping to be relieved of still more, but the people were shocked by the terrible fate of the *Wilhelm Gustloff* (see p. 290), and by the discouraging stories of crowding, hunger and air attack at Pillau and the intermediate station at Peyse.

For those who remained in Königsberg, or returned there, life assumed a semblance of peacetime conditions. Water, gas and electricity were restored, restaurants and cinemas re-opened, and cattle were driven in from the countryside, which assured supplies of milk and meat for the sick and the children. The weather was unusually mild for this time of year. Snow-drops and violets were in bloom, the grass turned green and women pushed their prams in the parks.

This interlude of calm gave Lasch no respite from the malice of his internal enemies. He had been a firm supporter of the new order in Germany, but his independent way of thinking, his humanity and his grasp of reality made him unpalatable to certain elements in Königsberg. East Prussian Gauleiter Erich Koch exercised a baleful influence from the safety of his post at Neutief, at the northern tip of the Nehrung, and he flew in periodically by Storch to encourage his party associates on the spot, notably Deputy Gauleiter Grossherr and Kreisleiter Wagner. A saying became current in both Party and military circles:

It is a bad omen for Königsberg to have a commandant called Lasch, and his chief of staff called Süsskind.

In German the word *lasch* means 'limp' or 'lax,' while the 'sweet child' (Süsskind) referred to the melancholy Colonel von Süsskind-Schwendi, some of whose officers were said to live well back from the firing line. 'Nowhere—not even in Breslau—did mistrust between Party and Wehrmacht generate such a gloomy and oppressive atmosphere as at Königsberg in its final weeks. Everywhere Koch and his associates were sniffing out weakness, lack of resolution, defection and treachery' (Thorwald, 1950, 192). The Volkssturm were retained under strict Party control, and the political authorities continued to build defensive works without any reference to the Wehrmacht engineers.

Much of the remaining authority of Lasch was destroyed by the intervention of General Müller (see p. 173), who at the beginning of April assumed overall command of the forces in Samland and Königsberg. Lasch knew that Müller was personally brave, but 'this man, in contrast to his responsible predecessor [Hossbach] had led an entire army to its certain destruction. He now meddled as commander in our imminent battle of encirclement, which deprived the troops and the leaders of their trust and confidence.' (Lasch, 1977, 80. For the similar feelings in the 5th Panzer Division, see Plato, 1978, 392.)

On 2 April Müller arrived at the headquarters of Lasch in the air raid shelter on the Paradeplatz:

> Incredibly enough, he was still in the grip of illusions, in spite of his experiences in the Heiligenbeil Cauldron, and he was incapable of understanding my pessimistic assessment of the state of affairs. He summoned an assemblage of divisional and unit commanders, together with a prominent representation of the Party leaders. He proceeded to address them in the university cellar, delivering an enthusiastic speech which was brimming with supreme optimism and confidence in final victory.

Müller outlined a scheme to bring the remnants of the Fourth Army from Samland to Königsberg, as a base for an offensive which was going to sweep the Russians from East Prussia:

> I objected that four or five battleworthy divisions would be needed to obtain even a partial victory of any value. He had to concede that he did not know where he could obtain these formations, but he was sure that everything would soon turn out well.

Afterwards Müller told Lasch that he was about to be relieved of his post at Königsberg, for there was an impression that he lacked confidence in the ability of the city to hold out:

> I asked him when I could count on being relieved. He replied that he still had to overcome a few snags, for the former commanders had pronounced such good opinions of me that he could not get the process under way just now. But he had 'a long reach,' and he would recommend my dismissal to the Führer. (Lasch, 1977, 84–85)

While these tragi-comedies were being played out in Königsberg, Marshal Vasilevskii built up a force of four armies in the immediate neighbourhood of the city, namely the Thirty-Ninth, the Forty-Third, the Fiftieth and the Eleventh Guards. The air support was on an unprecedented scale, since it comprised two air corps from STAVKA reserve and aircraft from the Baltic Fleet, as well as three full air armies, which gave a total of 830 fighters, 470 close support aircraft and 1,124 bombers. The whole came under the command of Chief Air Marshal N. Novikov.

For the war on the ground the staff of the Samland Group had to

> find solutions to a number of new problems, since it was the first time in the war that we were undertaking an assault

210

on such a large fortified city, an operation all the more awkward because Hitler regarded the need to retain the city as a matter of special importance. Preparing the troops was a difficult job, since they faced having to break through defences abounding in such engineering constructions as forts, pillboxes, large fortified buildings specially designed to ward off hardware and infantry. Training the commanders also raised numerous difficulties. Finding one's way in a besieged city is a problem, with the constant risk of clashes between friendly troops. Maintaining communications between advancing and support units is also difficult. (Bagramyan, in Erickson, ed., 1987, 228–29)

Bagramyan briefed the army and corps commanders with the help of a model of the entire defensive system, and the troops were rehearsed in their task on full-scale mock-ups of structures in Königsberg.

If the Soviet planning was meticulous in matters of technical detail, it was bold and simple in fundamental concept. Central and western Königsberg were to be cut open by a pincer movement coming

- from the south (the powerful Eleventh Guards Army) and
- from the north and north-west (Fiftieth and Forty-Third Armies).

Further west the Thirty-Ninth Army was to strike towards the Haff and threaten the communication with Samland.

A spell of rain set in on 1 April, and forced the Russians to postpone the start of their four days of preliminary bombardment, which was due that morning. The weather was no better when the marshal arrived to take charge in person:

Vasilevskii put a telephone call through to the supreme commander to report the situation. 'He wants us to make haste,' he said ruefully, after finishing his conversation with

Stalin. 'The Berlin Operation is close on our heels, you know . . .' Then, looking at the sheet of drizzling rain and the heavy clouds hanging over the muddy ground, he said with resolution in his voice: 'We must get going!' (Bagramyan, in Erickson, ed., 1987, 234)

The Second Siege of Königsberg, 2–10 April 1945

On 2 April Russian howitzers and heavy mortars opened the artillery preparation by raining shells and bombs on the earth covering of the forts. The heavy artillery was then directed against the pillboxes and the masonry of the forts, and finally, after this protracted softening-up, the main bombardment broke on the morning of 6 April, while aircraft flew in low with their guns blazing:

> The city fell into ruins and burned. The German positions were smashed, the trenches ploughed up, embrasures levelled with the ground, companies buried, the signals system torn apart, and ammunition stores destroyed. Clouds of smoke lay over the remnants of the houses of the inner city. On the streets were strewn fragments of masonry, shot-up vehicles and the bodies of horses and human beings. (Dieckert and Grossmann, 1960, 176)

Already on this first day the Russians smashed through vital sectors of the perimeter. The Eleventh Guards Army in the south pushed as far as the railway station, while the Forty-Third Army attacking from the north-west stove in the 548th Volksgrenadier Division, and severed it from the companion 561st Volksgrenadier Division and the forces in Samland. Lasch committed his reserves, without being able to hold the line, and forts and other strongpoints began to fall.

The events of the next day, 7 April, convinced Lasch that the end was near. Further ground was lost in the south, where the

Eleventh Guards Army broke through to the wharves on the left bank of the Pregel. In the north the Forty-Third Army widened its breach, while the Thirty-Ninth Army, attacking towards Seerappen, absorbed the attention of the 5th Panzer Division and prevented it from reopening the communication from Samland. Meanwhile the Volkssturm were breaking apart, and the German wounded were piling up in makeshift hospitals in the cellars of the city.

On 8 April forces of the Eleventh Guards Army crossed the Pregel by boat and united at Amalienau on the north bank with units of the Forty-Third Army, a stroke which cut the last possible avenue of communication between Königsberg and the forces which were fighting on the Samland side west of the breakthrough—the 5th Panzer Division and the 561st Volksgrenadier Division. It now dawned on Deputy Gauleiter Grossherr and the Party personnel that Königsberg was doomed, and they called on the military to organise some kind of mass escape to Samland. Lasch supported the idea in principle, and he wished to throw the main force of the garrison to the west, as he had done so successfully on 19 January. It was necessary, however, to refer the scheme to General Müller, who radioed from his headquarters in Samland that the first priority must be to hold the city, and that only a few specially designated units could be set aside to force open the necessary corridor for the civilian population.

To give the break-out some small chance of success, Lasch detached whatever forces he could spare from his eastern perimeter. The redeployments to the west were carried out under nightmarish conditions after darkness fell on 8 April, and Major Lewinski, who commanded the 192nd Grenadier Regiment, found that whole companies went astray even before they could reach the start line of the intended attack:

> Every company was furnished with guides who knew the ground. It later transpired that they were useless, for local knowledge ceased to be of any help in the inferno which had

once been the inner city of Königsberg. Ghostly lunar landscapes came into being in place of the great avenues which used to lead through the city. Paths could be reconnoitred, and just an hour later they were impassable. There was a continual crashing from the impact of bombs, shells, and heavy Katyusha rockets, while the remaining facades of the buildings collapsed into the streets and the ground was torn up by mighty bomb craters. (Lasch, 1977, 98)

Trucks, artillery pieces and assault guns came pressing in from north and south, and finally jammed immovably together.

The confusions of the night were compounded when at 0030 on 9 April the Party authorities, without reference to Lasch, passed the word for the civilian population to assemble on the old Pillau road. The whole mass set off westwards at 0200. Major-General Erich Sudau took the lead in an armoured car, which provided a semblance of military efficiency, but the civilian population and their vehicles occupied the whole width of the road behind. All this commotion attracted the notice of the Russians, who swamped the area with fire:

The enemy opened up with infantry weapons of all kinds, mortars, artillery and Katyushas against this ill-led and confused mob of soldiers, Party officials and civilians. The result was a frightful blood-bath. Sudau was badly wounded and shortly afterwards expired on the spot. Grossherr fell together with a number of other Party functionaries. Heartbreaking scenes were played out among the civilians. Many of them tried to drag their badly wounded relatives back into the city, and were themselves struck down. (Thorwald, 1950, 200)

Daylight showed that the city was enveloped in a bank of smoke, which was repeatedly pierced by the fiery tails of the Katyushas. German resistance was now reduced to seven main pockets in the centre of Königsberg, and by now women were hanging white sheets from their windows and trying to snatch the rifles from the soldiers' hands. It was clear to Lasch that the days of the Reich were numbered, that he had been abandoned by the High Command and that the situation in Königsberg was hopeless:

> But what proved conclusive in the judgment I now had to make was the recognition that fighting on would only result in the senseless sacrifice of further thousands of my soldiers and civilians. I could not justify such a conduct to God or my conscience. I therefore resolved to cease fighting and put an end to the horror. (Lasch, 1977, 106)

In the morning Lasch told all the accessible German commanders of his decision. After considerable difficulties he established communication with the Soviet command, and a Russian deputation eventually arrived at the Paradeplatz and negotiated the surrender, promising to take care of the wounded and guaranteeing good treatment of the prisoners as a whole.

Capitulation was intolerable to the diehards of the Polizeikampfgruppe Schuberth, forming a body of between 120 and 150 police and SS who threw themselves into the old castle. Here they sustained heavy casualties under Russian mortar fire, and towards midnight on 9–10 April Police Major Voigt ordered the survivors to break out to Samland. As far as is known, not a single man of the first group survived. Voigt was shot down almost immediately, and Police Major-General Schuberth (who had conceded the active command to Voigt) was run to earth in an abandoned bunker near Juditten, where he committed suicide or was eliminated by grenades. The remnants of the battle group were reduced still further when they made a second and equally unsuccessful attempt to break free, and the survivors and the wounded offered no resistance when a Russian party entered the cellars and invited them to give themselves up.

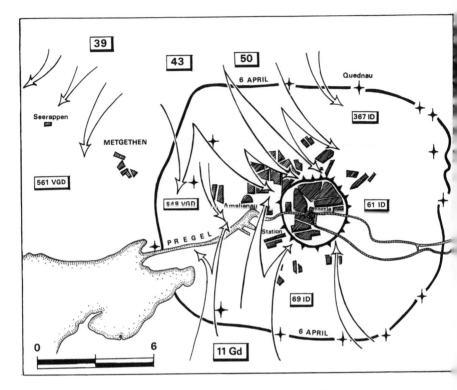

12. **The storm of Königsberg, 6–10 April 1945**

The technicalities of the surrender of Königsberg were completed at the Russian command post on the morning of 10 April:

Vasilevskii ordered the captured generals to be brought into the room. They came in and stood before us in silence with drooping heads. The fortress commandant [Lasch] looked particularly downcast and wretched. We knew that there was another reason for his gloom, quite apart from the fact that he was a prisoner of war. We had learned from radio monitoring that the imbecile Führer had declared him a traitor for the surrender of the fortress and ordered the arrest of his family. Obviously, General Lasch was depressed by this.

216

Only one of the prisoners, an engineer general, behaved as arrogantly as if we were his prisoners, not the other way round. His hatred for us lurked in every fold of his flabby and coarse brewer's face. (Bagramyan, in Erickson, ed., 1987, 242)

The 30,000 to 35,000 surviving German troops marched out to captivity amid demeaning scenes. Russian soldiers threw themselves into the column from all sides, snatching coats, caps and watches. The work of plunder was completed in the railway workshops, after which the prisoners were marched away to distant camps:

The houses burned and smoked. The Russians were adding to the stuffed furniture, musical instruments, kitchen utensils, paintings and china which they had already thrown from the windows. Shot-up cars stood between blazing tanks, and items of clothing and equipment were strewn about. Drunken Russians staggered around. They fired in wild abandon, or tried to ride bicycles—and then fell off and lay bleeding and unconscious in the gutters. Weeping and struggling girls and women were dragged into the houses, and children called after their parents. The sights were intolerable. We marched on . . . (quoted in Lasch, 1977, 115)

The End in Samland, 13–27 April 1945

Just three days after Königsberg had fallen, Marshal Vasilevskii turned the weight of the 3rd Belorussian Front against the Samland peninsula, where all the surviving German forces had been reconstituted into an Armee Ostpreussen under the command of a native Samlander, General Dietrich von Saucken, who took over the command from the incompetent Müller on 11 April:

Von Saucken had been carved from exceptionally hard and tough wood. He had been wounded in both world wars, and

217

he had proved himself a successful leader of men on many critical occasions. He was one of those generals who led their troops from the front rank, and his unimpeachable conduct earned him the unreserved trust of his men and his superiors alike. (Dieckert and Grossmann, 1960, 182–83)

However, von Saucken had been sent too late to save even this remaining corner of East Prussia, where six badly run-down German divisions were deployed on an irregular frontage across the Samland peninsula against an entire Russian army group.

On 13 April, the first day of the new offensive, the Russians broke through the two divisions on the German left and began to flood northern Samland with tanks. The Germans fought to hold a coherent front until the fifteenth, when they collapsed in the direction of the southern coast. The disintegration was almost total in the 5th Panzer Division, which had been a crack armoured formation but was now reduced to a loose collection of infantry combat teams. The main forces of the 5th Panzer now augmented the general confusion when they cut across the general axis of retreat, which was towards the narrow tongue of land leading to Pillau, and instead made south-east to their old base at Peyse. Colonel Hoppe, four officers and thirty-one men covered themselves with honour by halting the shipment of the wounded in order to make good their own escape: 'Here was further proof of the hopeless position of the troops and their desperation in the final days of the struggle —the fact that men of this battle-tested regiment could take it on themselves to abandon their comrades. . . . Nevertheless, the division as a whole kept up the fight in an exemplary way until the bitter end' (Plato, 1978, 397).

On 16 April the Russians broke into the northern part of Fischhausen, half-way along the coast between Peyse and Pillau. 'Sea, sun and springtime weather! . . . The guns were still thundering before Pillau, but the soldiers were already talking about a rapid end to the war, about home' (Beloborodov, 1978, 391).

Colonel Herzog had taken command of the 5th Panzer Division only a matter of days before. He had been a lawyer in civilian life, but in eight years of service in the division he had risen from private soldier to become one of its most respected officers. His confidence, however, was sapped because he knew that the war was being mismanaged at every political and military level, and now that the Russians were in Fischhausen he concluded that his forces in the Peyse peninsula were lost. At 1530 on 16 April he ordered a *sauve qui peut*: 'The division is cut off on the Peyse peninsula, and there is no prospect of restoring communications. I wish you the best of luck!' (Plato, 1978, 309).

A number of men were able to take the last craft to leave Peyse harbour. The rest tried to make rafts out of whatever materials were available, or melted into the wooded hinterland. Herzog and probably the greater part of his troops were captured almost at once.

The remaining forces of the Armee Ostpreussen fell back south-west to the narrow Pillau peninsula, where a comparable disaster was threatening. However, a band of assorted heroes held the Russians for four days at the improvised Tenkitten barrier, running across the base of the peninsula, which won time for most of von Saucken's command to be ferried the few hundred metres to the relative safety of the Nehrung sandspit. The last stages of the evacuation were covered by three permanent artillery emplacements in the neighbourhood of Pillau. The last to fall was Batterie Lehmberg, where Major Karl Henke and his little combat team fought on at bayonet point until they were wiped out by the Russians at 1530 on 27 April.

CHAPTER 18

Danzig and Gotenhafen

The Massing of Forces, 10–14 March 1945

THE SOVIET THREAT to West Prussia had materialised very quickly indeed (see p. 192). In the first week of March the Russians drove north through East Pomerania to the sea, whereupon Marshal Rokossovskii's 2nd Belorussian Front wheeled north-east like a giant gate, with its hinge on the Vistula near Marienwerder, and the outer edge sweeping clockwise along the Baltic coastlands. This movement jammed the Germans in West Prussia against the western shore of the Bight of Danzig in the area of Gotenhafen and the city of Danzig, where the mass of humanity comprised about 1.5 million German civilian refugees, 100,000 wounded troops, and what was left of the German Second Army (from north to south the 4th SS Police Division, the 7th Panzer Division, the 215th, 32nd, 227th, 83rd, 73rd, 389th and 252nd Infantry divisions, the 4th Panzer Division, the 12th Luftwaffe Field Division, the 542nd Volksgrenadier Division, and the 35th and 23rd Infantry divisions, with the 7th Infantry Division between the mouth of the Vistula and the Nogat branch).

Behind the retreating German field army, General Karl-Wilhelm Specht, the local commander of the Danzig military district, was doing all he could to turn the region of Danzig and Gotenhafen into a fortress which would hold out 'to the last round,' as Hitler has just decreed. During the period of Polish rule in West Prussia (1920–39), the Poles had built the new port of Gotenhafen (Gdynia) and furnished it with a series of coastal fortifications. However, less attention had been paid to the landward approaches, and the first task for Specht was to establish defensive positions along the wooded heights which ran to the west of Danzig and Gotenhafen.

Because the 2nd Belorussian Front came from Pomerania, the Russians were in the odd position of advancing east, while the Germans awaiting them faced west. Both the Russians (Babadzhanyan, 1981, 272) and the Germans found the reversal of front disconcerting. Some of the German soldiers were put to work thirty-two kilometres inland of the coastal resort of Zoppot:

> I had no idea where the enemy was, but it seemed to me that the positions that we were organising faced the wrong way. The anti-tank guns and anti-aircraft guns pointed west and south-west—the only directions in which retreat was possible. I couldn't understand it—but that made no difference! It wasn't the first time, and others were undoubtedly thinking for us. (Sajer, 1971, 444)

In the second week of March the contest for the fortified region began to assume a recognisable shape. The main force of the German Second Army was consolidating in the prepared positions in the tangled country inland of Danzig and Gotenhafen. The outer defences were probed by the enemy as early as 8 March, but the Russian armoured spearheads made little further progress until the rifle forces came up to support them, which took several days more. The going was difficult in this bosky and broken terrain, and the streams overflowed their banks in the thaw and rain: 'The infantry were in sodden, heavy greatcoats, and in mud up to their knees. The vehicles had to be towed along the disintegrating roads' (Ivanov, 1980, 23).

On 12 March General Dietrich von Saucken took over command of the Second Army from Colonel-General Walter Weiss, who was an Austrian and a stranger to this part of the world. We have come across von Saucken twice before—when he retreated across Poland with the Grossdeutschland Panzer Corps, and when he arrived in his native Samland in the closing stages of the defence of East Prussia. He was a first-class professional soldier, and he came to West Prussia with a clear sense of where his duties lay, which was not necessarily in obedience to orders: 'He was a son of East Prussia, and what mattered to him still more was his concern for the conglomerated mass of the refugees, whom he was determined to save from the grasp of the Russians' (Dieckert and Grossmann, 1960, 165). This principle guided all his dealings with the High Command and the Party authorities.

Von Saucken was repeatedly assured from Berlin that ammunition for the Second Army was 'on the way' by sea. Nothing materialised until a freighter bound for Kurland was immobilised by fire in Danzig harbour. For the best reasons of safety von Saucken took the cargo of ammunition on shore, where the Second Army naturally found good uses for it. The military bureaucracy threatened him with a dire fate if he attempted anything of the sort again.

Within the theatre of war von Saucken took direct control over all matters which concerned the welfare of the civilians. The Party leadership of the *Gau* of Danzig-West Prussia was in no state to offer effective competition, for it lay in the hands of that complex and not unsympathetic figure, Albert Forster. He was a fundamentally decent man (which could not be said of many of his fellow gauleiters), but one who was now breaking apart under a weight of contradictions.

Forster was a fervent Catholic, who nevertheless continued to find in Hitler an unfailing source of inspiration:

> I still believe in some kind of miracle. I still believe in Almighty God, who has given us our Führer, and destined him to make Germany free and turn it into a final bulwark of Western culture against the onslaught from the East. There can be no other explanation for the way God preserved him

on 20 July. All that is left is for the West to recognise where its real enemy lies. (quoted in Thorwald, 1950, 262)

The turn of events in West Prussia in 1945 reduced Forster to incapacity. He took refuge on the Hela peninsula, and he returned to the mainland for a single visit on 4 April, when the sights on the Vistula delta struck him literally dumb and precipitated a total collapse.

From the Opening of the Attack to the Breakthrough at Zoppot, 15–22 March 1945

On 13 March the Soviet 2nd Belorussian Front was concentrating in front of the Danzig-Gotenhafen fortified region, and Marshal Rokossovskii cast his plans for the assault. The action was going to be continuous along the whole frontage, with six armies converging from west, south-west and south, but Rokossovskii assigned a particularly important role to the Seventieth and the Forty-Ninth, which were ordered to advance shoulder-to-shoulder to the coast in the neighbourhood of Zoppot, thereby cutting the region in two, Danzig and Gotenhafen could then be reduced as isolated halves.

Heavy fighting raged on all sectors from 15 March. The Kriegsmarine continued to evacuate the refugees by day and night under heavy air attack, while the German troops contested the wet country south-east of Danzig and the wooded hills to the west of the fortified region. Forward observers directed the supporting fire from the old battleship *Schlesien*, the heavy cruiser *Prinz Eugen* and the light cruiser *Leipzig*, whose silhouettes were outlined clearly against the horizon of the bight, and when the shells arrived, 'the ground trembled and shook, and any window panes still in place fell out' (Sajer, 1971, 445).

The German commanders conducted the defence in a very aggressive way. They counterattacked the Russian gains, and if the Russians failed to come forward, the *Landser* were liable to be sent out to attack *them*. In such a way Guy Sajer and a few comrades of Grossdeutschland found themselves pitted in open ground against three Russian tanks. Two of the monsters were stopped by anti-tank rockets, but the third rolled forward:

> It had accelerated, and was no more than thirty yards from us, when I grabbed the last Panzerfaust. One of my comrades had already fired, and I was temporarily blinded. I stiffened my powers of vision and regained my sight to see a multitude of rollers caked with mud churning past in a dull roar of sound some five or six yards from me. An inhuman cry of terror rose from our helpless throats.
>
> The tank withdrew into the noise of battle, and finally disappeared in a volcanic eruption which lifted it from the ground in a thick cloud of smoke. Our wildly staring eyes tried to fix on something solid, but could find nothing but smoke and flame. (Sajer, 1971, 447)

On 19 March, however, the grinding Russian progress began to yield tangible results. On the Zoppot sector the Russian storm detachments mastered a height which gave them a view over the town of Zoppot and the shore of the bight. Further south Danzig came under artillery fire, and the 4th Panzer Division was pushed back to within two kilometres of the western edge. Von Saucken had once commanded this formation, and he now visited his old comrades, who demanded to know why they were expected to put up such a tough fight for 'an insignificant scrap of land' (Paul, 1978, 227). He explained that the army must cover the naval base at Hela and provide a shield for the evacuation of the civilians and the wounded from Danzig and Gotenhafen.

On 20 March the Russian tanks still encountered heavy opposition in the dripping woods west of Zoppot, but the German shipping came under artillery fire for the first time, and the Russians standing on the hills had a fine prospect of the supporting strike by Western bombers:

> They flew in above our heads, and proceeded to engage the town, the port and the Hitlerite naval squadron. The whole sky was flecked with tufts of detonating anti-aircraft shells, and a few of the planes exploded in the air. For the whole day the earth shuddered with the bursts of bombs and artillery rounds. (Gorb, 1976, 251)

22 March was the decisive day of the whole operation, for the Russians broke through to the sea north of Zoppot, and the Danzig-Gotenhafen Fortified Region was therefore reduced to two contracting bridgeheads.

The End at Gotenhafen, 23–27 March 1945

The Russians were now within artillery range of the centre of Danzig, and their commanders were now meditating how best to take Gotenhafen—an enterprise which demanded a very carefully planned attack. At this juncture the First Guards Tank Army was rewarded with a stroke of luck:

> A pretty young Polish girl reached one of the little villages not far from Gotenhafen and presented herself to I. F. Dremov, the commander of the VIII Guards Mechanised Corps. She delivered a map. Dremov scrutinised it narrowly, and realised that he had in his hands a map of the fortress of Gotenhafen, showing the entire German fire system. Dremov paused for thought; was this a happy chance, or was it some kind of fascist provocation?
> Mixing Polish words with Russian, the girl drew attention

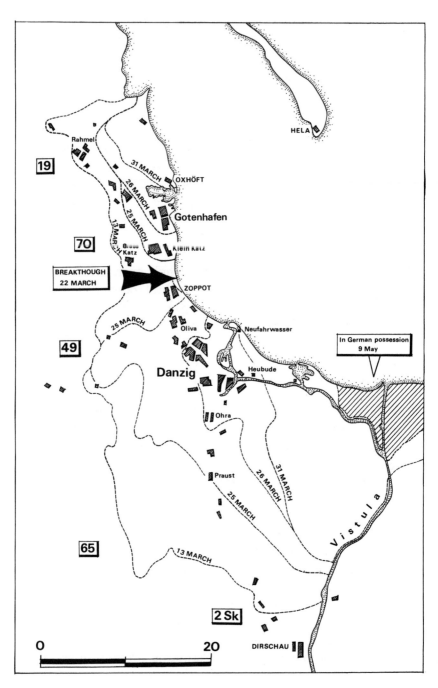

13. The siege of Danzig, 15–28 March 1945

to the most vulnerable locations of the fortress, and the sectors where it could be attacked to the best advantage. (Katukov, 1976, 385)

The map proved to be authentic, and storm detachments of the First Guards Tank Army proceeded to make their first penetrations of the town proper. The girl saved much Russian blood, and it transpired after the war that she had been a member of a Polish resistance network.

Between 24 and 26 March the Kriegsmarine put all its available resources into rescuing the refugees and the wounded, while the Russians fought their way through the town centre and brought the German steamers, barges and motor boats under direct fire. At first the storm detachments of the First Guards Tank Army made poor practice:

> Our observers were accustomed to directing fire on dry land, and to begin with, the range to the targets across water proved deceptive. Gradually, however, the tank gunners and the artillerymen learned to adjust their elevation. A gun would fire, then came the explosion of the shell, and another craft capsized and went to the bottom with its load of fascists. Another shot, then another—and a barge flared up and heeled over. (Katukov, 1976, 386)

On 26 March the artillery of the Russian Nineteenth Army heralded the final assault on Gotenhafen:

> We could see the houses where the Germans were hiding, and also the town cemetery, where the Hitlerites were likewise ensconced. The brigade signals commander Major Banit reported that the network for directing the fire was ready. Then, all of a sudden, the Katyushas opened up behind our backs and the rockets flew over our heads. The softening up by the tubed artillery then began, and the town was enveloped in clouds of dust and smoke. (Skorobogatov, 1976, 199)

The Germans had already begun to scuttle ships and blow up the harbour installations, and during the night of 26–27 March the last defenders and a few of the surviving civilians streamed northwards along to coast to a refuge on the Oxhöft peninsula.

The End at Danzig, 23–28 March 1945

The last act at Danzig was played out under a pall of sulphur-yellow smoke. Without authority from Forster or von Saucken the Feldgendarmerie and the SS *Sonderkommandos* roamed the streets, meting out summary justice to all those they considered to have failed in their duty. The victims ranged from shell-shocked *Landser* to terrified boys of the air-defence service, and whole rows of trees along the Hindenburgallee bore suspended forms. The placards slung around their necks announced the crime: 'I was too cowardly to fight,' 'I hang here because I abandoned my unit without permission' and so on.

The spirit of the front-line troops broke on 27 March, and the process was hastened when the men learned that the commander of the 4th Panzer Division, Lieutenant-General Clemens Betzel, had been killed by a shell. The division fell back on Langfuhr, and the dispatch rider Robert Poensgen was sent to inform the rearward elements about the move. At a cross-roads in Danzig he found that he was in the middle of a strike by Katyushas and tubed artillery:

> With all my strength I pressed on the brakes, I threw my motor cycle around on the street, and before it had come to a stop, I was crouching in the corner of a wall. Around me all hell broke loose. This whole area of the town was being thrashed by round after round of heavy and superheavy calibre. Houses broke apart like bundles of kindling, roof timbers were hurled high into the air and masonry crashed into the street. In an instant everything was shrouded in a red-brick dust. Yellow and red flames flashed and flared repeat-

edly through the veil, and the explosion of a round projected a column of fire up through the dust. (Schäufler, 1973, 231)

Worse, much worse, awaited Poensgen on the far side of the Vistula arm at Heubude:

> For kilometres on end the road was totally jammed with vehicles drawn up three or four abreast—petrol tankers, ammunition trucks, teams of horses, ambulances. It was impossible to move forwards or back. Russian combat aircraft now arrived in wave after wave, and threw bombs into that unprotected, inextricable mass. This is what hell must be like. Ammunition exploded, and burning petrol sprayed over dead, wounded and living, over men and horses. It looked like a heap of scrap metal in an annealing chamber of huge dimensions. It was the worst thing I have ever seen in all my years of active service—and I tell you I had already seen a lot. (Schäufler, 1973, 234)

Now that his front was caving in, von Saucken ordered the evacuation of Danzig to be completed on the night of 27–28 March. At midnight the staff of the 4th Panzer Division made for the arm of the Vistula delta which extended behind Danzig. Betzel's coffin was covered with the *Reichskriegsflagge* and was fastened to his old command tank. His Kubelwagen car followed behind, and the cortège made its way through the ruined moonlit streets. The column came to a temporary halt in the Hundgasse,

> and in front of us . . . we could see the dispatch riders of the various units. Girls from Zoppot and Danzig were sitting in some of the sidecars. They had been with the troops for some days now, and nobody objected to that. We noted the dearly beloved of the dispatch rider from the Pioneers—she was a pretty railway conductress, and he was determined to marry her at the first opportunity.

There was something sinister about the way the narrow gables of the old houses soared into the sky. They were thin, and they seemed to sway in the wind. The thought was still in my mind when someone yelled a warning from in front: 'Watch out! The wall's coming down!' I saw the motor cycles buzz into confused movement in a fraction of a second, and then the wall broke into several pieces in the air and crashed on the crowd. There was a roar, a crack, a violent gust of air—and then an impenetrable cloud of dust. I stood as if paralysed on the running board.

We all hastened to the scene of the catastrophe, where the debris lay nearly one metre deep over the motor cycles. All the soldiers were safe—for years now their reactions had been honed to lightning speed, and they had been able to leap to one side. But the girls had not moved from the sidecars and they were all buried. Cold sweat ran down our backs as we began to dig like madmen. The little Pioneer dispatch rider seemed to be out of his mind. We helped him to lift his dead bride from the sidecar. With extreme care he proceeded to wash her face, which was covered with a thick layer of dust. (Schäufler, 1973, 241–42)

The procession moved on and passed the Vistula bridge. Daylight showed the abandoned city of Danzig burning along the south-western horizon, and the wrecked vehicles of the Second Army which littered the woods along the bank of the river.

The Last Bridgeheads

By the end of March the German forces on the Bight of Danzig were holding three isolated pockets:

- The sandy Hela peninsula reached down from the north-west, offering a refuge which was secure against all but air attack until the end of the war, and the naval and fishing ports near the tip at Hela town received or transhipped hundreds of thousands of refugees during the weeks of spring (see p. 290).

- On the mainland eight thousand soldiers and many more civilians from Gotenhafen had assembled on the coastal plateau of the Oxhöfter Kämpe. Hitler now ordered the open Oxhöft headland to be defended as one of his 'fortresses,' which was patently absurd, and the Kriegsmarine and von Saucken colluded to ship all the troops and refugees to Hela. The Germans completed the work when the last craft left at 1600 on 5 April. Five hours later Hitler gave his consent for von Saucken to abandon the peninsula.

- The Danziger Werder, the marshy meadows of the Vistula delta, received the German troops and civilians who had escaped from Danzig. The long eastward extension, the Nehrung sandspit, offered salvation for those coming from Samland. The German pioneers had blown up the Vistula dykes on 27 March, releasing a flood of water which made the delta inaccessible to the Russian land forces. There was, however, no protection against the Soviet air strikes, and the German troops and civilians were pounded into such a state of insensibility that many of them had to be hauled from their foxholes when vessels arrived to take them off. All the civilians were evacuated by the beginning of May, and von Saucken decided that the troops must follow. The shipments were still taking place when, on 9 May, the High Command ordered that the whole remaining force must surrender to the Russians.

CHAPTER 19

Kolberg

KOLBERG was a small port which stood at the mouth of the Persante River in the centre of an otherwise empty stretch of the sandy East Pomeranian coast. It was famous in Prussian history for having undergone five sieges, most notably by the French in 1807 (see p. 287). In 1872, however, it was stripped of its military role. The fortifications were demolished in the course of the next year, and Kolberg survived undisturbed until it was again declared a 'fortress' in November 1944.

Little had been done to put Kolberg in a state of defence before Colonel Fritz Fullriede, an old colonial hand from South-West Africa, arrived on 1 March 1945 to inspect the progress of the work. He found that the railway station was jammed with refugees and trains waiting to leave for the West, and that a further twenty trains were stranded outside. Fullriede did what he could to relieve the congestion while the line to the Oder was still open, but the local kreisleiter refused to cooperate, saying that he had received no such authority from the Pomeranian Gauleiter Franz Schwede-Coburg (who was a notoriously brutal individual).

By now Russian commanders had unspread their maps of Pomerania and were jabbing with stubby fingers at Kolberg, for this little town was the terminal point of the formation boundary between the 1st and 2nd Belorussian fronts in the opening phase of their East Pomeranian Operation. On 4 March the leading units of the First Guards Tank Army reached the coast on either side of Kolberg, making it physically impossible for any more refugees to escape from the town by land. The

Russian army then turned east for some more urgent business in the direction of Gotenhafen (see p. 194), and its place before Kolberg was taken by an initial two divisions of the First Polish Army, which had a Soviet regiment of self-propelled artillery under its command.

Inside Kolberg the Germans had a feeble and motley force comprising broken units of the Wehrmacht, two poorly equipped Volkssturm battalions, and stranded personnel of the Luftwaffe and the Kriegsmarine. The total military personnel amounted to about 3,300, of whom around 2,200 were combatants. In fact, OKH regarded it as a near-miracle that someone was defending Kolberg at all, for the von Tettau corps group (see p. 197), which should have been defending this area, had been cut off to the west of the First Guards Tank Army's breakthrough. Fullriede himself had come merely to make an inspection, as we have seen, and it was only the force of circumstances which installed him as commandant. The garrison and town were swamped by 68,000 civilians, most of whom were refugees from the hinterland.

It was clear that Kolberg had to be defended at all costs. Most immediately, Colonel Fullriede had to provide a shield behind which the civilians could be evacuated by the Kriegsmarine. In a wider context he was supposed to draw the enemy away from the northern flank of the von Tettau group, as Guderian emphasised in a telephone conversation with the headquarters of Army Group Vistula on 3 March.

From 13 March the combined Polish and Russian forces began to attack in a more systematic way, and some particularly threatening thrusts developed in the direction of the harbour from both sides of the Persante. After a desperate scramble of a fight on the morning of 14 March, the Poles used the open radio at 1530 to demand the surrender of Kolberg. Fullriede had just managed to stabilise his front, and he was content to reply: 'The commandant has taken due notice.' A second summons at 1600 went unanswered.

The Germans had contrived to hold on thus far with the help

of two destroyers (Z 34 and Z 43) which stood off shore firing their 150-mm guns. Within the perimeter the Germans had only four tanks (Mark IVs), and even these eventually broke down and had to be hauled around by trucks. It was impossible to dig trenches, because the water table was so high, and the Germans were forced to hold out in shallow scrapes in the ground and in the collapsing houses.

Towards the end of the siege the losses through enemy action amounted to 40 per cent of the defenders as a whole, and 60 per cent of the Volkssturm, and yet the perimeter had contracted so much that there was scarcely room for the survivors to fight. Two companies of the 5th Fortress Regiment (Festungsregiment 5) were landed on 15 March, contrary to Fullriede's wishes, and these low-grade newcomers proved to be useless in the intense fighting in the burning town.

This dearly bought time allowed the Kriegsmarine to thin out the waiting masses of the civilians, who were suffering terribly from artillery fire and the effects of the foul water. Nearly all the babies fell ill and died, and whole families committed suicide so as to put an end to their collective misery.

From 11 March the two destroyers and the torpedo boat T 33 operated a shuttle service from Swinemünde, arriving off Kolberg to bombard the enemy, taking on board refugees from small craft, and returning to Swinemünde to replenish their ammunition.

The first lift by destroyer Z 34 involved 800 civilians and 120 wounded soldiers, and this cargo had the misfortune to arrive at Swinemünde simultaneously with the warning of a major raid by American B-17s and B-24s:

> There was a deathly hush on the bridge of the craft, and we could already hear the dull drone of a large number of heavy bombers reverberating from above the low-hanging clouds. Vessels of all kinds were fleeing in panic from the harbour. They rushed past us at full speed in an attempt to reach the safety of the sea before the raid began.

While the refugees were still below decks, Captain Hetz backed away from the dockside, turned in the fareway and made for the open sea:

> We steamed out again at fifteen knots. We had just passed the lighthouse when we heard the roar of a carpet of bombs landing on the town and harbour of Swinemünde. A high white wall signified where a line of bombs descended on the exact place where we had turned. The paralysing tension gradually relaxed, and while we were repassing the moles on the way out two refugee children appeared on deck. They were holding hands and laughing with joy. That made us happier than anything for a long time. (Kurowski, 1987, 287–88)

On 16 March the shipment of the refugees and wounded was completed. It was only just in time, for on that day the Poles were reinforced by the 6th Leningrad Rocket Artillery Brigade, and its Katyushas went into action immediately. By 17 March the Germans were reduced to holding a strip which measured 1,800 metres long and 400 metres deep. The Poles were about to break through to the west bank of the Persante, and in the afternoon Fullriede decided that he had done everything that was required of him, and that his last obligation was to save his men 'for further operations in Germany.' The evacuation went ahead overnight.

Lieutenant Hempel and a small rearguard beat off a final attack, and left by destroyer Z 43 at 0630 on 18 March, which set a seal on an operation which had been carried through to a successful end on the narrowest margins of resources and space. Goebbels kept the news of the fall of Kolberg out of the communiqués, which must have sharpened Fullriede's apprehension, but in the event, the last German commandant of Kolberg was rewarded with the Knight's Cross of the Iron Cross at the hands of the Führer on 26 March.

CHAPTER 20

The Altdamm Bridgehead

In GENERAL SHAPE, the Soviet East Pomeranian Operation may be compared with a monstrous fleur-de-lys. The head was directed at Kolberg and Köslin on the Baltic coastlands, while the right-hand petal extended towards the Bight of Danzig. To the left, or west, the flower curved towards the lower reaches of the Oder in the neighbourhood of Stettin, where we take up the sequence of events.

By the second week of March the only significant German forces remaining on the eastern side of the Oder were von Tettau's roving cauldron and the very diverse formations holding the Altdamm bridgehead, which extended for about eighty kilometres from Greifenhagen in the south to the area of Gollnow in the north. The town of Altdamm lay half-way between the two, and was an outlying east-bank suburb of the city-port of Stettin.

The Altdamm bridgehead was no beleaguered garrison, like Königsberg, Danzig or Kolberg, for it backed directly onto the heartland of the Reich, from where it received successive reinforcements. The defence was directed by the headquarters of the Third Panzer Army, which deployed about 105,000 men on its total frontage of rather more than 100 kilometres.

The terrain was excellent for purposes of defence. The high, wooded and heavily broken Bruchheide extended like a screen in front of the bridgehead, while the Oder River with its branches, marshes and inundations secured the flanks and rear. The Germans had good reason to stand their ground here, for as long as they held the bridgehead, they

- kept open a sanctuary for refugees and broken troops from East Pomerania;
- tied down large forces of the right flank of the 1st Belorussian Front;
- barred an important entry to north central Germany;
- maintained communication with the important naval base of Swinemünde and the open sea.

The first Russian effort against the bridgehead was a feeble affair, which developed from 6 March, when the Forty-Seventh Army pushed northwards down the Oder towards Greifenhagen, and the Sixty-First attacked frontally from the east (see p. 195). Zhukov ended the initial effort on 12 March, for he now recognised that the bridgehead could not be taken at a rush. He withdrew the Third Shock Army for use in the forthcoming Berlin Operation, but kept the Forty-Seventh Army, the Sixty-First and the Second Guards Tank Army in place and brought up four artillery breakthrough divisions, which permitted him to attain a density of 250 to 280 pieces and mortars per kilometre of breakthrough sector.

The Germans put the lull to good use, for it gave them time to strengthen their already formidable positions. Moreover, the Third Panzer Army had a new and energetic leader in General Hasso von Manteuffel, who replaced Colonel-General Erhard Raus on 10 March. When the Russians opened their new offensive on 14 March, they not only encountered the reinforced positions, but they came under fire from hitherto undetected shore batteries and were hit by heavy local counterattacks.

On 15 March, however, Hitler ordered a number of mobile units of the Third Panzer Army away from the front and redeployed them for operations in the direction of Küstrin, and on the nineteenth the Soviet Forty-Seventh Army and the Second Guards Tank Army broke through to the Oder south of Altdamm, cutting the bridgehead in two. Manteuffel presented Hitler with an ultimatum: 'Either withdraw everyone to safety on the west bank of the Oder overnight, or lose the whole lot tomorrow' (Murawski, 1969, 287). The evacuation was completed in the course of the following night, and the Germans blew up the Oder bridges behind them.

On 21 March the Russians eliminated the remaining pockets of resistance in Altdamm town, by which time they claim they had killed some 40,000 Germans in the area of the bridgehead and captured 12,000 more, together with 126 tanks and assault guns, over 200 artillery pieces and 154 mortars. More significantly still, the right wing of the 1st Belorussian Front as a whole was now free to redeploy for the Berlin Operation, which was going to end the war.

The harbour and channel at Stettin were now under direct Russian artillery fire, and therefore unusable, but the Soviets made no further advance against the line of the lower Oder until 25 April, by when the Berlin Operation was well under way.

CHAPTER 21

Küstrin

The Importance of Küstrin

THE FIGHTING in and around Küstrin occupied a central place in the history of the Reich in 1945. This episode accentuated the tensions in the German direction of the war, and led first to the removal of Himmler from active command, and finally to the downfall of the chief of staff, Colonel-General Heinz Guderian.

Küstrin was also central in the geographic sense, for this fortress was sited on an important crossing of the Oder just eighty kilometres east of Berlin, and was 'rightly called the gateway to the German capital' (Chuikov, 1978, 154). The place had a grim reputation which endured through the centuries, and Theodor Fontane, the poet of the Brandenburg landscape, could never bring it to mind without imagining the fortress under a leaden November sky. The core of Küstrin was a citadel which had been built on an island by Master Giromella in the sixteenth century. The future Frederick the Great had been confined there on the orders of his brutal father, King Frederick William I, and on 6 November 1730 the crown prince was dragged to the windows of his cell and forced to watch the scene on the Brandenburg Bastion, where his friend Lieutenant von Katte was beheaded by an executioner. Frederick came this way again in August 1758, after Russian howitzers had reduced the little town of Küstrin to smoking wreckage.

Küstrin in 1945 was a complex of works which spilled over the island and the adjacent banks of the Oder and the Warthe, and it comprised not just the reinforced citadel, but outlying forts, pillboxes and field fortifications. The ground nearby was low-lying and marshy, and the approaches were confined to causeways which were wide enough to accommodate only a single tank. These, however, were passive strengths, and the whole of Küstrin nearly fell at the beginning of February. The Russians won bridgeheads on the west bank of the Oder on both sides of Küstrin, and a regiment of the Fifth Shock Army actually penetrated to the interior of the fortress before it was thrown out again. *Sovinform*, the official news agency, rushed to declare that the Russians had taken Küstrin, and this supposed victory was greeted by salvoes of artillery in Moscow—a public-relations disaster which aroused a certain amusement in General Chuikov, the head of the rival Eighth Guards Army.

In fact, the Russians captured only some outer forts, and they were hard-pressed to hold their two bridgeheads on the far side of the Oder in the face of counterattacks by ground forces and incessant strikes by the Luftwaffe (see p. 120).

When the Vistula-Oder Operation ended, the Germans still held two bridgeheads on the 'Russian' bank of this stretch of the river. These were a southern bridgehead at Frankfurt-an-der-Oder and a more northerly one at Küstrin, which was sustained by a narrow corridor which led east from Berlin. The Küstrin pocket happened to be placed very awkwardly for the purposes of the Russians, for it was interposed between the Eighth Guards Army (Chuikov) in the south and the Fifth Shock Army (Bezarin) in the north, and prevented the Soviets from forming the single large bridgehead which they needed as a launching platform for their final drive against Berlin.

The Frankfurt and Küstrin bridgeheads fell within the sector of the German Ninth Army, which stretched for 120 kilometres down the Oder from the confluence with the Lausitzer Neisse to that with the Hohenzollern Canal. The term 'army' was in fact a misnomer for the congeries of units which the bespectacled and cantankerous General Theodor Busse was assembling from smashed forces from the old Vistula front, together with Volkssturm and all the other kinds of people who were being pressed into service in the last months of the Reich. The rest of the Oder down to the Baltic was the responsibility of the Third Panzer Army. The two armies together effectively made up Army Group Vistula, the Second Army being cut off in East Pomerania, and they had only about 482,000 troops to pit against Zhukov's 750,000.

The Crisis in German Command and the Removal of Himmler and Guderian, 12–29 March 1945

When so much was at stake for Germany, it seems almost incredible that there was nobody to direct the overall defence of the Oder until well into March. Himmler was the nominal commander of Army Group Vistula, but he had sunk completely from sight. At last, on 18 March, Guderian drove out in person to discover what was going on. He found that the great man had abandoned his headquarters at Prenzlau and retired to the care of his doctor in the sanatorium of Hohenlychen. Guderian ran him to earth later the same day, and was disgusted to find that he was suffering from no more than a bad cold. He was determined that Himmler must go, and he suggested that he had taken too much on himself, being simultaneously national leader of the SS, chief of police, minister of the interior, commander-in-chief of the Training Army and commander of Army Group Vistula:

> Each of these posts required the full-time activity of one man, or at least such had been the case during the early stages of the war; and no matter what respect I might have for his ability, such a plethora of offices was bound to be beyond the strength of one individual. Meanwhile he must have realised by now that command of troops at the front is no easy matter. I therefore proposed to him that he give up command of the army group and concentrate on his other offices.

Himmler was no longer so self-confident as in the old days. He hesitated: 'I can't go and say that to the Führer. He wouldn't approve of my making such a suggestion.' I saw my chance and took it: 'Then will you authorise me to say it for you?' Himmler now had to agree. The same evening I proposed to Hitler that the overburdened Himmler be relieved of his command of Army Group Vistula and that in his stead Colonel-General Heinrici, at present in charge of the First Panzer Army in the Carpathians [see p. 146], be appointed to succeed him. Hitler disliked the idea, but after a certain amount of grumbling finally agreed.' (Guderian, 1952, 422)

So it was that after men of action, careerists and Party functionaries had been found wanting, the defence of the core area of the Reich against Russian attack now rested on Colonel-General Gotthard Heinrici, 'a persevering, greying old soldier —a serious, taut little man' (Colonel Hans Georg Eismann, quoted in Ryan, 1980, 69).

Heinrici reached the Maybach camp at Zossen towards noon on 22 March:

Beneath the protective canopy of the forest, Heinrici's car followed one of the many dirt roads that criss-crossed the complex. Spotted among the trees in irregular rows were low concrete buildings. They were so spaced that they got maximum protection from the trees, but just to be sure, they had been painted in drab camouflage colours of green, brown and black. Vehicles were off the roads—parked by the sides of the barracks-like buildings beneath camouflage netting. Sentries were everywhere, and at strategic points around the camp the low humps of manned bunkers rose above the ground. (Ryan, 1980, 57–58)

Craters and other signs of the recent air raid (see p. 50) were all around, and the chief of the Operations Branch of OHK,

General Hans Krebs, was wearing a voluminous head bandage when he greeted Heinrici and introduced him to Guderian. Up to now Heinrici had retained his old image of the colonel-general, and he was struck by the changes which had overtaken him. Guderian was plainly under great stress, and his complexion had an unhealthy reddish hue.

Guderian briefed Heinrici on the resources of the Reich, such as they were, and he revealed that the Germans intended to thrust northwards from the Frankfurt bridgehead to take the group of Russian forces attacking Küstrin in the rear. He added in an alarmingly vague way that as far as he knew the offensive was due to open the day after next and that he wished Heinrici to take control.

A number of objections sprang to Heinrici's lips—the Frankfurt bridgehead was too small to accommodate the troops who were being sent there, the heights inland to the east were held by the Russians and the whole area between there and Küstrin was stuffed with enemy forces. Guderian could only agree, but said that Hitler was adamant that the attempt must be made.

The Soviets had no intention of allowing the Germans the necessary leisure. The 25th Panzer-Grenadier Division was being withdrawn from the Küstrin corridor to take its place in the counterattack, but before it could be fully replaced by the 20th Panzer-Grenadier Division, the Russians attacked the channel from both sides at 0915 on 22 March. Advancing respectively from the Kienitz and Lebus bridgeheads, the Eighth Guards Army and the Fifth Shock Army cut across the corridor and united in the area of Golzow.

Küstrin was now an isolated fortress which was garrisoned by a very small 'Police Army Corps,' amounting to four or five battalion equivalents. The commandant was SS Lieutenant-General (Gruppenführer) Rheinefarth, who was described as 'a good policeman but no general' (Guderian, 1952, 425). However, the Führer was looking for steadfastness rather than high technical skill, and it seemed to be a guarantee of a last-ditch defence that Rheinefarth and the police troops in general had a reputation for cruelty and were marked down for destruction by the Soviets.

We have not yet finished with the events of 22 March, for we must follow Heinrici to Prenzlau where he was due to take over the command of Army Group Vistula from Himmler, who had just returned from his clinic. 'Himmler was standing behind a vast writing table. A portrait of Frederick the Great hung on the panelled wall behind him. His face looked more bloated and weak than ever. He had evidently got over his 'flu, but he looked thoroughly seedy' (Thorwald, 1951, 23).

Heinrici hoped that the hand-over would be a brief formality, but instead Himmler picked up the telephone and ordered his deputy chief of staff and chief of operations to come to him with maps and documents to support his briefing. Himmler then launched into an exposition of the earlier history of the army group. After an hour the shorthand writer laid his pencil down in despair, and Heinrici was unable to find an opportunity to interrupt the monologue before the telephone shrilled. This was General Theodor Busse, who explained that the Russians had just attacked from their two bridgeheads and joined hands behind Küstrin. Himmler handed over the receiver: ' "You're the one who leads the army group now," he said with an air of relief. "Would you kindly give the appropriate orders" ' (Thorwald, 1951, 25). Heinrici unhesitatingly told Busse that he must put in a counterattack on the next day.

Even now Himmler was unwilling to let Heinrici leave, and he added in a quiet voice that he had taken personal steps to negotiate a separate peace with the Western powers. Heinrici did not know what to say, for what Himmler had just admitted was treason, and the tense silence ended when an officer came in to say that the staff of the army group was waiting to bid Himmler farewell.

The 20th and 25th Panzer-Grenadier divisions attacked on 23 March. They were halted by the fire of the overwhelmingly superior Russian artillery soon after they left their start lines, and a second assault met the same reception. Heinrici was convinced that the fighting for Küstrin was wasting fuel and ammunition to no purpose, and he went to Hitler on 25 March to put the case for the garrison to break out and leave the place to the Russians. Hitler recognised that there were difficulties in the way of the grand offensive that was still due to come from the Frankfurt bridgehead, but he argued that the only way for the Germans to gain time, and therefore accumulate stocks of ammunition, was to keep the Russians off balance by dealing blows of just this kind.

On the same day a much more productive meeting was taking place at the headquarters of the Soviet Eighth Guards Army, where Zhukov was conferring with Chuikov. They summoned General G. I. Khetagurov, and without further ado Zhukov asked him:

'How much time do you need to take the fortress of Küstrin?'

I was dumbfounded: 'But surely it has already been taken? We all heard it on the radio.'

Zhukov knitted his brows: 'You weren't asked that! Now answer my question. When do you reckon you can take Küstrin, and what do you need to pull it off?'

Under further interrogation Khetagurov conceded that his own division (82nd Guards Rifle) was suitable for the purpose, and he promised to prepare a plan of assault (Khetagurov, 1977, 188).

On 27 March the Germans undertook very nearly their last offensive actions in the entire war, in the shape of the Ninth Army's long-awaited attack northwards from the Frankfurt bridgehead by four divisions (20th and 25th Panzer-Grenadier, Führer-Begleit, and the scratch Panzer Division Müncheberg). The direction of the offensive took the Russians by surprise, and a number of tanks broke through to the outskirts of Küstrin, but the supporting troops were slaughtered by the artillery in the open ground before they had progressed three kilometres.

Heinrici cast aside his legendary composure when the news came to him. 'The attack was a massacre,' he declared. 'The Ninth Army has suffered incredible losses for almost nothing' (Ryan, 1980, 149). He blamed Guderian for sacrificing 8,000 men, and he paced up and down muttering the word 'Fiasco!' On this occasion Heinrici was unjust, for he was unaware that both he and General Busse were being defended by Guderian against Hitler, who was inclined to put the whole blame for the failure on them. The Führer criticised Busse in particular for the feeble level of artillery support, which he said was one-tenth of what had been available for comparable operations in the Great War.

Guderian knew that Busse had employed the Ninth Army's full available allowance of ammunition. He told Hitler as much in general terms, and then returned to Zossen to check the ammunition state in detail. When he had satisfied himself, he made ready to travel to the Frankfurt bridgehead, for Hitler was set on renewing the attack on a scale of five divisions, but he was forced to abandon his plans when he and Busse were ordered to appear at the Führer briefing on the next day.

The conference got under way at 1400 on 28 March. The discussion began quietly enough, but Guderian knew that Busse had worked untiringly to restore the Ninth Army as a fighting force, and he was determined to go to any lengths to protect him. Guderian's attitude reawakened all of Hitler's resentments against the professional officer caste, and the argument reached such a pitch of violence that the spectators cringed in horror. Hitler and his chief of staff might have come to blows if General Krebs had not drawn the purple-faced Guderian aside for twenty minutes and given everyone an opportunity to calm down. The meeting reconvened for only a very short time:

Hitler said: 'I must ask all you gentlemen to leave the room with the exception of the Field-Marshal [Keitel] and the Colonel-General.' As soon as the large gathering had withdrawn to the anteroom Hitler said to me, briefly: 'Colonel-General Guderian, your physical health requires that you immediately take six weeks' convalescent leave.' (Guderian, 1952, 428)

This was tantamount to a dismissal, and Guderian handed over his post as chief of staff to Krebs on 29 March.

The Reduction of Küstrin, 29–31 March 1945

At 1000 on 29 March the Russian air attacks against Küstrin gave way to a bombardment by the massed artillery, which served as the immediate prelude to the assault by units of the 82nd and 35th Guards Rifle divisions:

> From my observation post, I could see heavy shells fired point-blank slamming into the enemy pillboxes and dugouts on the dykes. It was an impressive sight. . . . Explosions hurled heavy stones and logs high into the air. At 1030 our assault groups disembarked from their boats on the island. Ten minutes later we heard the chatter of machine-gun and automatic fire and explosions of hand grenades and Panzer-fausts. (Chuikov, 1978, 169)

Acting on his own authority, Lieutenant-General Rheinefarth broke out shortly before midnight with a body estimated at between 800 and 1,600 men. The forces in the nearest German lines had not expected friendly troops to be approaching from the direction of Küstrin, and they were persuaded to cease fire only when they heard unmistakably German throats singing *Deutschland über Alles* through the darkness. Rheinefarth himself got through, but he was promptly arrested at the command of Hitler.

By the end of the month the Russians completed the mopping-up of the last survivors inside Küstrin:

The fascists were fighting with the fanaticism of doomed men. Looking back, we can say now that the seeds of the destruction of the Wehrmacht had already been sown in the battle in front of Moscow, but it seemed to us that it was only at Küstrin that we heard the unmistakable finale of the war. (Del'va, 1983, 176)

CHAPTER 22

Posen

ONE of the reasons why the Vistula-Oder Operation ran out of steam was that Zhukov had to detach significant forces to contain and eliminate the cut-off German strongpoints in his rear. The most significant of these was the fortress-city of Posen (see p. 99), where the siege absorbed four divisions of the Eighth Guards Army and two divisions of the Sixty-Ninth Army.

Inside Posen Major-General Ernst Mattern was relieved of the command on 28 January, making way for the newly promoted Major-General Ernst Gonell, an 'inveterate Nazi' (Chuikov, 1978, 137). Gonell imposed an iron hand on the numerically large (60,000) but very mixed garrison, and Chuikov himself saw how a group of German soldiers showed white flags and tried to surrender, only to be shot down by their own officers. The bodies rolled down the ramparts in twos and threes at a time.

The Russians enjoyed an overwhelming superiority in artillery, and they had so much ammunition that they could afford to fire their anti-tank guns at individual soldiers. They drove the Germans from the outlying works and the greater part of the city by the beginning of February, and from the twelfth the resistance was largely confined to the large citadel, which crowned a dominating height above the Warthe.

By 15 February Gonell had lost all confidence that Posen was about to be relieved, and his sense of betrayal was deepened when Himmler (commander of the new Army Group Vistula) refused to allow him to try to save the garrison by breaking out. On his own authority Gonell allowed the troops to the east of the Warthe to escape as best they could, and on the night of 16–17 February 2,000 men slipped through the Russian positions and broke into smaller groups, many of which actually reached friendly lines.

The Soviets opened a formal attack against the survivors in the citadel on 18 February. In the first onslaught the Russian infantry used assault ladders to descend the ditch and climb the rampart on the far side, but the follow-on forces were able to cross only in small groups under a lashing of enfilade fire from two redoubts which proved extraordinarily difficult to silence. At last on 21 February the embrasures of Redoubt No. 2 were swept by a flame-thrower, and small charges of explosives were dropped down the ventilators to eliminate the garrison. The German machine-gunners in the lower casemates of Redoubt No. 1 withstood a great exploding drum and an attack by flame-throwing tanks, and they kept up their fire until the Russians in their desperation threw down wooden crates, barrels and other articles which finally blocked their view.

At 0300 on 22 February Russian tanks and assault guns burst into the citadel across an assault bridge. The battle continued unabated inside the citadel, and the Russians sent in a captured German officer bearing a ferociously worded demand to surrender. Gonell gave his soldiers permission to break out as best they could, after which he retired to his bunker, spread the *Reichskriegsflagge* on the floor, lay down and shot himself through the head. In the event, none of his soldiers were able to make good their escape.

In the evening Chuikov was told at his headquarters in the city theatre that the enemy command desired to surrender. By then the German combatants had been reduced to 12,000 trooops, and they were all penned up in the citadel.

A quarter of an hour later a badly puffing Major-General Mattern—an incredibly stout man who must have weighed about 130 kg—squeezed his frame through the door. Regaining his breath, he handed me a brief note from the fortress *Kommandant*, General Gonell, asking the Soviet command to take care of the German wounded.

'Where is Gonell?' I asked.

'He shot himself.'

When asked how he himself felt, General Mattern shrugged: 'It is all the same to me; I am not a member of the Nazi Party and I would not have shed blood needlessly knowing that resistance is useless. Hitler is finished!' (Chuikov, 1978, 142–43)

CHAPTER 23

Breslau

The First Crisis, February to Early May 1945

THAT OVER-USED WORD 'EPIC' applies in full force to the German defence of Breslau, the capital of Lower Silesia. This city resisted for the remarkable term of seventy-seven days, which was beyond the lifespan of Hitler and Nazi Berlin. From the history of the other sieges we will be familiar with some of the basic ingredients of the story—professional but conscience-striken military commanders, a helpless civilian population, and a brutal and self-seeking Party leadership—but only in the telling do we encounter some of the strengths which prolonged the defence so far beyond the ordinary duration.

Breslau was a fortress only in virtue of a decree of August 1944, which set the Germans to work building an outer defence line about fifteen kilometres from the city centre. A couple of light field positions had been constructed outside the city in the Great War, but there were no rings of forts as at Posen or Königsberg, and no cleared fields of fire. Indeed all the connotations of Breslau had been peaceful ones. A pleasant assemblage of historic and modern buildings, it sat in the middle of the gently rolling Lower Silesian countryside, and in recent years it was famed as one of the few German cities which lay beyond the normal reach of the Allied bomber offensive. Almost 1 million German civilians were therefore sheltering in or around Breslau by the time the Soviets attacked on the Vistula in 1945.

The Russian armoured spearheads raced the three hundred

kilometres from the Sandomierz bridgehead with appalling speed, and from 14 January the Breslau railway station was swamped with thousands of civilians who sought places on board the trains leaving for Berlin, Saxony and Bavaria. Gauleiter Karl Hanke at first refused to allow any official movement from Lower Silesia, for this would have smacked of defeatism. The people tried to escape anyway, and when the trains and buses were unable to cope, loudspeakers blared down the streets on the twentieth and the twenty-first: 'Women and children must leave the city on foot and proceed in the direction of Opperau and Kanth!' It was an expulsion rather than an evacuation, for the defenceless folk were simply turned into the countryside. The snow lay half a metre deep in a temperature of minus twenty degrees centigrade, and the babies were usually the first to die.

On 24 January the sound of guns was heard from Oels scarcely thirty-five kilometres to the west, and by early February the area of Breslau emerged as an outlying bulwark stranded between the two Russian bridgeheads of Steinau and Ohlau. The approaches to Breslau were defended in a very energetic way by the 269th Infantry Division (from the Western Front) and the 17th Infantry Division (from the Vistula), but these formations were forbidden to run the risk of being cut off in Breslau, and on the night of 13–14 February they fought their way into the open country. Breslau was virtually isolated on 15 February (see p. 134), and a tight investment was completed on the following day.

The first axis of Russian effort was against the southern suburbs of Breslau, where it took the Soviets from 20 February to 1 March to advance the two kilometres from the Südpark to the Hindenburgplatz. On this sector the main symbolic and physical barrier was the great railway embankment which defined the city limit. Both soldiers and civilians were still confident that Schörner's Army Group Centre would shortly break through to them, and they hoped that by defending Breslau they were winning time which the Reich could turn to its advantage.

In early March the costly Russian effort in the south gradually died away, which offers us an opportunity to take stock of the means of the defence in general.

German Resources and Methods

In some respects Breslau was well provided. The garrison stood at an adequate 45,000 to 50,000 men, including about 15,000 Volkssturm, and this force was divided into twenty-six combat teams, ten construction battalions, two training battalions and a number of smaller units. Some 80,000 civilians remained in the city, and they might have presented a problem if Breslau, as a long-established sanctuary from Allied air attacks, had not been so well stocked with food.

The 'fortifications' included fortuitous barriers like the railway embankment, and the massive ferro-concrete warehouse near the harbour basin, but the Germans mostly had to adapt the ordinary office and apartment blocks as best they could. To begin with, the Russians employed a very successful tactic of setting corner buildings ablaze with incendiary shells and mortar bombs. The flames drove the defenders out, and the way was clear for Soviet combat teams to make their entry with the help of fire-fighting apparatus. The Germans in their turn countered by setting fire to the buildings in advance, which got rid of the inflammable material before the garrison moved in. Behind the front line Gauleiter Hanke had entire rows of houses along the Götenstrasse and the Sadowastrasse blown up, which created a no-man's land inhabited only by the rats which lived off the unburied corpses.

Public facilities functioned remarkably well for a city under siege. The fire brigade with its six hundred men and forty-four engines attained a higher rate of activity than the brigade of any other German city, and it suffered a loss of 26 per cent of its personnel. No less brave and industrious were the battalions of specialised workers who carried out demolitions, manufactured ammunition, repaired bridges and other communications and supplied gas, water and electricity. Medical care was the responsibility of the fortress *Oberfeldartzt* Dr. Mehling, who set up improvised hospitals in cellars, underground shelters, and the tall and massive concrete *Hochbunker*, which were proof against direct hits from artillery and aerial bombs.

The same spirit of resource and invention provided Breslau with a range of manufacturing facilities. The Aviatik cigarette factory continued to produce 600,000 smokes a day, 'which proved extremely welcome to all the fortress garrison, whether soldiers or civilians' (Ahlfen and Niehoff, 1978, 91). This detail was typical of the care which was taken to keep up morale. Private as well as service correspondence was dropped by parachute and bomb, and the postal service worked so well that there was a schoolmaster in the Volkssturm who received letters from his home in Vienna nearly every day. Entertainments were held for the soldiers whenever the tactical situation allowed, and the director of the Breslau Theatre, who had been enlisted into the Volkssturm, was particularly proud of a concert which he helped to organise in the pretty suburb of Villen. A string trio was included among the performers, and

> the waltz *Voices of Spring* by Johann Strauss accorded well with the swaying verdure of the fields, the blossoming apple trees along the roadside and the green of the young birches. Our mighty-voiced heroic tenor K. sang Italian arias, and these too seemed to match the deep blue sky of that day of early spring. We might have been able to forget the war and the siege for a little while if it had not been for the dreadful backdrop which extended behind the lightly coloured fields of spring—the city of Breslau, with its great fires and their black towers of smoke. (Hartung, 1976, 81–82)

The very considerable FAMO (Fahrzeug- und Motorenwerke Breslau Gmbh) was forced to abandon its premises in February, but it continued to manufacture and repair machines from a number of temporary workshops. The most spectacular single product of FAMO was the Eisenbahnpanzerzug Poersel, an armoured train mounting 88-mm, 37-mm and 20-mm anti-aircraft guns, and two MG-42 machine-guns. This fearsome assemblage was first taken into action by First Lieutenant Poersel on 20 March, and it went on to destroy seven tanks and three aircraft. Its presence was very comforting to the defenders, and particularly those in the area of Gandau airfield.

On 1 February the quantity of ammunition in Breslau was calculated at 130,000 rounds, which was alarmingly low. A search of the stores revealed forty 125-mm heavy mortars, for which it was easy to manufacture the 'low technology' am munition. Elsewhere the Germans came across about 100,000 empty shell cases for light field artillery. The necessary fuzes were flown in from the Reich, and the filling was extracted from unexploded Russian bombs—a delicate process, since the explosive became fluid only at 90 degrees Centigrade, but exploded at 102 degrees. Some of the duds contained notes from the German prisoners of war who had been forced to manufacture them: 'This is all we can do for you, comrades!' With this the Germans had reached the end of their technical resources, and the shortage of ammunition threatened to cripple the defence, to the extent that the artillery was forbidden to open fire without the permission of the commandant.

From the time the Russians had cut off Breslau on 15 February, the survival of the city hung to a great extent on air supply. On the next night the aircraft began their ferry service to Breslau, flying in artillery ammunition and other precious commodities, and leaving when possible with loads of wounded men. The classic Ju-52 trimotor was a strong and reliable machine, capable of carrying twenty-eight passengers or their equivalent in cargo at time, but the Germans had too few planes of this kind to meet the demands of Breslau, and the aircraft could not be risked in daylight against the batteries of anti-aircraft guns which the Russians massed along the approaches. Gandau field was too short for the fast tactical aircraft

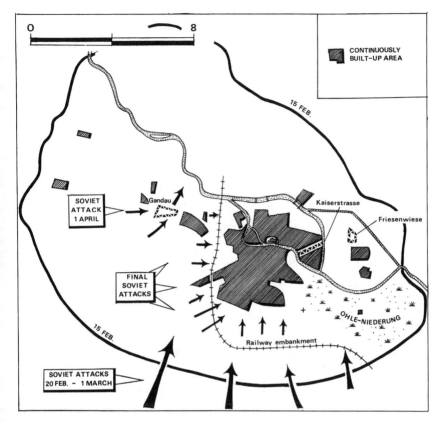

14. The siege of Breslau, 15 February–6 May 1945

which were employed to help with the transport, and their loads were therefore dropped by parachute. Some of the consignments fell behind the Russian lines, were lost in the Oder or suffered a variety of bizarre fates. Early one morning a party of Volkssturm were alerted by an agitated cry of:

'Alarm! Paratroops!' Large, dark aircraft were already thundering towards us in massive formation. They had no visible insignia, and red parachutes were floating down from them.

257

Those of us who knew how to work our rifles aimed at the planes and the descending parachutes, some of which were hit. It was a wild fusillade, rather like a shooting match.

All of a sudden an infuriated first lieutenant of the AA ran up and roared at us: 'Cease fire! You're shooting at our own planes!' (Hartung, 1976, 79)

The German Contest for Command—Gauleiter Hanke and the Commandants von Ahlfen and von Niehoff

The command of Breslau was split in a way we have encountered a number of times before. In this case the Nazi Party was represented by Karl Hanke, who was possibly the most infamous of the gauleiter breed. Hanke was youngish and energetic, and his connections extended far up the hierarchy of the Reich. He was *Reichsverteidigungskommissar* as well as gauleiter of Lower Silesia, and in virtue of this authority he was briefed by the commandant daily, and established communication by means of airborne liaison officers with Ferdinand Schörner, who was the overall commander of Army Group Centre. More important still, Hanke had control of a radio operated by naval personnel, which gave him direct access to Reichsleiter Bormann in the Chancellery in Berlin. In February, in a typical manoeuvre, Hanke 'generously' offered this facility to the commandant, Major-General Hans von Ahlfen, and then made sure that the transmissions with all their authentic military detail were passed under his own name.

Hanke put his personal brutality beyond all doubt when on 28 January he executed the second *Bürgermeister*, Dr. Spielhagen. His crime was that he had declared that it was useless to defend the city, and Hanke pronounced that 'he who fears an honourable death will die in disgrace' (Hillgruber, 1986, 37).

By such means Hanke won the reputation of being the om-nicompetent National Socialist hero in the critical days of the Reich. Goebbels was entranced. He heard a speech by Hanke on the radio on 3 March, and he entered in his diary:

> It was movingly impressive, demonstrating an acme of political morale worthy of admiration. If all our Gauleiters in the East were like this and acted like Hanke, we should be in better shape than we are. Hanke is the outstanding per-sonality among our eastern Gauleiters. (Goebbels, 1977, 35)

Breslau knew three military commandants during its long period of agony. Major-General Johannes Krause had arrived on 25 September 1944, and began work on the outer defences. His health was feeble, and he lacked the ruthlessness which Schörner hoped to find in Major-General von Ahlfen, who landed in Breslau on 1 February. However, the new comman-dant proved to be a very different kind of man from the one who had been expected, and von Ahlfen was soon at logger-heads with Hanke on a number of issues.

Not content with controlling the Volkssturm, Hanke wanted to build up an elite striking force, and over the protests of von Ahlfen two battalions of 'dismounted' parachutists were flown into Breslau on 25 February and 3 March respectively. The parachutists were lightly armed and not very well trained, but Hanke was set on using them to force a way to Schörner's outlying position on the Zobtenberg to the south-west. Von Ahlfen had to point out that several divisions would be needed to make such a breakout and to defend the corridor afterwards.

Von Ahlfen also disagreed strongly with Hanke on the ques-tion of finding an alternative airfield to Gandau, which was short and lay to the west of the city, exposed to attack. The general wished to complete an auxiliary airstrip on the Frie-senwiese, where work had already been in progress since the beginning of February. This field also had the advantage of being located just four kilometres east of the city centre and in a tactically strong position, for it was protected by a branch of the Oder to the north and east, and by the main channel and the Ohle inundation to the south. Hanke nevertheless resolved to push through a Führer order of 15 February, which decreed an entirely new site, the Kaiserstrasse, in the east centre of the city. The consequent gain in security did not match the great effort which had to be put into clearing this heavily built-up area by conscripted men, women and children who were forced to work under pain of death. The last day of the siege suggested that Hanke was motivated simply by the desire to save his own skin (see p. 267).

Now that von Ahlten had failed to live up to the hopes which had been invested in him, Schörner replaced him as commandant of Breslau by Lieutenant-General Hermann von Niehoff. For Schörner, the appeal of the new commander was that he seemed to be open to intimidation and blackmail. Von Niehoff was a family man with five children, and therefore vulnerable. He had also barely survived a charge of misconduct which Schörner had levelled against him, and something of the sort could always be resurrected. The army group commander sent him to Breslau with the admonition: 'If you fail in Breslau, you will answer for it with your head. I place the greatest importance on the closest and most cordial cooperation with the gauleiter' (Thorwald, 1950, 133).

When von Niehoff flew into Breslau on the evening of 5 March, he saw that flames and smoking ruins extended over the city, and he was able to distinguish the front line by the fire of the Russian artillery. On the ground von Ahlfen greeted him like the old friend he was, and spent several hours explaining the realities of the situation. Von Niehoff was impressed, and he replied: 'Schörner is bloody-minded towards you. In your place I wouldn't have acted any differently' (Thorwald, 1950, 133). Von Ahlfen was supposed to fly off immediately to answer for his failings, but he stayed in Breslau until 11 March to ease von Niehoff into the command.

Von Niehoff laid down clear lines of demarcation for his

dealings with Hanke, which helped to eliminate some of the friction, but the gauleiter's conduct reached new extremities. Always a lover of the extravagant gesture, he arranged at the end of March for eight large-calibre artillery pieces to be flown in by super-heavy gliders. Von Niehoff protested in vain that Breslau needed ammunition rather than guns, and in the event, seven out of eight of the lumbering gliders were shot down by anti-aircraft fire.

Hanke's concern for his personal safety (a typical gauleiter trait) was evident when he moved his headquarters from the military command post on the Liebigs Hill to the Sandinsel in the city centre, where he ensconced himself in the cellars beneath the University Library. He wanted to blow up the library so that the rubble would provide additional overhead cover, and he was deterred from burning the 550,000 books only by the fear that the flames would spread to the whole of the island.

The Continuation and End of the Siege, March to 6 May 1945

So far, the Russians had put their main effort into the attack from the south, but they were being contained by a line of defence which ran west from the extensive inundation of the Ohle hollow. Von Niehoff knew that he was inherently more vulnerable in the west, for on that side the open country extended over the Gandau field towards the city centre, and gave the Russians the potential of using their greatly superior artillery to the best advantage. He deployed the two parachute battalions on that sector, as well as the fine infantry regiment of Lieutenant-Colonel Mohr, and he allocated precious reserves of artillery ammunition for defensive fires.

As March progressed, the Russian attacks gained once more in ferocity, and on 1 April the Soviets subjected Breslau to a massive bombardment from the air and by artillery pieces up to a calibre of 280 mm. In the resulting firestorm the cathedral tower was destroyed, the pines in the botanical garden blazed like torches, and the population was driven from large areas of the south and west of the city. The long-awaited attack on Gandau was now made under cover of smoke shells, and the Russian tanks and infantry gained possession of the field after the German paratroopers had been badly mauled and several of the 88-mm guns destroyed by direct hits.

During the fight for Gandau Lieutenant Hartmann and Sergeant Maier drove up with their two assault guns to the edge of a park. Hartmann got out and tried to gain a better view:

> With my gun layer I crawled as far as a felled tree. We peered cautiously through the branches, and 150 or so metres away we espied a massive armoured vehicle standing in an avenue. It was a 152-mm assault gun. We got back into our own machine as fast as we could and drove on until the avenue lay before us. Over my throat microphone I ordered the driver to incline to the left. The gun was already loaded, and it was only a matter of seconds to lay it on the target. The NCO gun-layer called out: 'Ready!' I duly ordered: 'Fire!' By now the Russians had noticed us, and they began to depress their barrel, which had been pointing up into the trees. It was too late. The crack of our gun was almost painful, but it was as reassuring as always, and I saw the red flash of a strike immediately to the left of the barrel. We had hit with our first round. There were repeated bangs coming from somewhere close to my right, and when I looked through the hatch in astonishment, I saw that our comrade Maier had stationed himself to the right of my piece to give me supporting fire. But the Russian vehicle was already blazing to high heaven. (Ahlfen and Niehoff, 1978, 77–78)

Little actions like these limited the Russian progress in their Easter attack to just two or three kilometres, and it was lucky for the Germans that the enemy chose to exploit north-east to the Oder instead of due east—a direction which would have taken them into the city centre. The loss of the Gandau field was nevertheless a most damaging blow, for it made Breslau indefensible over the long term. Hanke's Kaiserstrasse airstrip was no substitute, being unusable by heavy aircraft.

The destruction in the interior of Breslau was now immense. One of the Volkssturm took a walk beside the Oder and noticed how

> pieces of charred wood were being carried on the dark and dirty water. Cathedral Island was now a dreadful sight—the towers of the cathedral and the Sandkirche had been reduced to burnt-out stumps, and only the elegant and slender tower of the gothic Kreuzkirche appeared to be intact. There were pools of blood and dead horses along the beautiful avenue which bordered the river. Large white bundles lay on the Holtei Hill. This was where many of the dead who had been killed over Easter were being buried. (Hartung, 1976, 79)

In the course of April the Russians compressed the defenders into the city centre, without ever managing to break the cohesion of the German front or to shake the resolution of von Niehoff in the face of the coming end. On 8 April a collapse of civilian morale threatened public order, and Hanke opened the stores of clothing in an attempt to divert the attention of the desperate crowds. Six days later Russian artillery fire made the military headquarters on the Liebigs Hill untenable, and von Niehoff had to join Hanke under the University Library. At the turn of April and May there was a significant change in the tone of the Russian loudspeaker propaganda, from lavish promises of good treatment to bulletins on the general progress of the war. The facts needed little enough varnishing, for the Americans and Russians had joined hands at Torgau on 25 April, and the garrison of Berlin surrendered unconditionally on 2 May.

On the morning of 4 May von Niehoff received a deputation of four clergymen—the Protestant pastors Hornig and Dr. Konrad, and the Catholic suffragan bishop and Canon Kramer. The general listened in silence while his visitors reviewed the situation as they saw it. At the end Hornig posed the question:

'General, in these circumstances, can you justify defending the city any further before your divine judge?'

After a long pause von Niehoff replied in a strangled voice: 'Gentlemen, what should I do?'

The clergymen gave the simple answer: 'Surrender!' (Thorwald, 1951, 316–17)

Von Niehoff then raised the possibility of breaking out with the garrison and civilians to Schörner's lines to the south. He could not have spoken with any great conviction, for he had already examined this project and found it quite impracticable. Possibly, he invited the rejection he received from Pastor Hornig, who had been a lieutenant of artillery in the Great War, and who pointed out that pitting the garrison against entire Russian army groups could only result in useless bloodshed.

The clergymen left towards noon without having received any further response from von Niehoff. It took some time for Dr. Konrad to pick his way through the ruins to his rectory, and he was met there by an officer who asked for Pastor Hornig. Konrad at first assumed that Hornig was going to be put under arrest, but the officer assured him that the commandant wished him to address the senior officers of the garrison. Hornig was contacted, and when he spoke to his audience of thirty or so military men, he sensed that the majority were on his side.

The next two days promised to be the worst in the history of Breslau. Hanke had been infuriated by the news of the meeting between von Niehoff and the clergy, and on the morning of 5 May his fortress newspaper made slighting references to defeatist elements and demanded resistance to the last man and woman. The men and women concerned were terrified by a Russian threat to level the city to the ground, and rather than undergo a new firestorm many of them determined to flee to

the Russian lines—it is difficult to imagine a more desperate ex-
pedient. Mercifully, von Niehoff assembled his commanders before daybreak on 6 May and announced that he had decided to
end the battle. At the close of his address the officers reached out
their hands in a spontaneous gesture of recognition and thanks.

When the clergy called again on von Niehoff on the morning
of the same day, he was able to tell them: 'Gentlemen, the issue
has been decided according to your wishes' (Thorwald, 1951,
319). Later von Niehoff went out to meet Lieutenant-General
Gluzdovskii, the commander of the Sixth Army of the 1st
Ukrainian Front, and gained guarantees for the life, personal
possessions and eventual return of all the defenders, the SS included. The surrender was concluded on these
terms, and on the night of 6–7 May Russian storm detachments
penetrated as far as the bridges leading to the Sandinsel: 'Red
and green flares rose in the night sky. Music resounded from
the Russian loudspeakers. The artillery had fallen silent and
the final bombs had landed on the city, but the Germans had
scarcely time to draw breath before the plundering and the rape
began' (Thorwald, 1951, 320).

In the course of the siege between 80 and 90 per cent of the
city was destroyed. There were 6,000 killed and 23,000
wounded among the 50,000 combatants and the 80,000
civilians—or about 22 per cent of the total of 130,000 souls. The
Russian losses are difficult to establish, though one of their
own communiqués put the number at 60,000 dead and
wounded, and it is known that a cemetery for 5,000 officers
was laid out to the south of the city. About six Russian divisions
had been engaged in the immediate neighbourhood of Breslau,
and seven more in reserve, and the seventy-seven days of resistance had helped to take the pressure off the 1.6 million
German refugees who were in the process of escaping from
Silesia by way of Czechoslovakia.

Shortly after he went into captivity an officer of the fortress
staff penned a memorandum which explained that the endurance of Breslau was due to three factors:

1. The vicissitudes of fortune had the effect of binding soldiers and civilians together. Their common determination was to preserve our beloved Breslau, the jewel of our German homeland, for as long as humanly possible from the Russians, who would bring us nothing but brutality, captivity and death. This resolve was reinforced again and again by promises of relief.

2. The leadership succeeded in mobilising the moral, material and technical resources which were latent in Breslau, and while the fighting was actually in progress it created fortress troops who grew progressively in quality and number. In other words, the command managed to turn the 'air-raid shelter of the Reich' into a fortress. The leadership also defended that fortress with increasing skill until the final capitulation.

3. The enemy were clumsy, and they neglected to launch concentric attacks against the fortress from several directions at the same time. (Ahlfen and Niehoff, 1978, 112)

The final point is confirmed by the fact that on 6 May the Germans still held almost the entire built-up area of the inner city, as shown on our map. The accessible Soviet sources are virtually silent about the conduct of the attack, from which it is possible to conclude that the siege of Breslau has not been counted among the more glorious Russian feats of arms. It is known, however, that Gluzdovskii had more than once asked Konev for permission to carry out a full-scale storm.

During the final days in Breslau individuals had responded in typical ways when they learned that von Niehoff was about to surrender. Some of the troops tried to break out into open country, while others threw their weapons into the Oder and changed into civilian clothes. General Herzog, the commander of the Volkssturm, committed suicide. On 5 May Gauleiter Hanke heard a number of compelling items of news—that Hitler was already dead (30 April), and that he himself had been made minister of the interior, national leader of the SS and chief of police in place of the disgraced Himmler. He now had a justification of sorts for abandoning the city which he had so often demanded must be defended to the last.

A Fieseler Storch landed on the Kaiserstrasse airstrip to carry away von Niehoff. The general, however, preferred to stay with his men and share their captivity. Hanke had no such scruples, but changed into the uniform of an SS NCO and flew away. His fate is still unknown. More worthy of what had been achieved in the city was the radio message which arrived on the same day from the headquarters of the Seventeenth Army:

It is with feelings of pride and sorrow that the banners of Germany are lowered in tribute to the steadfastness of the garrison and the self-sacrifice of the people of Breslau.

PART VI

1945 and Germanic Eastern Europe

CHAPTER 24

The Catastrophe

The Germanic East Before the Catastrophe

God forbid that the land should ever relapse into its former state, that the Slavs should ever drive out the German settlers and again undertake its cultivation.

(Prince Wizlaw of Rügen, 1221)

BEFORE THE DISASTERS of the 1940s the German presence in Eastern Europe was rich and varied, and all the more because it was the product of peaceful settlement and trade more than outright conquest. Even in the 'Prussian' heartland of Brandenburg and Pomerania, the mixing of races was more far-reaching than Nazi theorists cared to admit.

North-east along the Baltic coastlands the architecture of towns like Danzig, Königsberg, Libau, Revel and Dorpat expressed a Germanic trading life which went back hundreds of years. In Czechoslovakia the University of Prague counted as the second German university of Europe, and along the northern borders of the provinces of Bohemia and Moravia the Sudetenland formed a deep belt of German settlement, where the style of life differed in no way from that in political Germany.

In Russia Catherine the Great (herself a German princess) invited German settlers to farm the rich lands of the Volga in the second half of the eighteenth century. By the twentieth century the number of their descendants reached the millions, and Lenin respected their culture by forming a German Republic within the Soviet Union. By then German influence had penetrated the Russian bureaucracy, professions and army so thoroughly that it is difficult to establish whether such a tradition can be accounted Russian or Germanic.

South-eastern Europe contained both the communities of 'Saxons,' who had been invited to Transylvania in the twelfth century, and the Germans of the sandy Banat of Temesvar, who were the descendants of the Catholic Swabians and Viennese prostitutes who were settled there by the Austrian monarchy in the eighteenth century. A variety of still quainter communities was to be found in out-of-the-way places like Slovakia (the old Upper Hungary), Galicia, Bessarabia and Dobruja.

Certain unities could be discerned among all this diversity, and they came from a general reputation for hard work, distinctive styles of architecture (like the stepped gables of the Baltic ports, or the railway stations, opera houses and coffee salons of the old Habsburg lands) and the German language— and above all the variety called Yiddish, which was employed by the Jews of Poland and western Russia, who made up the largest German-speaking group in eastern Europe.

It is curious to reflect that the Nazis qualified in two respects as the greatest enemies of the Germanic presence in the East —as the authors of the destruction of the Jews, and the ones who led Germany to war and defeat.

The Cycle of Revenge

In our time the cruelty of man towards man is the result of the lack of religion.

(Tolstoy)

There is something indecent about trying to explain, let alone justify, the atrocities which contributed to the unimaginable scale of suffering in the Second World War. Millions of the

272

victims were innocent civilians, and the word 'innocent' applies just as well to the further millions of frightened, powerless soldiers who themselves died in dreadful circumstances.

Perhaps it requires a training in philosophy, like that of Ernst Nolte, to qualify one to pronounce whether hideous deeds in one time or place may be equated with hideous deeds in others. However, the historian cannot avoid an obligation to set his tale in context, and in this case he must try to establish why the Russians behaved so savagely in the Germanic lands in 1945.

Racialism, ideology and nationalism combined to make Hitler's war aims very wide-ranging indeed when he went to war with the Soviet Union in June 1941, for the Nazis intended to drive more than 30 million Russians into Siberia and open the four *Reichskommissariaten* of the Baltic Coast (Ostland), Muscovy, the Ukraine and the Caucasus to German colonisation. West of the Urals the surviving Russians were to be reduced to slaves and vassals, and their children were to be given only as much education as fitted them for their menial tasks. The German forces began to massacre civilians as soon as they crossed the border (as had happened in Poland in 1939), and the work of the SS *Einsatzgruppen* in the captured areas, together with casual slaughters by the other forces, already accounted for hundreds of thousands of deaths even before the industrialised murder of the Holocaust opened in 1942.

By 1945 Russian military men of every rank went to war with personal scores to settle. Stalin knew that his son Yakov, a prisoner of the Germans, was as good as dead (see p. 19). Colonel-General Rybalko, the commander of the Third Guards Tank Army, led his forces with such notable energy not just because he was a good soldier, but because his daughter had been carried away by the Germans from the Ukraine in 1942. In a single regiment (the 242nd Rifle) it was established that 158 of the men had close relatives who had been killed or tortured. The families of fifty-six had been deported to forced labour, and 445 of the troops knew that their homes had been destroyed or ruined (Kartashev, 1980, 99). In Silesia a group of Russian officers encountered one of those herds of cattle which had been rounded up on German farms and were being driven to the rear:

> A lieutenant unsheathed a knife, walked up to a cow, and struck her a death-blow at the base of the skull. The cow's legs folded under, and she fell, while the rest of the herd, bellowing madly, stampeded and ran away. The officer wiped the sharp edge on his boots and said: 'My father wrote to me that the Germans had taken a cow from us. Now we are even. . . .' (Koriakov, 1948, 67)

Further evidence of the character of the Nazi state was uncovered on 24 July 1944, when the Russians overran the concentration camp at Maidanek, near Lublin. When the Soviets continued their drive across Poland, they discovered Treblinka, Auschwitz-Birkenau and other massive establishments which served to fuel the Red Army's mission of hatred. Almost as revolting in their way were the little camps in the woods which stood next to the comfortably furnished villas of their overseers (see p. 193).

The urgings of the propagandist Ilya Ehrenburg reached extremities of excitement early in 1945, lest there should be any flagging in dedication. He reminded the troops of the blood-soaked soil of Belorussia when they were advancing through Pomerania, and at the gates of Danzig millions of leaflets fluttered from the air bearing a message which had been composed by him and signed by Stalin:

> *Soldiers of the Red Army! Kill the Germans! Kill all Germans! Kill! Kill! Kill!*

One of the defenders of Danzig unhesitatingly declares that the majority of the Soviet combat troops were too humane to put this order into literal effect (Schäufler, 1979, 67). It must also be conceded that the Russians had nothing to compare with the SS special groups, which combed the country systematically in pursuit of a policy of mass extermination. We are left, however, with cruelty on a scale which far exceeds that which might have been expected from men who had been brutalised by a pitiless war. While many of the atrocities must be laid to the account of low-grade rear-echelon troops such as released prisoners of war and newly conscripted peasants, it is clear that the lead was often taken by the best-trained and best-equipped elements of the armoured spearheads. Again and again we hear of the Russian tank forces opening fire on trains, or driving straight down columns of civilian refugees, crushing people and animals and machine-gunning the survivors in the ditches and fields.

Massacre, rape and plunder contributed to the very marked decline in discipline that was evident in the last ten days of January, when the Russians moved into German territory. The marshals were appalled, and in his ferocious order of 27 January Konev cited a number of spectacular lapses and gave a long list of commanders who had been consigned to penal battalions. One of his officers remarked on a tank battalion where

> the tanks were so tightly packed with loot and plunder that the members of the crew could not move inside and would have been unable to go into action in case of emergency. . . . I heard a story about the members of one tank crew who were so drunk that they took their tank into the front line, opened fire on Russian units, destroyed four gun emplacements, and crushed one gun. (Koriakov, 1948, 61)

The Russian barbarities were also important because they stiffened the German resistance and contributed to the survival of the Reich until the early summer of 1945. The Russian way with German civilians first became known after the Germans recaptured the town of Nemmersdorf in East Prussia, which was the scene of a wholesale massacre of the population in

October 1944. This experience was relived on every theatre of the Eastern Front, and on every occasion it provoked in the German troops an intense desire for revenge. In Silesia the grisly findings extended into March. At Sagan the Germans beat Russians to death with shovels and rifle butts; at Striegau, which was cleared by the 208th Infantry Division, the few surviving civilians were wandering around literally out of their minds. 'After Striegau there was no question of giving quarter. When the soldiers were asked to hold themselves back, they replied in words to the effect that: "After what we saw and lived through at Striegau, you can't ask us to take prisoners" ' (Ahlfen, 1977, 169; see also Neidhardt, 1981, 379).

In notable contrast to their behaviour on the Western Front (see p. 54), the Volkssturm in the East fought with real determination, and without their help the defence of Breslau and the other 'fortresses' would have been impossible. Commanders did not need to be members of the SS or devotees of Hitler to be convinced that they were now fighting a 'just' war, motivated by the mission to save the millions of refugee civilians. In truly desperate situations the troops formed a protective shell and tried to fight their way through the enemy forces, as was attempted by Hossbach in the Heiligenbeil Cauldron in late January, and actually accomplished by the von Tettau group when it broke through to Dievenow on 11 March. More typically, the troops held a contracting bridgehead, and fought on to gain time for the civilians, wounded and combatants to be evacuated by sea. General von Saucken described his task in the Gulf of Danzig:

We . . . formed a shield for all the people who were seeking to reach the West from the area of Danzig, Pillau and Hela. Well over a million Germans—children, women, old folk, wounded and sick—had found protection behind that shield. As the commanding general, I assumed personal control of the whole operation, for I had refused to accept a subordinate position under the gauleiter. (Kurowski, 1987, 300. For similar sentiments concerning Königsberg, see Lasch, 1977, 82.)

The Experience of the Catastrophe

As early as 28 January 1945, the Wehrmacht calculated that 3.5 million German civilians were on the move in the East. By the end of the war the number of German non-combatants fleeing from the Russians had nearly doubled to about 7 million. Most of those who tried to stay in their homes were evicted after the war, a process which by 1950 brought the number of Germans displaced by the Russians and their clients to a final total of 11 million. More than 610,000 ethnic Germans were killed by local regular or irregular forces in Romania, Poland, Czechoslovakia and Yugoslavia, and a further 2.2 million from Eastern Europe generally remain unaccounted for, many of them undoubtedly killed. The rest of this chapter will seek to convey a little of what these figures mean.

It was only at the beginning of 1945 that the peoples of the Germanic lands as a whole began to learn some of the common experiences of war in a mechanised age. As had happened in Poland, France, Belgium and western Russia, we find crowds of shoppers staring at columns of tanks in unfamiliar livery which were unaccountably driving away from the battlefront. Again we encounter dedicated civilian telephone operators, plugging and unplugging at their switchboards after the military men had disappeared.

The ordeal of the eastern Germans in 1945 nevertheless had some remarkable features of its own. The suffering was augmented to a significant degree by the complacency and brutality of most of the gauleiters, who would have agreed with Erich Koch of East Prussia that 'it is cowardice to consider even the possibility of misfortune' (Gaunitz, 1987, 19). Since Nazi Party credibility was bound up with the pretence that everything in the Reich was stable and under control, the gauleiters did what they could to prevent the Wehrmacht from building defences in depth, and almost everywhere they kept the civilians in place until after the Russians had effected their breakthroughs and made an orderly escape impossible. When Karl Hanke executed the mayor of Breslau, or the SS *Sonderkommandos* left rows of corpses dangling from the trees in Danzig, it was further proof of how far the Germans had now become the victims of their own masters.

None of this deterred the gauleiters from going to considerable lengths to save their own skins. The most notorious example was again provided by Hanke, in the episode of the Kaiserstrasse airstrip at Breslau, but there were several others. In Pomerania Franz Schwede-Coburg demanded that every village be made into a fortress, but he himself moved his headquarters several times to avoid capture, and on 4 May he made good his escape by sea from the island of Rügen.

Help was forthcoming from some remarkable quarters. Eighteen French prisoners of war were among the fifty-six people murdered by the Russians at Krenau in East Prussia, and for a large number of ex-Allied soldiers the prospect of 'liberation' became distinctly unappealing. Many of the refugee columns were led to safety by French, Poles and Russians, and Lieutenant Hans Schäufler testified to

> something which struck me again and again, how nearly all the peasant households from East and West Prussia were accompanied by French prisoners of war, who took sedulous care of 'their' families, and were much concerned not to be separated from them in the turmoil. They were usually the only males in the column, apart from some sick old men. They were attached above all to the welfare of the children, and these in turn were exceedingly fond of their 'Jean.' (Schäufler, 1979, 120. See also Dieckert and Grossmann, 1960, 102.)

278

The same Panzer lieutenant tells in circumstantial detail the story of thirty-two British officer prisoners of war who had been abandoned by the Germans in the camp at Schlossberg in easternmost East Prussia. The Russians tried to transport them east to some unspecified destination, but the British broke free and made their way across the width of East Prussia until they reached the 35th Panzer Regiment of the 4th Panzer Division at Heiderode:

> In the polite English way, and with all proper courtesy, they emphasised that they wanted to come back and stay with us. Without any prompting they assured us that, if necessary, they would be willing to fight on the German side.
>
> We had been sunk in gloom, and you may imagine how their request gave a mighty boost to our morale. Naturally we took them in, and we willingly shared our rations and cigarettes.

It transpired that four of the party had been captured by the 4th Panzer Division at Béthune in 1940. The last that was seen of the officers was in late March or early April, when they were waiting with thousands of German soldiers and civilians to be shipped from Oxhöft (Schäufler, 1979, 119–20; see also Schäufler, 1973, 245). This episode invites further investigation.

On the far side of Danzig was the Vistula delta. It was one of the enclaves which were held by the Germans until the end of the war, and for the historian Andreas Hillgruber it was significant that even this little patch of ground held a concentration camp, the one at Stutthof, which therefore remained 'a symbol of the essential nature of the National Socialist regime' (Hillgruber, 1986, 39). It is perhaps churlish to add that the 6,000 inmates had been turned loose by their SS guards, but preferred to wait with the Germans on the coast for evacuation to Schleswig-Holstein rather than take their chance with the Russians.

The OKW War Diaries describe the retreat of the German forces from the East in an entirely dispassionate tone: 'Plessin has been lost . . . the suburb of Kietz at Küstrin has been lost,' and so on. What was being 'lost,' however, was not just terrain in the military context, but homes, familiar landscapes and hundreds of years of Germanic history and culture. The timing of these events was significant, for German imaginations were still borne on the tide of historic romanticism, which had set in early in the nineteenth century and reached its last flood in the Third Reich. The Soviets too were open to sensations of the sort, after Stalin had invoked the spirit of the patriotic Russian past in 1941. For that reason something that was composed and ritualistic emerged amid all the squalor, heartbreak and suffering.

It was noticed that when German families abandoned their homes in East Pomerania for what they knew would be the last time, they left everything in immaculate order, as if they expected to return from a shopping expedition to town. Decorum was no less important to Prince Louis Ferdinand of Prussia, who made a final visit to the church on his estate at Cadinen near Elbing, where he played the organ, lit the candles on the altar and closed the door behind him. On 25 March Colonel Christern was on his way through Danzig to take command of the 4th Panzer Division, which was a reasonably urgent commission at that time. Greatly to the surprise of his lieutenant of signals, he turned aside into one of the few intact churches:

> The colonel looked about inquisitively, and then a delicate smile lit his battle-scarred face. He shot a silent glance at me to indicate that I was to seat myself on a bench, whereupon he and the driver climbed a steep flight of steps to the loft. The bench was massive and dark brown with age, and I was somewhat uncomfortable sitting there while the rumble of combat carried from outside. Then I nearly jumped out of my skin . . . the organ roared into music, subduing the sounds of killing and enabling me to forget the war about

us. . . . Naturally, I knew that the colonel was devoted to music, and could perform on a number of instruments. But this was the first time I had heard him on the organ—and he played it like a master. (Schäufler, 1979, 102)

In detail, the experience of the catastrophe was shaped by the history and geography of the lands in question, the degree of readiness of the civilians for their flight, and the speed with which the territory was overtaken by the military operations. We must accordingly enter into specifics.

The Soviet Union and the Remoter East

There was no chance of escape for most of the Volga Germans, who were treated as real or potential collaborators from the beginning of the war. The Volga Republic was abolished without further ado, and the population was deported to Siberia. The post-war years brought little relief, for the Germans were removed from Siberia to Soviet Central Asia. In time, many of the younger generation began to grow up in near-total ignorance of the German language, and it was to recover the links with the homeland, as well as to improve their material circumstances, that in 1989 Volga Germans in their tens of thousands began to avail themselves of the freedom to emigrate to West Germany.

Rustic Germans from the Balkan fringes had already contributed to the first waves of refugees who fled before the Soviet armies in 1944 and 1945. With their strange garb and swarthy features they were a world removed from East Prussian landowners and Silesian burghers, and Goebbels commented that 'the type of people entering the Reich calling themselves Germans is not exactly exhilarating. I think there are more Germanic types entering the Reich from the west by force of arms than there are Germanic types coming in peacefully from the east.' (Goebbels, 1977, 70)

The Sudetenland, Bohemia and Moravia

'Czechoslovakia' lived in walled-off seclusion from the war as a whole. In terms of international politics Hitler had been undeniably brutal in his treatment of that country. In virtue of the Munich Agreement the Reich annexed the largely German-speaking Sudetenland in northern Czechoslovakia in the autumn of 1938. Then in March 1939 German forces marched into the remainder of Czechoslovakia, whereupon Bohemia and Moravia became a 'protectorate' under German rule, and Slovakia emerged as a right-wing client state.

The history of the German occupation of Czechoslovakia is stained by the horror of Lidice, a village which was destroyed along with its people on the direct orders of Hitler, after the *Reichsprotektor*, Reinhard Heydrich, was assassinated in 1942. However, that killing was not the culminating point of some great saga of national resistance, but an isolated deed which was carried out by a small party of highly trained and highly motivated Czechs who had been parachuted in by the British. The everyday reality of life in 'Czechoslovakia' was still one of cohabitation of Czechs, ethnic Germans and occupying German forces. The Czechs had lost their country and their political freedoms, but few of them suffered any significant infringements of their personal liberty or property, and in the gross material sense their standard of living was higher than that of the civilians in the historic Reich. The contribution of the Czech economy to the German war effort has still to be assessed, but it was undeniably great, and when we compare what happened to Warsaw to what did not happen to Prague it was incontestably better to have been a 'betrayed' Czech than a 'saved' Pole.

This peaceful if hardly idyllic existence came to an end early in May 1945, when Soviet forces burst into the heart of Bohemia and Moravia. On the ninth the first Russian forces penetrated Prague and attacked a column of German troops and civilians who were about to leave the city. Some were killed on the spot, and others perished over the following hours:

> Can we apply the word 'men' to those creatures who car-ried out the atrocities on 9 May on the Wenceslas and Charles squares and along the Road of the Knights, when they poured petrol over the Germans (and not just SS men), hung them feet upwards from poles and lanterns, set them alight and stood mocking at the sight of the burning torches? Their agony lasted all the longer, because they were deliberately hung head downwards so that they would not be suffocated by the smoke. They were not real men who tied together civilians and women, as well as German soldiers, with steel wire, then shot them and threw the human bundles into the Moldau. (Thorwald, 1951, 383)

This was the opening scene of months of massacre and bru-tality which extended beyond Prague to all the areas of Czecho-slovakia in which ethnic Germans were living. What is extraordinary in this grisly episode is that the initiative was taken by the Czech civilians rather than the Soviet troops, who indeed had the best of reasons to hate the Germans. Not until 1989 was the Czech government prepared to admit that some shameful episodes had taken place.

The Baltic Provinces—East Prussia, West Prussia and East Pomerania

In so far as the spread of Germanism to the East had a military character, it was associated with the crusading order of the Teutonic Knights, who won East Prussia from the pagans in forty years of warfare in the thirteenth century. The political power of the Teutonic Order suffered a mortal blow at the hands of a Polish army in the battle of Tannenberg, on 15 July 1410. However, the advance of the Poles was checked at the Marienburg castle in West Prussia, and a lenient peace left the German presence in East Prussia essentially intact. In 1525 East Prussia became a secular duchy in fief to Poland, but Königsberg and the other towns remained as distinctly Germanic in character as ever, and in 1701 East Prussia became the legal seat of the new Prussian monarchy, when the Elector Frederick had himself pronounced king 'in' East Prussia, in the peculiar wording of the formula.

In 1758 East Prussia was occupied by the army of Empress Elizabeth of Russia, and (although German historians did not like to mention it) the local Germans were more than content under the subsequent five years of enlightened Russian rule. The Russians came this way again when two armies broke across the border in August 1914. By that time nationalistic romanticism had elevated East Prussia from the status of a backwoods province to a symbol of the austerity of the Prussian character and of the German presence in the East. General Paul von Hindenburg and his chief of staff, General Erich von Ludendorff, proceeded to rout the invading armies at a second battle of Tannenberg (24–31 August) and at the battle of the Masurian Lakes (5–15 September).

In the German consciousness the East Prussian type which survived such ordeals was wholly admirable. General Otto Lasch, who defended Königsberg in 1945, was not a genuine East Prussian by birth, but he was proud to count himself as an honorary East Prussian in virtue of his marriage and the time he had spent there in his military and sporting career:

This was where an upright Germanic race of men had, though centuries of laborious effort . . . brought a barren soil under cultivation. That ground evoked in them feelings of immutable love and remarkable loyalty. They are reserved and reticent towards all strangers, but they show exemplary hospitality and attachment to those they recognise to be honourable and worthy of trust. (Lasch, 1977, 8)

For the Soviets in 1945 East Prussia was the seat of the militaristic Junker class. In the days before the great offensive the soldiers of the 3rd Belorussian Front were reminded:

Comrades! You have reached the borders of East Prussia, and you will now tread on that ground which gave birth to those fascist monsters who devastated our cities and homes, and slaughtered our sons and daughters, our brothers and sisters, our wives and mothers. The most inveterate of those brigands and Nazis sprang from East Prussia. For many years now they have held power in Germany, directing this nation in its foreign aggressions and its genocide of other peoples. (Beloborodov, 1978, 98. See also Dragon, 1977, 95; Koyander, 1978, 231)

The memory of the events of 1914 survived into the final years of the Second World War. Churchill wrote to Stalin on 20 February 1944 to explain that in his view the two wars against Germany formed a single struggle, and that the Russian sacrifices in 1914 had established a moral right to Königsberg and the adjacent part of East Prussia. By the second half of January 1945 the Germans on their side were faced with the imminent loss of the holy ground of Tannenberg. They blew up the massive Tannenberg Memorial before it could be desecrated by the Russians, and on the twentieth Lieutenant-General Oskar von Hindenburg supervised the evacuation of the colours of the Prussian regiments and the coffins of his mother and father on board a cruiser.

Further towards the heartland of the Reich, the *Gau* of Danzig-West Prussia corresponded with the former free city of Danzig and the Polish Corridor. The region as a whole was one of bitter memories for Poles and Germans alike. West Prussia had been annexed from Poland by Prussia in 1772, and remained a predominantly Slavonic area under alien rule until it was returned to Poland after the Great War. Danzig was a different case, for this prosperous trading city had always been Germanic in character. It was annexed by Prussia in 1793, and by 1914 96 per cent of the population was German. After the Great War Danzig was declared a free city, a state of affairs which was just as displeasing to the Germans as it was to the Poles, who from 1924 built up Gdynia (Gotenhafen) as a rival port in Polish territory. The disputes over the status of the Polish Corridor and Danzig led directly to the outbreak of war between Germany and Poland on 1 September 1939.

Such was the inheritance of the new Gauleiter Albert Forster, a humanitarian and idealist who believed that Germany had a civilising vocation in the Slavonic lands: 'We can fulfil our great cultural mission in the East only if we win the Polish people over to us. Accommodation and trust will generate accommodation and trust in their turn. Mistrust just sows hostility' (Thorwald, 1950, 262).

The task was inherently impossible, and Forster was broken by the speed and magnitude of the events which overtook his *Gau* in February and March 1945. The coastal strip on the western side of the Bight of Danzig, with Danzig, Zoppot, Gotenhafen, Oxhöft and the Hela peninsula, became the refuge of the German Second Army and the million or so civilians who were awaiting rescue by sea (see p. 230).

The eastern barrier of the region was the Nogat branch of the Vistula, with the Marienburg bridgehead. This castle had been the last stronghold of the Teutonic Knights, and for the Germans in 1945 it became the last base from which an attempt might yet have been made to break through to East Prussia. The order to abandon the Marienburg castle reached the defenders on 8 March, but a group of officers lingered for a while in a corner of the castle. The battle was raging outside, and the light from the flares 'spread a magical illumination over that dark hall, revealing its mighty supporting pillars and the steep curve of the ribbed vaulting' (Paul, 1978, 190).

To the west of the Polish Corridor the territory of East Pomerania was an old Prussian possession. Here the centre of military historical tradition was the port of Kolberg, which had undergone repeated sieges since the seventeenth century, and notably the fifth and most recent in 1807, an episode which provoked Goebbels into the ultimate excesses of romanticism. Thousands of metres of colour film, thousands of still more precious troops, a budget of 8.5 million marks, and the talents of Veit Harlan (the director of *Jew Süss*) were devoted to recreating the events of 19 March to 1 July of that year. When the rest of Prussia had fallen to Napoleon, little Kolberg had been inspired to successful resistance by the sturdy townsman Joachim Nettelbeck, and by the energetic young Major von Gneisenau, who took over the military command in April.

Goebbels, as gauleiter of Berlin, identified himself with Nettelbeck, and wrote the final stirring speech which was put into Nettlebeck's mouth. Gneisenau represented National Socialist leaders in the style of Schörner, and it was just as easy to find modern parallels for the deadbeat old military governor Loucadou, and the violin-playing defeatists who had favoured giving up to the French in 1807.

The completed film *Kolberg* was premiered in Berlin on 30 January 1945, and prints were flown to Küstrin and other beleaguered fortresses. The critic Theo Fürstenau admired the lively depiction of the burning roofs, the collapsing walls and the panic among the townspeople, and Vice-Admiral Schirwitz radioed Goebbels from La Rochelle to testify how he had been 'deeply impressed by the heroic defence of the fortress of Kolberg, and the unsurpassable artistry with which it has now been represented.' This was the day when the Russians were establishing some of their first bridgeheads on the direct path to Berlin.

Kolberg was never shown in Kolberg itself, where the Poles and Soviets arranged a sixth siege with still more impressive visual effects in March 1945. As a professional soldier and responsible individual, Colonel Fullriede interpreted his task as being to hold off the enemy for just as long as he needed to evacuate the civilians and the garrison (see p. 232). Fullriede's operation was completely successful, but it did not suit Goebbels and Hitler to let the world know that Kolberg had fallen, and this truly notable episode passed without any reference in the communiqués. Once again fantasy was preferred to reality in the last weeks of the Reich.

Meanwhile the people of East Pomerania were paying for the mismanagement of their affairs by the Nazi regime. In late January Himmler, as commander of Army Group Vistula, barred an escape route by rail from Schneidemühl by parking his command train *Steiermark* in the Eastern Station at Deutsch Krone. In February he forbade the evacuation of civilians from East Pomerania altogether, with the full support of the Gauleiter Franz Schwede-Coburg. The result was that when the Russian tanks first reached the sea near Kolberg on 4 March, between 1,116,000 and 1,302,000 German civilians were cut off to the east of the breakthrough, and were left with no escape except in the direction of Danzig.

The Baltic provinces as a whole extended as a 'balcony' along the coast, and they were segmented into progressively smaller fragments whenever Russian columns drove north. The sequence is probably best shown in diagrammatic form

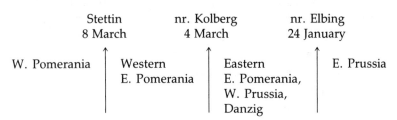

	Stettin 8 March	nr. Kolberg 4 March	nr. Elbing 24 January
W. Pomerania	Western E. Pomerania	Eastern E. Pomerania, W. Prussia, Danzig	E. Prussia

Long before these dates it was clear that escape by sea remained the only resort for the majority of the Germans of the Baltic lands.

288

The ordeal of the civilians almost invariably began with a flight across the frozen countryside. In northernmost East Prussia the people instinctively made for the temporary refuge of Königsberg, or the Samland peninsula beyond, which contained the hideously crowded camp at Peyse and the little port of Pillau. In West Prussia and East Pomerania the civilians were drawn to the major ports of Danzig and Gotenhafen, where the facilities for shipment were much greater.

In between, another 450,000 civilians were cut off in the area of the Heiligenbeil Cauldron and were forced to flee across the frozen Frisches Haff to the Nehrung sandspit or Pillau. The ice held until the end of February, and the Wehrmacht marked the passages to Pillau, Narmeln and Strauchbucht with poles and lamps, but the crossing remained a dangerous and harrowing business. One of the women recalls how

> the ice was breaking up, and in places we had to make our way through water twenty-five centimetres deep. We constantly sounded the depth of the water in front of us with sticks, and the innumerable bomb holes compelled us to make detours. Frequently, we slipped and gave ourselves up for lost. Our clothing was wet through and through, and we could move only with difficulty. . . . Household effects were strewn all over the ice. Wounded men dragged themselves towards us on sticks, gesturing for help, and their comrades drew them the rest of the way on little sledges. (Gaunitz, 1987, 51)

The Kriegsmarine pressed all available naval and merchant shipping into service to take the refugees, combatants and wounded from the principal ports of Libau (Kurland), Memel, Pillau and the Nehrung (East Prussia), Danzig, Gotenhafen, Oxhöft and Hela (the *Gau* of Danzig-West Prussia) and Stolpmünde, Rügenwaldermünde, Kolberg, Swinemünde, Stettin, Stralsund and Sassnitz (East and West Pomerania).

The total of civilians and troops saved by the Kriegsmarine

came to more than 2 million. Some of the ships made directly for the safety of German-held Denmark and Schleswig-Holstein, but most of them acted as ferries, carrying their human cargo to intermediate ports for later transhipment. Little Hela was the main collection point for the troops and refugees in the Bight of Danzig, and 387,000 souls were shipped from there in the course of April alone. Likewise the Pomeranian ports received 851,735 soldiers and civilians from 15 January to 10 May, and forwarded 340,710 over the same period. The business was managed by the two relevant commands of the Kriegsmarine:

- Admiral of the East Baltic (Burchardi) who commanded the waters of Kurland, East Prussia and the Bight of Danzig.
- Admiral of the West Baltic (Lange, then from 31 March Schubert), responsible for Pomerania and the Baltic further west.

Considering the numbers involved, the losses to enemy action were very low, but a place on board ship was no absolute guarantee of safey. There was little danger from the surface craft of the Red Banner Fleet, which were deterred by the German minefields and the German superiority in destroyers, cruisers and battleships. However, the large German passenger ships and freighters were vulnerable, for their bulk made them easy marks for Soviet aircraft and submarines, and adequate escorts could not always be provided.

On 30 January 1945 the *Wilhelm Gustloff* left Gotenhafen with 5,000 of the refugees who had been waiting in snowstorms on the quays. Shortly after 2100, when the ship was twenty-five nautical miles off shore, she was shaken by a dull blow. Second and third blows announced hits by two more torpedoes, and the vessel listed to port. The crew lost control of the crazed passengers, and only a few of the lifeboats made good their escape before the interior partitions of the lower decks broke and the ship plunged to the bottom. There were 937 survivors.

The reports of the sinking of the *Wilhelm Gustloff* terrified the refugees still stranded on the Baltic shores, and there were yet further horrors in store. The white-painted hospital ship *General von Steuben* was torpedoed on the way from Pillau on 11–12 February. The vessel swam for only twenty minutes, and although 630 of the refugees and crew were taken off, there was nothing to be done for the 2,680 military wounded, all of whom drowned.

The greatest single loss of life in maritime history was sustained in the sinking of the *Goya*, which steamed from Hela with every space, including the companion-ways, jammed full. The *Goya* was a fast, modern freighter, but she was torn apart by two torpedoes shortly after midnight on 16 April. A battle for personal survival broke out inside the ship, and for possession of the life rafts, where the first-comers defended their places with blows and kicks. Only 165 individuals were saved by the escorts and the light craft, leaving about 7,000 refugees and soldiers to the Baltic on that cold night.

Brandenburg and Silesia

Brandenburg east of the Oder (the Neumark) and the province of Silesia were familiar to generations of German schoolchildren as the stamping ground of Frederick the Great of Prussia in his struggle against the Russians and Austrians in the Seven Years War (1756–63). Goebbels recalled the setting when he addressed the victorious troops in Lauban on 8 March 1945, and he shared with Hitler a delight in Carlyle's biography of the soldier-king, whose example seemed fitting in so many ways in the last stages of the war. Frederick's way with failing generals was brutal but salutary, and he provided a model of philosophical steadfastness when everything about him had fallen into apparently irreversible decline (see p. 39).

Soviet generals and political officers drew inspirations of their own from the Seven Years War. When Babadzhanyan established the headquarters of his XI Guards Tank Corps at Kunersdorf, he admired the commanding observation post which had been adopted by Marshal Saltykov on 12 August 1759, the day that the Russians and Austrians gave Old Fritz the greatest beating of his career (Babadzhanyan, 1981, 253; see also Yushchuk, 1962, 137).

In the next campaign of the Seven Years War the old-time Russians had proceeded to capture Berlin and hold it to ransom. In April 1945 a large symbolic key was duly dropped by air to the 82nd Guards Rifle Division of the Eighth Guards Army. It was inscribed on one side with the date '1760,' and on the other with '1945':

The report that the key to Berlin was in the possession of our division awakened in our Guardsmen a new surge of warlike enthusiasm. Our political workers took the cue and helped to improvise meetings, where they expounded on the theme of how our distant ancestors had stormed the capital of Germany 185 years before. (Khetagurov, 1977, 196)

When the German front collapsed in January 1945, the refugees from the Neumark needed only to cross the Oder to find safety in the region of Berlin. Silesia received many fugitives from the Warthegau and contributed 3.2 million natives to the hosts which were seeking safety. Untold thousands were crushed by the Russian tanks or massacred by the Soviet rear-echelon troops, but the great saving mercy was that the refugees had the potential of overland escape south to the intact positions of Army Group Centre along the wall of the Sudetens, or west across the Oder and the Lausitzer Neisse to Upper Saxony. Saxony had been largely spared from the Allied air offensive, and as the war drew on, it received refugees, hospital patients, military wounded, and precious archives and art collections. By the late winter of 1944–45 it was jammed with 500,000 Silesians, as well as 400,000 civilians who had been made homeless by air attacks on the interior of the Reich, and this sanctuary was violated only by the British and American bombing raids on Dresden on 13 and 14 February.

CHAPTER 25

The End of the War and Beyond

The Military Termination of the War

The Danube Theatre

HITLER REGARDED the Nagykanizsa oilfields, just to the south-west of Lake Balaton, as the most strategically vital area on the Eastern Front. His order of priority was demonstrated in the way the German forces were deployed in January and February 1945. Out of the eighteen precious Panzer divisions on the Eastern Front, seven were fighting in Hungary, two in Kurland, four in East Prussia and only five on the Berlin axis.

The Soviet forces progressed rapidly up the Danube valley in the late summer of 1944, but for more than five months from 29 October the campaign in Hungary stuck fast in operations for or around Budapest. On 24 December forces of the 2nd and 3rd Ukrainian fronts joined behind the city, cutting off 188,000 German and Hungarian troops. The IV SS Panzer Corps was moved south from Army Group A (leaving the Germans dangerously weak in Poland), and on 1 January 1945 it opened the first of the four successive German counteroffensives on the Hungarian theatre. The same corps renewed the attack on 18 January, and this time it penetrated to within two kilometres of the suburbs of Buda, but the twin city of Pest had already fallen, and Hitler was less interested in retrieving the garrison of Buda than in letting it fight on and tie down Russian forces.

Buda fell on 13 February, but four days later the IV SS Panzer Corps opened a useful spoiling operation (17–24 February) which eliminated the Russian bridgeheads over the Hron River and thereby lessened the immediate threat to Bratislava and Vienna.

It was significant that Hitler committed his last operational reserve, the Sixth SS Panzer Army, not in the defence of Berlin but to a fourth and final offensive in Hungary. This was the Lake Balaton Operation (Frühlingserwachsen, or Spring Awakening, 6–15 March), when the German forces burst from the area east of Lake Balaton, with the Sixth SS Panzer Army attacking north in the direction of Budapest, and the Second Panzer Army thrusting east and south-east.

The Soviets contained the onslaught in one of the largest but least-known battles of the Second World War, and in the third week of March they opened their grand offensive in the direction of Vienna (3rd Ukrainian Front in the north, 16 March, and 2nd Ukrainian Front in the south, 17 March). Hungary was cleared by 4 April, and the Russians fought their way into possession of Vienna (5–13 April). The advance halted at Stockerau in Lower Austria.

Moravia, Bohemia and the End of Schörner's Army Group Centre

We resume the story of Ferdinand Schörner's Army Group Centre, which formed the 'balcony' on the left or southern flank of the Russian forces operating on the Berlin axis. Schörner (promoted to field-marshal 5 April) deployed the Fourth Panzer Army along the border hills with Silesia to the north, the powerful First Panzer Army (Heinrici's old command) in the Mährisch-Ostrau industrial region to the north-east, and the Seventeenth Army prolonging the line to the south-west.

The ethnic 'Czechs' were quiescent until 3 and 4 May, when the railways were paralysed by strikes, and red flags began to appear at house windows. Communist partisan groups took the initiative in the open combat which broke out in Prague on 5 May, and on the next day the struggle took a bizarre but decisive turn when a force of Russians in German uniforms fought their way into the city. This was the 1st Division of General Andrei Vlasov's Army, which had been recruited by the Germans from Russian prisoners of war, and had new turned against its new masters. Vlasov's double turncoats were now in the position of being at war with both the German and Soviet armies, and the 1st Division retreated from Prague on 7 May before the Soviet forces could arrive on the scene.

The last two days of the war found about 1 million German troops still in 'Czechoslovakia.' The general direction of their movement was towards the west, for they hoped to be received as prisoners by the Americans. Their rearguards meanwhile executed a fighting retreat in the face of the Soviet forces, of which the most dangerous were the armoured spearheads of Konev's 1st Ukrainian Front, thrusting into Bohemia from the north. The authority for this 'organised flight to the West' was given on 7 May by Army Group Commander Schörner at the suggestion of his chief of staff, Lieutenant-General Oldwig von Natzmer, who had received an order from the OKW telling him that a cease-fire must come into force at midnight on 8–9 May.

The Germans were naturally ignorant of the radio conversations which had opened late in April between the Soviet chief of staff, General Antonov, and the Allied commander-in-chief, General Eisenhower. The Soviets were anxious to rein the Americans back in the Böhmerwald and western Bohemia, and so leave the Russians with a clear run to Prague and the open country behind. On 4 May Eisenhower agreed to hold the American forces behind the line Karlsbad-Pilsen-Budweis, and when at the end of hostilities the German troops approached the Böhmerwald, they found that the Americans refused to take any more of them under their wing. A number of small parties infiltrated through, but most of the Germans had to resign themselves to being taken into captivity by the Russians.

We do not know with complete certainty what happened to

Field-Marshal Schörner until he was recognised on 18 May by some civilians in eastern Austria, where his light aircraft had crash-landed. He was taken into custody by German officers acting under American authority, and he was duly passed to the Russians. Schörner was imprisoned as a war criminal in the Soviet Union until 1955, when he was released and returned to his native Bavaria. He was now confronted by angry German veterans seeking revenge for the thousands of their comrades who had been executed on his orders in the last stages of the war. In 1957 Schörner was sentenced to four and a half years of imprisonment on a specimen charge of manslaughter. He lived for ten years after his release and died in 1973.

There are two contradictory versions of what had happened to Schörner in that mysterious second week of May in 1945. According to Lieutenant Helmut Dirning, his aide-de-camp, Schörner had made good his escape in direct obedience to an order from Hitler to take command of an ultimate 'National Redoubt' in Bavaria. It should be noticed, however, that Dirning was a cousin of Schörner, and that he had not accompanied him on his flight from Bohemia.

A much more circumstantial account was left by his chief of staff, Lieutenant-General von Natzmer. The story began at Josephstadt on 7 May, when Schörner stuffed his briefcase with money and told von Natzmer that he was going to escape by light aircraft, for he was too compromised to allow himself to fall into the hands of the Soviets. He offered some of the money to von Natzmer in case he too decided to run, but 'in a cold and dismissive voice von Natzmer drew Schörner's attention to the fact that on the next day the army group would be marching for its life. At such a juncture the commander should not abandon his troops, for never was higher direction more necessary than now' (Thorwald, 1951, 362). Schörner replied that he had already given everyone in the army group freedom to escape to the west, and he was now merely claiming the same liberty for himself.

On the morning of 8 May Schörner's car took off at such

speed that von Natzmer's vehicle was hard-pressed to keep up. There was no sign of the promised Fieseler Storch at Saaz, and the party remained there until a number of Russian tanks appeared on the northern side of the airfield and opened fire. The mad chase was resumed, and continued to Podhorsan, where it was discovered that a Storch had landed in a nearby meadow. Von Natzmer needed the aircraft desperately as a means of establishing communication with the Seventeenth Army and the First Panzer Army, which were out of radio contact, but when he addressed himself once more to Schörner, he found that the field-marshal had dosed himself very heavily with alcohol and had contrived to change into Bavarian national costume. Early on 9 May Schörner browbeat the elderly sentries into handing the Storch over to him, and he took off for the west.

The Berlin Operation

The last German defensive line immediately in front of the heartland of the Reich ran down the Lausitzer Neisse and the Oder to the lagoon of Stettin. For the Soviets the war was as good as won, but they mounted their final offensive in an atmosphere of some urgency—Stalin was desperate to reach Berlin before the Western Allies, and he put Konev and Zhukov on their mettle by making the city the target in a race between their two army groups, the 1st Ukrainian Front and the 1st Belorussian Front. Rokossovkii's 2nd Belorussian Front closed up the line in the north, facing the lower Oder.

The Berlin Operation began on 16 April 1945, and involved 2.5 million troops, 6,250 tanks and 42,000 artillery pieces and mortars. Zhukov laboured under the disadvantage of attacking from the crowded Küstrin bridgehead against the multiple defences of the Seelow Heights. He broke through only on 19 April, but he proceeded to make up time so successfully that Stalin placed the symbolic prize of the Reichstag within the boundaries of the 1st Belorussian Front. The two Russian army groups surrounded Berlin on 25 April, and the fighting for the city centre began on the next day. On 30 April Hitler committed suicide and the Reichstag fell, and on 2 May the surviving Germans surrendered.

The Last Days

When Hitler committed suicide, his *Political Testament* came into force, and Grand-Admiral Karl Doenitz was appointed president of the Reich and supreme commander of the Wehrmacht. On 2 May he made his first and most significant entry in his war diary: 'At the present stage of affairs the principal aim of the government must be to save as many as possible of our German men from destruction by Bolshevism.'

At that time substantial bodies of German troops were still scattered over Eastern and Central Europe. Many of the Germans were assured of falling into Western captivity, such as the divisions in Schleswig-Holstein, Bavaria and the Tyrol. Others were doomed to be taken by the Russians, like the 190,000 men of Army Group North in Kurland (surrendered 10 May), the troops still holding out in the Vistula delta to the southeast of Danzig and the embattled garrison of Breslau (surrendered 6 May). All the rest were imploding from the line which up to now had been holding firm eastwards along the Sudetens to the region of Mährisch-Ostrau, then south across eastern Moravia, the Danube valley and the Austrian Alps to northeastern Yugoslavia. Out of these forces about 1.5 million troops were able to disengage themselves from the Eastern Front between 1 and 9 May, and throw themselves on the mercy of the Western Allies, from whom they expected to have basic guarantees of their lives and welfare. Such hopes were not always fulfilled.

The official end of hostilities came on 9 May 1945, though some fighting continued east of Prague until the eleventh, and the surrender of the German forces in Yugoslavia was not completed until the fifteenth. The last remnant of the Third Reich was eliminated on 23 May, when a British armoured brigade captured Grand-Admiral Doenitz and his provisional government in their refuge on the Baltic.

Despoliation, Occupation and Partition—The Yalta Period in German History, 1945–90

Behind the 'spirit of Yalta' . . . lay the reality of the Soviet military victories, the epitome of which was represented by Poland.

(John Erickson)

Only towards the end of the twentieth century was it possible to appreciate that Germany and Central Europe had lived through a distinct historical period, which had its starting point in the final Yalta communiqué of 10 February 1945. That statement was conditioned by the conquest of western Poland in the Vistula-Oder Operation, and enshrined essential principles relating to the loss of German territory to Poland and the Soviet Union, and the occupation and effectively the partition of the rest of Germany.

In a wider context the expulsion of the Germans from the East and the partition of Germany had been not just 'some kind of "answer" to the crimes of German despotism—the full extent of which was not actually recognised while the war was on. They also corresponded to objectives which had long been harboured by the main enemy powers, and which were put into effect during the war' (Hillgruber, 1986, 9–10).

The British aims as they evolved during the war were strongly inimical to 'Prussia,' and inclined British statesmen to favour territorial arrangements which would break that entity. Both Britain and the United States consented to the Soviet annexation of the north-east corner of East Prussia with the city of Königsberg, which became 'Kaliningrad.' On 5 February 1945, while the Yalta Conference was still in progress, the Soviet-dominated Provisional Government of Poland announced that Silesia and the rest of East Prussia would come under Polish civil administration, thereby anticipating or surpassing the final communiqué, which spoke merely about a 'considerable accession of territory' to Poland in the north and west. In the subsequent Potsdam Conference the West consented to the Poles' extending their administration to the area of Germany east of the Oder and the Lausitzer Neisse, and the final communiqué on 2 August 1945 approved the transportation of surviving ethnic Germans from Poland, Czechoslovakia and Hungary.

The realities were still more far-reaching than the wordings suggested. The Poles helped themselves to Stettin (Szczecin) together with a sizeable tract of land on the west bank of the lower Oder, and upstream the administrative line of the Oder and the Lausitzer Neisse hardened into a permanent state border, which advanced the boundaries of the Poland of 1939 about 130 kilometres to the west, offering a compensation of sorts for the large Russian annexations in eastern Poland. It now emerged that the acquired territory, much of which had been wholly Germanic in character, was to be included in the 'Poland' as defined in the Potsdam communiqué. East Prussia, East Pomerania, the Neumark and the whole of Silesia were thereby added to the Sudetenland of Czechoslovakia as territory which was to be cleared of Germans. More than 2 million people, amounting to most of the German ethnic stock, were therefore uprooted from their homes after the Second World War. The Potsdam communiqué had talked about an 'orderly and humane transportation,' but the process was inherently violent in character, and was attended with killings and much brutality.

By 1955 the three Western zones of occupation had become West Germany (the Federal Republic of Germany), and the Soviet zone East Germany (the Germany Democratic Republic). East Germany together with Czechoslovakia provided the base for a massive standing concentration of Soviet forces, which as late as 1989 amounted to some 505,000 personnel, 9,500 tanks, 3,950 artillery pieces and 490 multiple-rocket launchers. The Soviet Union did not desire hostilities, but if it had gone to war, it would have given the absolute priority to the offensive, carrying the conflict away from the Russian homeland and driving westwards to great depths.

The appropriate military doctrines were projected from the experience of the Great Patriotic War, and especially the great offensives of 1944 and 1945, in which the Vistula-Oder Operation had pride of place. Military history was ranked as one of the six branches of military science, on an equal footing with other components like training and technology, and the Military Historical Directorate applied the most rigorous statistical methods to the study of the Great Patriotic War, updating its findings with reference to the extra speed, range and destructive power of new weapons systems, but always with reference to the base line of 1941–45. This heroic labour yielded 'scientific' norms from which a commander in the field could calculate, for example, the likely incidence of casualties, the consumption of fuel and ammunition, rates of advance, or the precise results of such and such an application of firepower.

By an extraordinary irony the forces which profited most by this work were those of the British in the Persian Gulf in 1991, when their planners addressed the unfamiliar problems of breaking through fixed defences. The Soviet experience was consulted in relation to both the initial bombardment of the Iraqis and the expected 'meeting engagement' in the open country behind, and in the actual fighting (24–28 February) the British 1st Armoured Division acted very much like a Soviet tank army or tank corps in 1945, exploiting through the gap which was opened in the defences by the American 1st Mechanised Infantry Division. The logistic norms were based heavily on the British experience in North Africa (1940–43).

The Challenge to the Verdict

Analysts were overwhelmed by the changes which overtook Eastern Europe with bewildering speed, starting in 1989. In January 1990 near-anarchy broke out in East Germany, which had hitherto been a model of Socialist order, and on 3 October was accomplished the reunification of Germany, or, rather, the West German takeover of the decrepit East. The Soviet garrisons became islands marooned in the capitalist world. The corresponding forces of the Americans and British, already under financial and environmental pressures, were now deprived of most of their raison d'être for remaining on German territory, and by the end of that year they had despatched some of their best troops and equipment to the Persian Gulf.

As far as it concerned the division of Germany, and a significant foreign military presence, the Yalta period of German history came to an end in 1990. It had lasted forty-five years, during which the former Allied forces were deployed more or less where they had ended up in 1945, just as if the order of battle of Waterloo had been preserved by British and Prussian troops stationed in France at a comparable remove of time in 1860.

One potentially troublesome legal problem was resolved much more quickly than was expected. It had not been generally recognised outside West Germany that the Federal Republic had never accepted the *de facto* borders established by the Poles at the expense of Germany after the war. The Potsdam final communiqué of August 1945 had drawn a provisional line along the Oder and the Lausitzer Neisse, and declared that 'the final delimitation of the western frontier of Poland should await the peace settlement.' The settlement in question was never reached, for the Cold War succeeded the hot war without a break, and the peace was not concluded. In the view of the West German Constitutional Court the frontiers of Germany still extended to those of 1937—in other words, taking in the western part of Poland and the area of the Soviet Union around Kaliningrad (Königsberg). To the surprise of some observers the government of reunited Germany renounced claims in this direction, and in virtue of a treaty of 14 November 1990 it recognised the Oder-Neisse line as its permanent eastern boundary.

However, a challenge to the moral verdicts of 1945 still remained, and it is significant that it was the historians of Germany who had meanwhile begun to question whether the Germans should always labour under a burden of guilt for what happened under the Third Reich. Germans take the study of history most seriously, for the profession of historian has its origins in German universities in the nineteenth century, and historical writing about Germany almost inevitably assumes a political character.

The opening shots in the *Historikerstreit* were delivered by the philosopher-historian Ernst Nolte in his article 'The Past That Will Not Go Away' ('Vergangenheit, die nicht vergehen will') in the *Frankfurter Allgemeine Zeitung* of 6 June 1986. Nolte was classified, rightly or wrongly, as a 'neoconservative' along with Andreas Hillgruber and the prolific Michael Stürmer. Their central thesis, though disputed in matters of detail, is not easy to contest—that the misdeeds of the Third Reich were not unique among the atrocities of the twentieth century.

CHAPTER 26

Summary and Conclusions

HUMAN LIFE came to count for less and less as war developed in the twentieth century. Within the boundaries of the technology of the time, Hitler's aims approached totality in the war he opened against the Soviet Union in 1941. The Germans nearly captured Moscow and Leningrad in their first campaign, but the disaster at Stalingrad, where the Sixth Army surrendered on 2 February 1943, and the costly failure of their attack at Kursk (5–12 July 1943) indicated that the war was turning against them. In the summer of 1944 the Soviets made important gains, driving the Germans from eastern Poland and progressing up the Danube valley.

Two army groups, the 1st Ukrainian Front under Marshal Konev, and the 1st Belorussian Front under Marshal Zhukov, were given the task of advancing across western Poland and into Germany early in 1945. The Soviets had overwhelming superiority in numbers, the quality of their equipment was outstanding, and they had acquired a mastery of mechanised warfare. The offensives opened on 12 and 14 January respectively, and by the sixteenth the Russians had broken through the German tactical zone of defence and were exploiting into the open country.

On the way to the Oder Konev's army group freed Czestochowa and Krakow, and manoeuvred the Germans out of the main part of the Upper Silesian Industrial Region. On the right, Zhukov's army group cleared Warsaw and Lodz, and penetrated the Meseritz Fortified Region. By 2 February the Soviets had advanced well into eastern Germany, to the upper and

middle stretches of the Oder—at one point only seventy kilometres from Berlin.

For many reasons the Russians were unable to crown this
Vistula-Oder Operation by pushing the short distance to
the German capital—the Germans were fighting hard on the
Oder, the thaw interfered with Russian movement and the flow
of supplies, the Soviet command experienced a lack of confidence, and indiscipline reduced the effectiveness of the Russian
troops. Finally, the Russians were forced to engage in large-
scale operations to safeguard the two flanks of their forces on
the 'Berlin axis.'

On the southern flank Konev had to launch the Upper Silesian Operation (8–24 February). He surrounded the city of Breslau, but was checked on the line of the Lausitzer Neisse. In the
subsequent lull the Germans gained local successes in counterattacks at Lauban (2–5 March) and Striegau (9–14 March).
In a second clearing campaign, the Upper Silesian Operation
(15–31 March) Konev made small gains at high cost, and the
Germans were able to hold the industrial region of Mährisch-
Ostrau until 28 April.

We turn to events on the northern flank, where two further
Soviet army groups, the 3rd and 2nd Belorussian Fronts, had
been under orders to fix and destroy the German forces in East
Prussia and on the lower Vistula. In the north Chernyakovskii's
3rd Belorussian Front attacked on 13 January, but ran into heavy
opposition in front of Königsberg. The advance was resumed
after a week of bitter fighting, and the Russians subjected Königsberg to a first siege (27 January–26 February). However,
the Soviet plans had been disrupted, and the consequences
were far-reaching. Most immediately, Rokossovskii's 2nd Belorussian Front was turned aside from the lower Vistula and
directed north-east into East Prussia, so as to reduce the pressure on Chernyakovskii. This move cut off the German Fourth
Army in central East Prussia, but reduced the flanking support
which the 2nd Belorussian Front was supposed to give to Zhukov in his advance on the Berlin axis. The Germans now built

up a powerful new force, Army Group Vistula, in the angle between Rokossovskii and Zhukov, and they delivered a counterattack (Operation Sonnenwende, 15–21 February). Although the Germans failed to reach their objectives, the Soviets were now thoroughly alarmed by the vulnerablity of their flank facing Pomerania, and they were forced to undertake a full-scale campaign in this direction.

In the first phase (24 February–4 March) of the East Pomeranian Operation, elements of the 1st and 2nd Belorussian Fronts drove north through East Pomerania to the Baltic. The Russians then peeled off to right and left. The 2nd Belorussian Front turned east and drove the isolated German Second Army into the Danzig-Gotenhafen Fortified Region, while the 1st Belorussian Front shattered the Third Panzer Army and advanced to the lower Oder in the direction of Stettin.

The East Pomeranian Operation was a victory for the Soviets in its own terms, but like Konev's campaigns in Silesia it weakened the forces facing the German heartland and helped to prolong the existence of the Third Reich for more than three months after the Russians first reached the Oder.

Meanwhile a number of isolated German armies and garrisons were fighting desperately. The Fourth Army, isolated in central East Prussia, was virtually annihilated in the Heiligenbeil Cauldron (13–28 March). The Soviets reduced Königsberg in a second siege (2–10 April), and captured the adjacent Samland peninsula (13–27 April).

Another sequence of operations eliminated the centres of German resistance which had survived the Russian victory in the East Pomeranian Operation. These were the attacks on the Danzig-Gotenhafen Fortified Region (15–28 March), Kolberg (4–18 March), and the Altdamm bridgehead on the east bank of the Oder opposite Stettin (6–21 March).

Further up the Oder the Germans put a great effort into sustaining the fortress of Küstrin, which lay directly in front of Berlin. The tensions precipitated a crisis in the German leadership, which led to the resignation of Himmler from the command of Army Group Vistula on 18 March and the dismissal of Guderian as chief of the OKH on 28 March. Küstrin fell at the end of the month, and the Russians now had a wide bridgehead as one of the bases for their final attack on Berlin.

Other garrisons had been under threat or siege since the early days of the Russian offensive in January. The reduction of Posen (27 January–22 February) cleared a major obstacle to Russian communications. The city of Breslau was isolated on 15 February, but offered an epic defence until 6 May.

The great Berlin Operation had opened on 16 April. Hitler committed suicide on 30 April, and the city fell on 2 May. By 9 May the German forces throughout Europe had surrendered or were about to do so.

The Allied conference at Yalta (4–10 February) was conducted under the influence of the first spectacular Russian victories, and led directly or indirectly to the seizure of German territory by Poland, the expulsion of millions of ethnic Germans from Eastern Europe, and the occupation and effective partition of the remainder of Germany. The division of Germany, and of the continent as a whole, lasted until 1990, when the Communist order collapsed in Central and Eastern Europe, and Germany was reunified—developments which put an end to a period of history which opened when the Soviets attacked on the Vistula on 12 January 1945.

The German defeat in 1945 was inevitable, given the weight of Allied material superiority, especially on the Eastern Front, and the fact that the Alliance held together politically. It remains to ask why the Germans lost in the particular way they did, and here every line of enquiry leads to the conclusion that the Germany of the Third Reich, for all its banners and stamping, fell short of being a united community in many fundamental respects.

As Colonel-General Guderian was aware, Hitler and some of his closest associates were men of the Danube or the Rhine, who awakened too late to the mortal danger to the old Prussian heartland of the Reich. It is striking how at the lower levels of command also the Germans attached so much importance to a man's roots as part of his qualifications for such and such a task. It was judged important, for example, that General Krappe was a Pomeranian, Schulz a Silesian, von Saucken an East Prussian, and that Greiser hailed from the Warthegau. *Panzerknacker* Rudel arranged for his wing of Stukas to be moved from Hungary as soon as he learned that his native Silesia was under attack.

Real or supposed local origins account for the fate of Colonel-General Erhard Raus, who was dismissed from the command of the Third Panzer Army on 10 March. His end was welcomed by some elements of regional opinion, for he was 'a native of Austria, and therefore alien to the land and people of Pomerania' (Murawski, 1969, 72). The immediate cause, however, was a ludicrous episode in Hitler's bunker, where Raus had gone to deliver a report on the state of his army. Guderian writes that he himself found the exposition

> outstandingly lucid. When he had finished Hitler dismissed him without comment. Raus had scarcely left the Chancellery shelter, where this conference had taken place, before Hitler turned to Keitel, Jodl and myself and shouted: 'What a miserable speech! The man talked of nothing but details. Judging by the way he speaks he must be a Berliner or an East Prussian. He must be relieved of his command at once!' I replied: 'Colonel-General Raus is one of our most capable Panzer generals. . . . And as for his origin, Raus is an Austrian and therefore a compatriot of yours, my Führer.'
> HITLER: 'Absolutely impossible. He can't be an Austrian.'
> JODL: 'Oh yes he can, my Führer. He talks exactly like Moser, the actor.'
> Hitler's opinion of him remained unfavourable. When I pointed out that we had no surfeit of good generals my re-

mark was ignored. Raus was relieved of his command. (Guderian, 1952, 420–21)

The fundamental disunity of the Reich was also evident in matters of organisation. Competition for authority and resources was shown in the lack of coordination in the development of weapons, the hoarding of ammunition and fuel, and the tardy and broken-backed mobilisation for Total War in 1944. Likewise the dissensions between Party and Wehrmacht were responsible for the lack of effective defence in depth on the Eastern Front, and for the deaths or needless misery of millions of civilian refugees.

When the Reich neared its end, it became clear that leaders had been fighting for different 'Germanies.' On the one side the moral contagion of those closest to the Nazi system became unmistakable. Field-Marshal Schörner, and those brown-jacketed heaps of filth the Gauleiters Greiser, Schwede-Coburg, Koch and Hanke were unsparing of the lives of others as long as there was a Nazi order to defend, and they then attended with great speed to their own safety. In contrast, Germany was honoured by the devotion of men like Hossbach, Reinhardt, von Tettau, von Saucken, Lasch, von Ahlfen, von Niehoff and many others, who proved that human responsibility could still be reconciled with soldierly duty.

The Conduct of War: Soviet Science and German Art

The Soviet Style

The Evolution of Soviet Mechanised Warfare

IT IS UNFORTUNATE that nobody has come up with a neater term than 'blitzkrieg' to apply to a style of war which is familiar to every student of twentieth-century military history. Blitzkrieg is an offensive way of fighting, which uses the combined efforts of tanks, mechanised infantry, mobile artillery and combat engineers, and calls on the greatest possible close air support. Concentration of force and a brief but intensive application of firepower secures breakthroughs on one or more narrow sectors, after which the emphasis shifts to fast-moving operations in great depth. Victory is attained as much through achieving psychological disruption as through inflicting physical damage.

The great disadvantage of the word 'blitzkrieg' is that it suggests that the Germans were the sole pioneers and practitioners of mechanised warfare in the second quarter of the twentieth century, whereas in fact the Soviets proceeded at least as fast on parallel lines.

Russian-built tanks were first shown to the public on Red Square on 23 January 1923, which was the fourth anniversary of the Red Army. However, the origins of Soviet mechanised warfare are not to be found in the tank forces as such, but in the notion of the 'interworking' (*vzaimodeistvie*) of infantry and artillery, which was explored by General (later Field-Marshal) Mikhail Nikolaevich Tukhachevskii and two associates (M. N. Tukhacheveskii, N. E. Varfolomeev, E. A. Shilovskii *Armeiskaya Operatsiya*, Leningrad, 1926). This essential principle of combining the action of the various arms was expressed in a rudimentary way in the *Field Service Regulations 1929* (*Polevoi Ustav R.K.K.A. 1929*, or *PU-29* for short).

In the Soviet version of mechanised warfare derived from a collective effort on the part of the Operational Faculty of the Frunze Military Academy, and the Operational Directorate of the General Staff under V. K. Triandafillov. The various notions, as they emerged, were put to the test in field exercises and command staff games, which did much to obviate the gap between theory and practice which plagued the development of armoured warfare in the West.

Having established the basic 'combined arms' principle, the Soviets studied how it was to be applied at the grand tactical level in the 'deep battle' (*glubokii boi*). From there they moved onto 'deep operations' (*glubokaya operatsiya*) at the army and army-group level. They knew that European Russia was open to new forms of mechanised attack, and in 1933 the chief of staff, E. I. Egorov, reported to the Revolutionary War Council that it was technically possible for an invader to penetrate up to six hundred kilometres, disrupting the Soviet mobilisation, overrunning military bases, and seizing economically important regions. The Soviet answers were expressed in the *Instructions for the Deep Battle* (*Instruktsii po glubokomu boiyu*, 1935), and in the very significant *PU-36*. The preferred option in both publications was offensive, and *PU-36* enshrined principles which remained unchanged for years to come.

The first task was to 'achieve the simultaneous destruction of the whole enemy deployment to its full defensive depth' (Kir'yan, 1982, 116). Wide sectors of the enemy frontage were to be amused and held down by the weak forces of the 'pinning group' (*skovyvayushchaya gruppa*), while at least two-thirds of the combat strength was focussed in the 'shock group' (*udarnaya gruppa*), where the Russians concentrated up to forty tanks per kilometre. These machines were mainly the tanks of the Direct Support Group (Gruppa NPP), which worked in close association with the infantry, artillery and air forces to break through the enemy tactical zone of defence.

The second phase was exploiting into the open country in the enemy rear, which was carried out by mechanised infantry, horsed cavalry and the tanks of the Group for Further Operations (Gruppa DD).

The essentials of Soviet mechanised warfare were now complete. There followed, however, a period of disruption which extended for six or more years. This was partly the result of the Great Purge of 1937–38, which eliminated Marshal Tukhachevskii along with 35,000 fellow officers, and partly a consequence of misguided reorganisations of the mechanised forces which were ordered in November 1939, July 1940 and February 1941. Communist armour fared disappointingly in the Spanish Civil War and in Poland in 1939, and downright disastrously during the first period of the Great Patriotic War.

Old principles now had to be rediscovered or extended, and they were enshrined in the draft *PU-41* and the fully fledged *PU-44*. In general, the Soviets learned to strike a better balance between the tanks and the infantry in their key formations, and they relied more and more on artillery to make up for the declining quality of their manpower:

> We saw a well-organised artillery as the embodiment of our army's power. We held that whatever we would do with gunpower rather than the bayonet would be to our great advantage and would safeguard our troops against superfluous losses. Hence we should spare neither time nor effort in preparing the artillery attack. In the final analysis, if we looked at it from the moral point of view, such work was, under war conditions, a specific expression of concern for the human being in the highest sense in which the words 'concern for the human being' are at all compatible with the word 'war.' (Konev, 1969, 10–11)

* * *

Soviet Organisation in 1945

Fronts

Soviet 'Fronts' were the equivalent of Western army groups—literally, groupings of ten or so armies which could reach a combined strength of about 1 million men. For the Vistula-Oder Operation the 1st Ukrainian Front and the 1st Belorussian Front formed what was in effect a double Front attacking on the same axis, and they comprised 2.2 million troops, 33,500 field guns and heavy mortars, over 7,000 tanks and assault guns, and 5,000 tactical aircraft (see p. 24).

Tank and Mechanised Formations

Tank Armies

The main exploitation force of the Fronts was concentrated in the tank armies (Konev and Zhukov had two each in 1945). The first Soviet tank armies began to appear in May 1943, but they soon took a tremendous battering, for they were weak in artillery and the component rifle troops were not properly integrated with the armoured forces. By January 1945, however, the establishment of the individual tank armies had risen by one-third in personnel, about twice over in tanks and assault guns, and four times in towed artillery. The tank army was now a well-balanced mechanised force, which normally included two or three corps of tanks, and a single corps of mechanised infantry. This produced

35,000–50,000 troops
500 (two tank corps) or 900 (three tank corps) tanks
850 artillery pieces and mortars.

The mechanised infantry travelled in trucks or on top of the tanks, and their role was never more important than towards the end of the war, when they helped the tanks to winkle out parties of Panzerfaust-armed German infantry in broken or built-up terrain.

It was the infantry component which enabled the Fourth Tank Army to batter its way a short distance into the heavily industrialised region of Upper Silesia in the spring of 1945. This army was already 'infantry heavy,' since it had just one corps of tanks (X Guards) to partner its corps of infantry (VI Guards Mechanised), but Lelyushenko was delighted to receive an additional corps of infantry (V Guards Mechanised) on 24 March:

> I had long striven to obtain a third corps for the army, but it was particularly fortunate that it was a [further] corps of mechanised infantry which was added to our establishment. This increased the general military effectiveness of the army, but especially its capacity as regards artillery, mechanised infantry and tanks. Two mechanised corps and one tank corps—in my view that was the most advantageous organisation for a tank army at that time. (Lelyushenko, 1970, 306–7)

Tank Corps

Lelyushenko's comment reminds us of a central principle of blitzkrieg—that the Russian tank and mechanised formations all comprised a mixture of tanks and mechanised infantry; it was just the weighting of the two elements which was different. Tank corps (usually to the number of two or three) were an important ingredient of tank armies, as we have seen, but under enterprising leaders they were capable of acting as miniature armies in their own right, thrusting and weaving well ahead of the main body of the first echelon (wave) of the Soviet armies. This degree of independent life would have been unthinkable without the brigade of mechanised infantry being at hand to support the three brigades of tanks. A tank corps numbered approximately

11,700 troops
220 tanks
40 assault guns
152 towed artillery pieces and mortars, and eight BM-13 Katyusha multiple-rocket launchers.

Mechanised Corps

The mechanised corps was almost as fast and useful as the tank
corps. Its organisation was a mirror image of the latter, for it
was made up of three brigades of mechanised infantry and one
tank brigade. The following figures show in addition the importance of the artillery component:

16,000 troops
180 tanks
60 assault guns
252 artillery pieces and mortars, and eight Katyushas.

Tank Brigades

These little entities were highly versatile. As well as working
directly with the parent tank corps, they could find themselves
detached to all-arms (i.e. rifle) divisions, corps or even armies.
Tank army commanders also liked to employ them as personal
reserves, and they were particularly fond of packaging them
with supporting forces and sending them forth as the fighting
advance guards ('forward detachments'; see p. 340) of the army.
In 1945 the tank brigade was formed of three battalions of tanks
and one of mechanised infantry, and held

1,354 troops
65 tanks.

Mechanised Infantry Brigades

These forces each owned the respectable number of thirty-nine tanks, and they were used for much the same purposes as the tank brigades.

All-Arms (Rifle) Formations

All-Arms (Rifle) Armies

These formations took shape from April 1943. The organisation and size varied greatly from one army to another, but they had great numbers of tanks and guns to compensate for the wretched quality of the rifle troops. All-arms armies included from two to four rifle corps, together with brigades of tanks, tank-destroyers and mortars, and all the supporting services. In round terms we are talking of

40,000 troops
400 or more tanks
1,100 or more artillery pieces and mortars.

For the Radom-Lodz Operation in January 1945 the Sixty-Ninth Army fielded three rifle corps (altogether, ten rifle divisions), one tank corps, 512 tanks and assault guns, 2,400 towed artillery pieces and mortars, and 195 Katyushas (Danilov, 1958, 200).

Rifle Corps

The impressive structure (three rifle divisions) was belied by the weakness of the component infantry. Typical figures are

9,000–16,000 troops
300–400 artillery pieces
450–500 heavy mortars (the very high proportion of artillery is significant).

Rifle Divisions

The division was the basic building brick of military calculations, and although the Soviet rifle division was composed of three rifle regiments, it is perhaps useful to remember that a Russian infantry division reached only about half the strength of its German counterpart. The establishment of the Soviet rifle division provided for 11,780 men, but the average was in the range of 3,000 to 7,000 troops.

On 1 January 1945 the 83rd Guards Rifle Division of the Eleventh Guards Army held 6,642 men, thirteen assault guns, sixty-eight towed artillery pieces and sixty-two mortars.

Artillery Organisation

The Soviet artillery was formed into formation- and unit-level 'groups,' according to whether it supported armies, corps divisions or regiments.

Aviation Organisation

The air army was the level of aviation command which corresponded to the ground Front (army group). Thus in January 1945 the Second Air Army (2,583 aircraft) supported the 1st Ukrainian Front, while the Sixteenth Air Army (2,190 aircraft) supported the 1st Belorussian Front.

Air armies in turn comprised specialist divisions of bombers, close-support (*shturmovoi*) aircraft and fighters.

Notes on Some Key Weapons

Tanks

The classic T-34 medium tank was put into mass production early in 1941. It was an excellent fighting vehicle, combining a heavy (76-mm) gun for its time, well-sloped armour, useful range, reliable starting in cold weather, and wide tracks which contributed to its exceptional mobility. The Germans were so impressed that they considered building a direct copy, but they settled instead on the more complicated Panther (Mark V). Partly as a result of the lessons of the battle of Kursk (July 1943), the Soviets introduced an up-gunned and redesigned machine in 1944. This was the

T-34/85
Weight: 32 tons
Armament: one 85-mm gun, two 7.62 machine-guns
Armour: 45–75 mm

The standard Soviet heavy tank in the first years of the war was the KV-1, which was furnished with the same calibre (76-mm) gun as the original T-34, but had thicker armour and a high (and therefore vulnerable) silhouette. A new version was delivered from 1941, and was employed in particular for specialised artillery support:

KV-2A
Weight: 52 tons
Armament: one 152-mm howitzer, two or three 7.62 machine-guns
Armour: 75–110 mm

A much better heavy tank in general confirmation was the first fully fledged machine of the Stalin line, the IS-2, which came into service in April 1944:

IS-2
Weight: 45 tons
Armament: one 122-mm gun, three 7.62 machine-guns, one 12.7-mm anti-aircraft machine-gun
Armour: 60–160 mm

The IS-3, essentially a version of the IS-2 with redesigned and very heavily sloped armour, saw action in Germany in the final weeks of the war. A German testifies that 'our otherwise excellent L48 75-mm tank gun could do little against the super-heavy Russian Stalin tanks. Only what we called a "Sunday shot" was capable of penetrating that thick armour' (Schäufler, 1979, 26).

Artillery

Self-propelled and assault guns combined well-tried tank chassis with artillery gun barrels, from the standard 76-mm upwards. The SU-85 and the SU-100 were effective tank-destroyers which utilised the T-34 chassis. The chassis of the heavy tanks was in turn the basis of two assault guns of almost identical design, the ISU-122 and the still more formidable ISU-152 (also called the M-43 howitzer):

ISU-152 (M-43)
Weight:	46 tons
Armament:	one 152-mm howitzer
Armour:	60–90 mm

'The 152-mm Model 1943 howitzer brought together in a splendid way the power of a heavy six-inch shell with the mobility of a tank-destroyer system' (Ivanov, 1980, 23). It looked like a great metal box on tracks, with a trunk-like barrel projecting from the front, and it became one of the most powerful images of the end of the war, as it pushed down the rubble-strewn streets of German cities.

The conventional 76-mm and 122-mm towed artillery pieces offered the main fire support for Soviet operations in the field, with valiant help from the 120-mm heavy mortar. The guns of heavier calibre came into their own when the Soviets began to break into the defences of the Reich, for these massive tubes were increasingly employed in the direct-fire role against forts, pillboxes and other strongpoints. The Katyusha (BM-21) multiple-rocket launcher, however, was the type of ordnance most directly associated in the popular mind with the Soviet way of war. It was a direct expression of military doctrine, for it was designed to deliver the greatest possible weight of explosive in the shortest possible time (see p. 333). Katyusha fire was delivered in salvoes which distributed 4.35 tons of ordnance over an area of ten acres for a span of between seven and ten seconds.

Aircraft

Soviet strategists, like their German counterparts, saw aircraft primarily as a means of lending close support to the ground forces rather than as an instrument of strategic bombing. It was no coincidence that the Il-2 Shturmovik fighter-bomber became the classic Soviet aircraft of the Great Patriotic War. It was very effective against the lighter German tanks, and by 1943 it accounted for one-quarter of all aircraft production.

The Storm on the Reich

General Concepts

For their offensive in Poland and East Prussia in 1945, the Soviets intended to smash the crust of the German forces in one mighty blow, then exploit to a great depth. The tank and mechanised forces had the task of fragmenting the German deployments rather than encircling them, and they were under orders to press on at any price to objectives in the deep rear and to leave the business of mopping up to the forces of the second echelon (wave). In earlier campaigns some of the momentum of the offensive had been lost when the first echelon carried out short-range pincer movements, like the envelopment which the Germans now expected in the Vistula bulge (see p. 61), but this time, fully in accordance with the situation as it developed, STAVKA used in the operation the concept of mighty bisecting thrusts being struck deep into enemy-held territory. This made it possible first to divide the Vistula defence line into isolated pockets, following which it was imperative to press tank corps and armies onwards into the breakthrough sectors, which advanced at full speed deep into enemy-entrenched areas, spending no time in crushing his centres of resistance behind. (Larionov et al., 1984, 400)

In the same way, the offensives of the 2nd and 3rd Belorussian Fronts were intended to drive straight to the Baltic on parallel rather than converging forces. Only when the 2nd Belorussian Front was unexpectedly diverted to the north-east was the campaign in this theatre converted into a close envelopment of East Prussia.

Making Ready

Maskirovka

Maskirovka, literally 'masking,' is a term which cannot be rendered exactly into English, for it embraces every activity from physical camouflage on the battlefield to campaigns of political 'disinformation.' *PU-44* upheld *Maskirovka* as an essential ingredient of surprise, and consequently a

mandatory form of combat support for each action and operation. The missions of *Maskirovka* are to secure concealment of the manoeuvre and concentration of troops for the purpose of delivering a surprise attack, to mislead the enemy about our forces, weapons, actions and intentions, and thus force him to make an incorrect decision.

The techniques of *Maskirovka* had reached a high stage of development by the end of 1944, but the Soviet planners had to employ every trick of the trade if they were to attain any useful degree of surprise. The Russians had already set out their bridgeheads beyond the Vistula and the Narew, and they could not hide the fact that they intended to attack some time in the middle of the winter. 'To solve these problems, Soviet planners sought to develop a *Maskirovka* plan which concealed primarily the scale of the attack rather than its location, timing, or their overall offensive intent' (Glantz, 1989, 475).

Negative measures of *Maskirovka* involved hiding the approach and emplacement of forces (movement at night, camouflage screens and nets, etc.), and applying the 'need to know' principle in a very literal way. Precious secrets were confided only just before the men concerned had to act on them, and even then they were carried in the head rather than set down on paper.

Positive *Maskirovka* was more difficult to obtain in the circumstances of 1944–45, but it was not altogether out of the question, providing the Russians could identify the expectations of the Germans and reinforce them. The most successful enterprise of this kind was the elaborate hoax by which Konev persuaded the Germans that he had powerful forces massing on his left flank south of the Vistula, ready to attack in the direction of Krakow (see p. 32).

Beyond doubt the greatest achievement of *Maskirovka* on a larger scale was to leave the German intelligence under Colonel Reinhard Gehlen in ignorance that Stalin had moved nine armies and a tank corps from STAVKA reserve to strengthen the central push in Poland, namely:

- To the 1st Ukranian Front:
  Sixth, Twenty-First, Fifty-Second and Fifty-Ninth armies, Third Guards Tank Army, VII Guards Tank Corps.
- To the 1st Belorussian Front:
  Thirty-Third and Sixty-First Armies, Third Shock Army, First Guards Tank Army.

The Germans calculated that the Soviet forces in the bridge-heads had odds of 3–3.5:1 in their favour, whereas the superiority was in the order of 5–7:1 (Glantz, 1989, 498).

On the sector of the 3rd Belorussian Front a large proportion of the Russian forces had already declared themselves in the fighting for northern East Prussia, and the German intelligence estimates were substantially correct. This helps to account for the slow progress which Chernyakovskii made at the beginning of his offensive. To the south-west, however, the 2nd Belorussian Front kept the Fifth Guards Tank Army well back from the front line, after it had arrived from STAVKA reserve, and the presence of this striking force remained completely unknown to the Germans until after the Front had begun its attack.

Intelligence, Reconnaissance, Maps

By now the Soviets were fighting well beyond the historic borders of Russia, and the planners were denied the wealth of information which had once come to them from agents and partisans behind enemy lines (see p. 34). Intensive aerial photography helped to make up for the deficiency, as did the little surveillance patrols which operated forty or so kilometres in the enemy rear, recording the movement of German forces and identifying their daily routines. Chuikov had a lieutenant and seven men emplaced for months in the heart of the forest twelve kilometres south-west of Warka, and they relayed their observations to the Eighth Guards Army by radio or by means of the light PO-2 aircraft which flew in by night. However, a lot of valuable information was obtained simply by keeping a close watch from observation posts in the Soviet forward positions, and personal reconnaissance was regarded as an important obligation for commanders at every level from sub-unit to Front.

The amount of intelligence that reached the Russian staffs was cumulatively impressive, and helps to account for the excellent standard of Soviet military cartography. Cooperation between armies was worked out most conveniently on maps on a scale of 1:100,000 (Yushchuk, 1962, 208). Large-scale base maps were prepared for battery and company commanders, and these

> told them all they needed to know about the enemy engineering fortifications, fire systems and targets in the given sector. In principle, this enabled the artillerymen to fire without wasting a single round. Similarly, every infantry commander had a complete idea of the engineering and fire obstacles he might encounter. The base maps contained information on the entire enemy tactical zone, thus enabling the artillerymen to see everything the enemy had for about ten kilometres ahead. (Konev, 1969, 11)

The Germans conceded that the enemy maps of German territory were often better than their own, and they detected evidence in episodes like the accurate artillery and air strikes which were delivered against the port of Rosenberg in the Heiligenbeil Cauldron on 24 March:

> Hundreds upon hundreds of vehicles of every description were jammed together in a minute space—trucks, cars, private vehicles and horse-drawn carts. The bursting bombs and shells now turned them over, smashed them into pieces or hurled them through the air. (Dieckert and Grossmann, 1960, 148. See also the Führer briefing on 19 January, Schramm, 1982, IV, 1,023)

War Games

These sessions were not remotely recreational in character, but were designed to establish and firm up plans of operations, to brief officers in their tasks and to work out every last detail relating to cooperation across formation and unit boundaries, and the support from the artillery, engineers and logistic services. Planning and training therefore went hand in hand, and war games or presentations in one form or another were carried out at every level of command above sub-unit. Colonel Antonov describes the final session at the headquarters of the Fifth Shock Army on 11 January:

> The war game was carried out on the sand table, where real circumstances were reproduced in miniature. Looking at the model, we could see a representation of the various operational tasks of Bezarin's Fifth Shock Army, together with the sector of attack of each division. The commanders of the corps and divisions, and the chiefs of the arms and services were summoned in turn to the model where they reported their operational task and their state of readiness for the attack. Here we were able to make all the detailed arrangements concerning the cooperation between the infantry, tanks, artillery and aviation, and between the formations of our army and the neighbouring forces—the Second Guards Tank Army and the VII Guards Cavalry Corps.
>
> Our commander, Nikolai Erastovich Bezarin, was in a composed frame of mind, and when the report was clear and logical, he was content to look up and say 'Good, that's how you will conduct the action.' But he invariably levelled reprimands at commanders who happened to stumble.' (Antonov, 1975, 193. See also Kon'kov, 1983, 35; Lelyushenko, 1979, 272; Katukov, 1976, 338; Babadzhanyan, 1981, 225–26)

Political Education

Great efforts were made to raise motivation and standards among the troops through political indoctrination. Members of the Communist Party and the Komsomol (League of Young Communists) were committed activists who formed substantial elements in each army at the beginning of the offensive (15, 946, for example, in the Thirty-Eighth Army, and 9,769 in the Sixty-Ninth Army). In addition, the full-time political deputies (commissars) carried on political work with the battalions and companies. They distributed pamphlets and newspapers, organised political *mitings*, and got veterans to circulate among the green troops with cheering stories. Chuikov expressed particular admiration for the work of Junior-Lieutenant Vassily Vybornov, a company political organiser who came out to the trenches every nightfall with the latest news of the war, and stopped to inspect the weapons and tell the soldiers how to improve their living conditions. He took one Private Skvortsov to task because he had found sand in the breechblock carrier of his machine-gun. 'He did not report the oversight to the commander, but demanded that within an hour Skvortsov put his machine-gun into ideal working order. Such comradely warnings were more effective than any punishment' (Chuikov, 1978, 68).

Logistic Preparations

Some indication has already been given (p. 33) of the quantity of materials of every kind which were amassed to support the offensives in January 1945. The Soviets based their provision of ammunition on the *Boekomplet* (set), which for each weapon corresponded with the number of rounds which was carried on the individual man or vehicle. In January 1945 this represented about 1.5 to 2.5 *Boekomplets* per infantryman, and 3 to 10 for every tank and artillery piece.

On the same principle fuel was calculated according to the *Napravka* (fill), which signified the quantity of liquid which was carried in the internal and external fuel tanks of the armoured vehicles, assault guns and trucks. In January 1945 the two Fronts on the central axis in Poland embarked on their offensive with 4 to 4.5 fills per vehicle (which in the event was going to fall far short of consumption).

At the level of a tank army these calculations produced a weight of *Boekomplets* of about a thousand tons, and of *Napravkas* of some six hundred tons (First Guards Tank Army). The two definitions were likewise employed to work out the units of replenishment, once the original ammunition and fuel had been exhausted.

Command and Control

Before the offensive opened in January 1945, Stalin had taken on the role of 'Front co-ordinator' (see p. 16), and from his headquarters at STAVKA he was in continual telephone communication with the army-group commanders, adjusting their tasks as was dictated by the changing military and political face of affairs. As a rule, the management of business within the army group was left to the judgment of the Front commander concerned.

Konev wrote:

> I have always held that in decisive moments, especially during frequent and sudden changes in the situation, the Front commander (and the army commander too) must be closer than usual to the troops and make the necessary decisions on the spot. I have never regarded visits to the troops, however short or long, as personal bravery, and certainly not heroism. To my mind they are merely an inseparable part of the work of commanding modern mobile operations. (Konev, 1969, 76)

The memoirs of Soviet officers leave us in no doubt that the Front commanders were often to be seen at the forward edge of the battle area, where they didn't hesitate to take control at the operational or even the tactical level. On 1 March Zhukov climbed a church tower in Pomerania and revived a stalled attack by ordering the forward detachment of the First Guards Tank Army to be committed to the battle (Katukov, 1976, 378; see also Bokov, 1979, 54, 114). More strikingly still, at the end of January his rival Konev had used the facility of a single radio to adjust the advance of the Third Guards Tank Army around the flank of the Upper Silesian Industrial Region (see p. 92).

The structure of the Russian headquarters in fact favoured a personal style of leadership. The principle was explained by Lelyushenko:

> Our experience demonstrated convincingly that the most effective way of directing armies in the course of operations was by having two groups acting in parallel—an operational group, managed directly by the commander—and a second group, namely the actual staff of the army, situated right next to the command post. (Lelyushenko, 1970, 273)

The operational group (*Operativnaya gruppa*, or *Opergruppa*) of the army, corps or division was a very small and very mobile directing organisation which centred around the formation commander, the chief of the artillery, three or four operational officers and a small complement of drivers, radio operators and escorts. The advantage of immediacy was particularly important for the commander of tank forces:

> It's not just a question of personal bravery and presence of mind. . . . He cannot count on having timely or accurate information on the strength of the enemy. The situation changes from one moment to the next. Uncertainty lies in ambush for him at every step, especially when he is operating in the operational rear of the enemy. (Katukov, 1976, 353)

The 'actual staff' mentioned by Lelyushenko formed the administrative headquarters of the formation, and was situated at the misleadingly named 'command post.' The command post was not quite as quick on its feet as the operational group, but in fast-moving operations the command post of an army moved about once a day, and those of corps and divisions about two or three times.

331

The Breakthrough Battle

Concentration on the Breakthrough Sector

SUCCESS in blitzkrieg, whether Soviet or German, depended crucially on the quantity of force which could be amassed against the target sector of the enemy defences. This led to a massive concentration of striking power on the 'breakthrough sectors,' in the Russian parlance, and a correspondingly weak spread of forces along the 'passive sectors,' where the intention was just to keep the enemy occupied. In January 1945 the following densities were the result:

Lengths and Proportions of Frontages and Breakthrough Sectors

	Total Frontage	Breakthrough Sector(s)	Breakthrough Sector(s) as proportion
1st UKF	250 km	36 km*	14.4%
1st BRF	230 km	30 km†	13.0%
2nd BRF	285 km	28 km	9.8%
3rd BRF	170 km	24 km	14.1%

*Excl. the 3-km breakthrough sector of the Sixtieth Army.
†Excl. the 4-km breakthrough sector of the Forty-Seventh Army.

The same principle of concentration applied within the individual armies. Thus the seven-kilometre breakthrough sector of the Sixty-Ninth Army amounted to only 13 per cent of the frontage, but contained 80 per cent of the infantry, 90 per cent of the artillery and mortars, and all the tanks and assault guns.

When they came to choose the breakthrough sectors, the commanders bore in mind considerations like good approach routes, the availability of woods or other cover where they might conceal their forces, and any opportunities which they might detect in the areas held by the enemy—firm going, weak defences and forces, formation boundaries and so on.

Echeloning of Forces

For purposes of attack Soviet forces were deployed in one, two or three echelons (waves or lines) according to the circumstances of the case. Multiple lines, which were capable of sustaining a prolonged and heavy battle, were indicated where the Germans were themselves arrayed in depth. Conversely, a shallow defence suggested an attack in a single echelon, which would enable the maximum number of weapons to be employed in the first blow. (Danilov, 1958, 27–28)

The Artillery Strike

In the Great War the typical artillery preparation fired off hundreds of thousands or even millions of shells to no great effect. One of the reasons was that the bombardment usually extended over several days, which sacrificed the element of surprise and attenuated the effect of shock. Moreover, the ground was churned up by the vast quantity of shells and became a significant obstacle to the attacking forces.

The 'lightning bombardment' was based on different principles. It was lighter in overall weight than the cumulative preparations, but it directed a much higher density of fire against pre-registered targets in a very short span of time. Key installations like command posts and artillery batteries were likely to be knocked out in a matter of minutes, the enemy troops were stunned if they were not physically destroyed, and yet the ground remained relatively untouched.

The first of the lightning bombardments were directed by German Colonel Bruchmüller at Riga in 1917. They contributed significantly to the surprise which the Germans achieved in their offensive on the Western Front in March 1918, and they became part of the stock-in-trade of Soviet and German warfare in the Great Patriotic War.

As practised by the Soviets in January 1945, the opening bombardment was comprised of

- an initial strike (*ognevoi udar*) of very high intensity, and then, if necessary
- a steady and more prolonged bombardment;
- a single or double rolling barrage (*ognevoi val*) descending like a curtain at specified intervals ahead of the attacking troops.

On the 1st Ukrainian Front (12 January) the initial strike lasted five minutes and prepared the way for the attack of the 'forward battalions.' After this reconnaissance in force had probed the German defences, a bombardment of 107 minutes softened up the remaining strongpoints for the attack by the main forces.

On the 1st Belorussian Front (14 January) much more emphasis was put on the first strike, which lasted twenty-five minutes and delivered 315,000 artillery rounds weighing 5,540 tons, of which 825 tons (15 per cent) were devoted to counterbattery fire. The strike reached to a depth of eight kilometres, overthrew eighty-six shelters, and twenty-five observation posts, and destroyed or 'suppressed' eighty-two artillery batteries, forty-nine mortar batteries and 347 machine-guns. Zhukov had a further strike of 107 minutes in store, but did not find it necessary to employ it.

All the targets had been carefully surveyed beforehand, and by shooting from their excellent maps the Russian gunners were able to defy fog, blizzards, smoke and darkness.

The artillery in general was by now highly responsive to command, thanks to effective field radio (which had not been available in the Great War), and to the useful way the Soviets reorganised the structure in 1944. Hitherto the artillery had been organised rigidly for specific missions—infantry support, deep strike, counterbattery fire and the like. Now the ordnance in the breakthrough sectors was arranged in 'groups' at the army, corps, divisional and regimental levels (see p. 320), and placed directly at the service of the relevant field commander. The kind of flexibility that was possible was demonstrated at the opening of the offensive by the 1st Belorussian Front on 14 January. Zhukov was present at the command post of the Fifth Shock Army, and

> the corps commanders reported one after another that the fighting reconnaissance was proceeding successfully. Marshal Zhukov authorised General Bezarin to bring the first echelon of the corps into action twenty minutes earlier than had been stipulated in the timetable, and to switch the artillery from preparation to fire to support the attack by the main force. (Bokov, 1979, 54)

The Grinding Process

In the Vistula-Oder Operation the evolution of tactics made considerable advances, and especially in perfecting the means of breaking through the enemy tactical zone of defence.

(Kozlov, 1975, 81)

One of the lesser-known features of blitzkrieg is the bitter, close-range and often slow-moving battle which was necessary to clear avenues through the enemy fixed defences and open the way for the exploitation forces.

On the 1st Belorussian Front (14 January) each rifle corps of the first echelon was assigned two or three battalions of assault engineers, who helped to lift more than 90,000 anti-tank and anti-personnel mines and clear over 800 passages. Just as vital was the role of the close-support tanks and assault guns. Their original brigade structure was dissolved, and they were split into battalions or companies, which were assigned to the rifle battalions, or subdivided still further for cooperation with platoons: 'This improved to a considerable extent the teamwork between the tanks directly supporting the infantry and the rifle units, and promoted their rate of advance' (Larionov et al.; 1984, 402).

As always, the Front commanders were free to determine how they intepreted the general principles. Zhukov, like most of the others, was willing to divert sizeable proportions of his assets in tanks and assault guns to support the infantry in the grinding match. Konev was stingy in comparison. Thus:

Assignment of Armour to the Grinding Battle on the First Day of Assault

	Total of tanks and assault guns	Number devoted to infantry support	Density of tanks and assault guns per km of frontage
1st BRF (Zhukov)	3,220	1,448 (46%)	25–30
1st UKF (Konev)	3,660	820 (23%)	21

It was also significant that Zhukov deployed up to seventeen engineer companies per kilometre of his breakthrough sectors, whereas Konev committed only between five and thirteen.

The Commitment of the Tank Armies to the Breakthrough

Most of what we have considered so far was the product of sound doctrine, and industrious staff work and training. There came a point, however, when the outcome of the battle hung directly on the informed instincts of the Front commander. This was when he judged that the time had come to release the tank armies, which on most Fronts were awaiting the signal where they stood just before the all-arms armies of the first echelon.

Zhukov held back until the infantry, the engineers and the close-support tanks and assault guns had chewed a way clear through the tactical zone of defence to the open country, and he did not commit his tank armies until the second and third days of the offensive—namely the First Guards Tank Army at 1400 on 15 January, and the Second Guards Tank Army early on the sixteenth. Konev, on the other hand, economised on his close-support tanks, as we have seen, and by way of compensation he sent in his full tank armies on the first day. This was his practice at the opening of the Vistula-Oder Operation (12 January), and at the start of the Upper Silesian Operation (15 February). He writes

> Had we, in this case [Upper Silesia], sent in only the infantry, the offensive would have slowed down still more, and our already depleted infantry divisions would have suffered much greater losses. Quite apart from a commander's purely moral responsibility for excessive human losses, I had no right to take risks at that time for practical reasons, i.e. in anticipation of such an important and responsible operation as the Berlin Operation.
>
> In general, it seems to me that in 1945 it was in principle inadmissable to throw infantry into an offensive without tanks. That would have been a step back. By that time we had already become used to the fact that a modern offensive involves the closest cooperation of all arms of the service, the tanks playing the leading role. . . . That our tankmen should have suffered considerable losses during the first day of the Upper Silesian Operation was distressing, but unavoidable. It was dictated by extreme necessity. Under the circumstances we would not have advanced a single step without tanks. (Konev, 1969, 72)

This is tendentious. If he had given due weight to the work of the close-support tanks, there would have been no need to commit the tank armies to close-quarter fighting.

Zhukov had the better of the argument, for post-war analysis showed that it was advisable to give the tank armies a clear run into the open country:

The tank armies, which were brought into action to complete the breakthrough, had, as a rule, lower rates of press in the subsequent advance into the enemy depth, since their shock capabilities had been considerably reduced. That was why the STAVKA of the Supreme Command and a number of Front commanders, especially G. K. Zhukov, K. K. Rokossovskii and I. D. Chernyakovskii sought to complete the breakthrough of the enemy tactical zone of defence by means of infantry formations, powerfully strengthened by close-support tanks and artillery, and also the mobile groups of the all-arms armies. The intention was for the tank armies, which formed the mobile groups of the Fronts, to be introduced into ready-made breakthroughs and rush directly into the enemy rear so as to destroy their complete operational defence. (Radzievskii, 1977, 123–24)

Exploitation

The Action of the Tank Armies and Tank Corps

The main and decisive force in exploiting the success after the breakthrough were the tank armies and the detached tank and mechanised corps. In cooperation with the air force, like a fast-moving ram of colossal power, they cleared the way for the field armies.

(Zhukov, 1971, 579)

In the Vistula-Oder Operation the tank forces advanced at an average rate of 45 to 70 kilometres every 24 hours, and the rifle forces 25 kilometres. This produced an overall penetration of up to 500 kilometres in 22 days, though the individual tank armies travelled considerably further when we take into account all their twists and turns (First Guards Tank Army, 600 kilometres; Second Guards Tank Army, 700 kilometres). Likewise the overall frontage (including the flanks) of the two Fronts expanded from 73 kilometres in three isolated sectors at the outset, to a united 500 kilometres by the fourth day, and to 1,000 kilometres by the end of the operation.

Progress of some sort was made day and night, though for action in darkness in Upper Silesia in March Konev

> picked out the men who were best adapted to it and organised special battalions. These battalions, fighting only at night and withdrawing for rest at daybreak, played a very important role. In night fighting their operations were supported mainly by point-blank artillery fire, the guns being moved forward as far as possible before nightfall. (Konev, 1969, 73)

In general, the high Soviet rates of advance depended on:

1. Bold and enterprising leadership.
2. Beating the enemy to their own prepared positions. This was achieved again and again, and prevented the Germans from making a firm stand anywhere east of Posen.
3. Avoiding action in built-up areas:

> In January 1945 we accumulated sufficient experience to prove that the liberation of populated localities was in no respect the chief task of tank forces. To cut the communications of the enemy, reduce their defence to chaos, bar the routes by which their forward forces might retire, or the paths along which they might throw their reserves— those were the missions that we gave first priority. (Katukov, 1976, 353)

4. Using the hard-frozen ground to travel cross-country when necessary, by-passing towns and strongpoints. Conversely, the thaw helped to reduce the progress of the Upper Silesian Operation in March to a virtual standstill:

The situation was aggravated by the spring flooding which forced the tankmen to fight along the roads and for possession of them, and to break through built-up areas. And it was precisely from behind buildings and shelters that it was very easy for the enemy to operate with Panzerfausts. (Konev, 1969, 73)

It was much the same story in East Pomerania.

Mobile Groups and Forward Detachments

The momentum of the Soviet forces as a whole was sustained by systems of 'mobile groups' and forward detachments' which were identical in principle with the fighting advance guards employed by Fredrick the Great of Prussia in the Seven Years' War.

'Mobile group' was the designation for a large and immensely powerful formation which acted as the operational spearhead of the offensive. For the Vistula-Oder Operation the two Fronts had their two tank armies each (the 1st Ukrainian Front's Third Guards Tank Army and Fourth Tank Army; the 1st Belorussian Front's First and Second Guards Tank armies), while the all-arms armies had their independent tank corps (the Fifth Guards Army's IV and XXI Guards Tank corps; the Third Guards Army's XXV Tank Corps; the Sixty-Ninth and Thirty-Third armies' XI and IX Tank corps).

Forward detachments were small but hard-fighting battle groups which were sent out by their parent tank armies or tank corps. Their tasks were to beat the enemy mobile forces in 'meeting engagements,' and anticipate the Germans on defensive positions, road junctions, river crossings and the like, and hold them until the main body arrived on the scene.

The forward detachment was usually formed around an independent tank brigade (see p. 318), with its sixty-five or so tanks, and with an accretion of infantry, conventional tubed artillery, assault guns, mortars and Katyushas, anti-aircraft guns and supporting services. As a typical example, we may cite the forward detachment of the Fifth Shock Army, consisting of the 220th Independent Tank Brigade, the 89th Independent Heavy Tank Regiment and the 1,006th Rifle Regiment. It got under way on 19 January, and

> one after another the tanks set off down the glassy road, followed by three hundred trucks. Although it might seem strange, Colonel Esipenko placed the main force, including the heavy tank regiment, not at the head of the column but at the tail. He calculated that the enemy, in the process of retreating under the impact of our army, would appear behind the detachment, and it was there that the greatest danger was to be expected. Concealed under tarpaulins, the Katyushas were travelling in the middle of the column. It was an imposing sight as the column moved along the road—the trucks filled with troops, the tanks, the guns, and the anti-aircraft pieces. (Bokov, 1979, 74)

Within three days (20–23 January) Esipenko seized the crossing over the Warthe at Wolow, and captured Strezelno and the important strongpoint of Wagrowiec. Shortly before the end of the Vistula-Oder Operation, the same forward detachment crossed the ice of the Oder to Kienitz and planted itself on the west side of the river directly in front of Berlin (see p. 111).

The all-arms armies had forward detachments of their own, which helped to keep contact with the faster-moving armoured and mechanised forces in front. The result was a straggling chain of formations which is represented here in a simplified form. All of the intervals are very approximate:

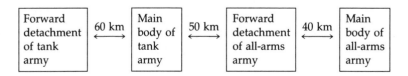

Forward detachment of tank army	60 km ⟵⟶	Main body of tank army	50 km ⟵⟶	Forward detachment of all-arms army	40 km ⟵⟶	Main body of all-arms army

The regulations required artillery commanders to 'direct fire from mobile observation posts from tanks equipped with radio sets.' It was usual for artillery observation officers to be attached to every tank battalion of the spearhead forces, so as to direct the gunners to lay down carpets of fire in front of the attacking armour. In the case of the XI Guards Tank Corps of the Sixty-Ninth Army the artillery concentrated its fire in successive rolling barrages falling at intervals of 1.5 to 2.5 kilometres to a total depth of 12 kilometres.

By 1945 large numbers of assault guns and tank-destroyers had come into service, and they were able to provide a particularly fluid kind of fire support. Among the partnerships which resulted was the one in the 2nd Belorussian Front between the 1,989th Self-Propelled Artillery Regiment and the 239th Guards Rifle Regiment. These comrades-in-arms survived all attempts on the part of superior officers to have the guns assigned to other regiments or divisions:

> A specified group of soldiers, under the command of a sergeant or an officer, was attached to every assault gun for the whole duration of combat. The group never left the gun, whether in action or during our short periods of rest. They helped the gun detachment in every way, and protected it valiantly from the enemy armour-piercing guns and Panzer-fausts. (Gorb, 1976, 245)

Close Air Support

In the Russian way of thinking, the military aviation was very much the servant of the ground forces. Thus more than three-quarters of the 54,000 sorties of the Second and Sixteenth Air armies in the Vistula-Oder Operation were committed to immediate support of the Russian spearheads. Liaison between the two elements had long been bad, but the aviation began to address itself to the problem seriously after STAVKA issued a sternly worded instruction on 30 November 1944.

Ground and airborne radio relay stations helped to extend the chain of communications, and aviation officers with staffs and radios were attached to the headquarters of armies, corps and the leading brigades: 'This made it possible to set supplementary tasks for the air forces, and enabled them to strike at new targets as they happened to appear' (Lelyushenko, 1970, 273). When the aviation radios failed, it was technically possible to restore communications with the aircraft by means of the radios of the tank commanders. On 16 and 17 January liaison was re-established in this way between the IX and XI Tank corps and their assigned close air support aviation division.

It was nobody's fault in particular that air support often failed during the Vistula-Oder Operation. The snowy and foggy weather in the middle of January limited the number of planes which could take to the air at the beginning of the offensive. Thereafter, the main problem was to secure enough airfields within close range of the fast-moving ground battle. The Russians tried to help themselves out by utilising stretches of road like the highway near Posen or the Breslau-Berlin autobahn. In the same way, the semi-combatant airfields service battalions moved with or immediately behind the foremost troops to seize German airfields and make them operational as soon as possible. The speed and urgency of the thing was demonstrated soon after the offensive had opened, when the fighters of the III Aviation Corps landed on the airfield at Sochaczew while fighting was proceeding on the western perimeter between the Germans and a tank brigade of the Second Guards Tank Army. The field was still insecure when the 402nd Fighter Aviation Regiment was rebased there on 18 January.

Even heroic measures like these were inadequate to support the ground forces in the later stages of the Vistula-Oder Operation. The thaw rendered many of the grass airstrips unusable and left the Sixteenth Air Army, for example, with only three airfields within efficient flying range of the ground fighting. While many of the Russian aircraft had to make round trips of up to four hundred kilometres, the Luftwaffe was able to keep up a high rate of sorties from the airfields around Berlin and win a temporary but crucial command in the area of the Oder bridgeheads (see p. 118).

Long spells of clearer weather arrived in the spring, and the Russians could at last bring their great numerical superiority in aircraft into play. In the fighting for Danzig 'the Soviet aircraft were in the air all day long. The strike planes with the red stars on their wings shot up every vehicle which appeared on the roads and flogged our front line repeatedly with their rockets' (Schäufler, 1979, 86). Air support reached its apogee in the siege of Königsberg, where the air forces carried out more than 20,000 sorties, and on occasion had 300 planes in the air at the same time.

Engineering Support

The main contribution which the military engineers made to speeding the advance was to bridge the rivers. During the Vistula-Oder Operation, for example, water obstacles were encountered every fifty to ninety kilometres, and were defined as 'wide' (over 300 metres), 'medium' (100 to 300 metres) and 'narrow' (up to 100 metres). The ice on most of the rivers lay 10 to 25 centimetres thick, which was strong enough to permit the passage of infantry and light artillery, if necessary with the help of plank causeways, but was too weak to bear tanks. It is not surprising that nearly one-third of the operations of the tank armies were concerned with mastering these awkward obstacles.

The highest level of engineering organisation was that of the Front reserve. This was particularly large in the case of the 1st Ukrainian Front, for the Oder on its sector of advance slanted away to the north-west, and the component armies could be expected to reach the river at intervals, with those on the left arriving first. Konev therefore assigned his reserves to each sector in succession. The formations of the 1st Belorussian Front, on the other hand, approached the lower Oder perpendicularly, and Zhukov decentralised his engineering assets to the armies.

When it came to crossing rivers, much depended on the adroitness of the forward detachment and its accompanying companies of engineers. The leading battalions or the core tank brigade of the detachment arrived hard on the heels of the preliminary reconnaissance parties and tried to effect two or three passages. The forces then fanned out on the far side and held the bridgehead until the main force arrived with the heavier bridging equipment. A full-scale passage by a tank army involved about five planked ice causeways for the infantry and light artillery, and three or four girder bridges, at least two of which would be capable of bearing sixty tons. Such a bridge could be built in as little as seven and a half hours, like the 60-ton 120-metre-long bridge over the Pilica near Palchev.

In their river crossings, as in so much else, the Russians found that old solutions no longer applied to the unfamiliar terrain of the Reich. When it exploited from the Steinau bridgehead, the 53rd Guards Tank Brigade of the Third Guards Tank Army reached the Bober on the night of 9–10 February after a rapid advance, but found that it could make no progress to the far side, for the Germans were playing tricks with the five locks upstream: 'The experience we had of building low-lying bridges, which we had amassed during the offensives in the Ukraine and Poland, no longer held good here. Every time we tried, the enemy raised the level of the water and the bridge was swept away by the current' (Nersesyan, 1964, 175). The Russians were forced to build a much higher bridge than usual, and they finally crossed the river only on the morning of the twelfth.

Logistic Support

The Russians launched the Vistula-Oder Operation on the following margins of foodstuffs:

Rations by Days

	1st Ukrainian Front	1st Belorussian Front
Bread	21.8	14
Groats	20	65
Fats	28.8	33
Sugar	35.5	66

During the operation detachments were sent out to herd back the cows, pigs and sheep which had been abandoned by the German refugees:

> They were of prime importance to the Red Army because for a long time Russia had been so impoverished that she could not feed her soldiers and had to depend on American food supplies and Polish grain, and because during the January advance the supply lines had become over-extended. (Koriakov, 1948, 67)

Otherwise, hungry soldiers were left to forage for themselves.

The Russians were rarely embarrassed by any shortage of ammunition, even in the Third Guards Tank Army, which had the highest expenditure of all in the Vistula-Oder Operation. The First and Second Guards Tank armies did not consume as much, and so came nowhere near exhausting the initial *Boekomplets* (see p. 329) which they took with them on that campaign:

Ammunition Expenditure in *Boekomplets*

	Rifle	Mg	82-mm mortar	120-mm mortar	76-mm art'y	76–85-mm tank
1GTA	.5	.6	.6	.4	.5	.7
2GTA	.5	.6	.2	.5	.4	.65

	Rifle	Mg	82-mm mortar	120-mm mortar	76-mm art'y	76–85-mm tank
3GTA	.6	.8	.6	2.5	1.4	1.5
4TA	.54	1.25	.57	1.11	1.22	.59

The 1st Belorussian Front was helped in the final phase of the Vistula-Oder Operation by a mighty lift by road which moved the artillery dumps 150 to 200 kilometres forward on 24 January. By the time of the siege of Danzig in March, a German noted that his forces had almost nothing left to fire,

> whereas the troops of the Red Army had ammunition in enormous quantities, and expended it lavishly. They unloaded their stocks almost under our eyes in the station at Zuckau [eighteen kilometres east of Danzig], since they knew we could not disturb them. Acting with astonishing speed, their service troops had restored the German railway network up to this point in a matter of days. (Schäufler, 1979, 80)

It was much more difficult to supply fuel. The consumption of the spearhead tank and mechanised formations was proportionately much higher than that of ammunition, with the tank armies in the Vistula-Oder Operation gobbling the equivalent of the initial *Napravkas* between 3 and 7.6 times over. Thus:

Consumption of Fuel

	Diesel		Petrol (gasoline)	
	Tons	*Napravkas*	Tons	*Napravkas*
1GTA	1,175	3.9	2,535	6.5
2GTA	885	3	2,182	4.0
3GTA	1,920	6	3,519	7.6
4TA	1,214	4.7	1,739	6.7

The direct line between the Vistula and the Oder was a formidable 500 kilometres or so, but the actual journeys of the tank armies were much greater still (see p. 338) on account of the changes of axes of advance, of which the most famous were probably those of the Third Guards Tank Army. Again in the East Pomeranian Operation the First Guards Tank Army changed its fundamental direction of advance four times.

The Russian transport system was unable to meet the demand, and towards the end of the Vistula-Oder Operation in particular, the tanks and mechanised forces proceeded by fits and starts according to the availability of fuel. In sixteen days of offensive action the Second Guards Tank Army had to halt for no less than five days (30 per cent) and the Fourth Tank Army for six (33 per cent). The fuel of the Third Guards Tank Army was almost exhausted by 24 January, during its move to the south-east to cut off the Upper Silesian Industrial Region, and General Rybalko kept the manoeuvre from coming to a complete stand still only by diverting all his remaining resources to General Sukhov's IX Mechanised Corps.

The captured dumps of fuel were very welcome, and accounted, for example, for 25 per cent of the consumption of the Second Guards Tank Army in the Vistula-Oder Operation; the trucks were making journeys of 500 kilometres or more from the distant dumps and railheads behind the Vistula, and they returned in pairs, one towing the other, so as to economise on fuel; the 1st Belorussian Front denuded several regiments of all their fuel-carrying trucks, and centralised the vehicles in two Front supply battalions of 130 and 160 vehicles respectively. But nothing seemed to help. The Soviets concluded in their post-war analyses that road transport is unable to sustain an operation in great depth, and they proceeded to set up field pipeline brigades which were each capable of laying about thirty kilometres of fuel pipe every twenty-four hours.

*   *   *

348

Mechanical Recovery and Repair

Out of all the Russian tanks and assault guns which were lost temporarily or permanently in the Great Patriotic War, about one-quarter bogged or broke down, and three-quarters were knocked out by enemy action. More specifically:

Losses to Categories of Weapons During Soviet Offensive Actions

Weapons	Losses
Aircraft	1.5–17.7%
Anti-tank mines	2.0–14.0%
Panzerfausts	Up to 24.0%
Art'y and tank gunfire	58.8–94.8%

The estimate for Panzerfausts, however, does not include the great increase of kills by these weapons towards the end of the war. Out of all losses, tanks made up about 65 per cent, and assault guns 45 per cent.

On 11 November 1944 STAVKA put all the facilities for mechanical repair under unified command, a measure which increased their productivity by 50 per cent. A significant role was played by the recovery tractors and workshops of the damaged vehicle assembly points (*SPAMS*), which attended to running repairs. The more difficult cases were left for repair at the army, corps or Front level.

The results were quite remarkable. In the first six days of the Vistula-Oder Operation, the Eighth Guards Army (1st Belorussian Front) had a total of 159 tanks and assault guns disabled, but only 71 of them permanently inoperable. In January as a whole the 1st Belorussian Front carried out 3,786 successful repairs of tanks and assault guns, and the 1st Ukrainian Front 4,267. This means that many of the vehicles were patched up more than once.

The rate of repair undeniably fell off towards the end of the Vistula-Oder Operation. There were a number of reasons. The *SPAMS* themselves began to suffer heavy losses, they were now three to four hundred kilometres from their depots of spares, and they scarcely began to set themselves down and start work before the fighting far outran the distance of forty to fifty kilometres within which they operated most efficiently. However, these failings are only relative, and the work of the Soviet mechanical repair teams helped to extend the 'sustainability' of the Russian offensives beyond the twenty or so days which had been the limit in 1942 and 1943.

Medical Services

The Soviets applied to shattered human beings the same basic principle which they applied to broken vehicles, that is, they gave their first priority to the units which could be put together with little delay and returned to the front line. In the case of the soldiers the category of such 'lightly wounded' covered about 40 per cent of all casualties. Medium cases made up 37 per cent, and the severely wounded about 23 per cent.

Army by army, the casualties in the tank formations did not differ greatly from one campaign to another:

Losses in Tank Armies

		Casualties as proportion	Proportion of casualties returned to service
Vistula-Oder Op.	1GTA	14.5%	27.0%
	2GTA	7.2%	31.5%
	3GTA	8.7%	24.0%
East Prussian Op.	5GTA	17.5%	24.0%
E. Pomeranian Op.	1GTA	12.4%	23.0%
	2GTA	14.5%	16.0%

These casualties among the tank forces do not correspond to the Soviet losses as a whole, which display great variations. When measured against what was achieved, the Russian losses in the Vistula-Oder Operation were astoundingly low, at around 15,000 dead and 60,000 wounded (see p. 114). Furthermore, a high proportion of these casualties was sustained in the early stages, when the offensive was breaking through the fixed defences. However, the grinding process went on much longer in East Prussia, which helped to bring the Russian casualties there to a grisly 200,000 to 250,000.

Such figures reflect the role of the infantry, which was much greater in East Prussia than between the Vistula and the Oder. In fact, it was much safer to be inside a tank than out of it, and tank forces in general suffered only about 10 per cent of the losses of the accompanying motor rifle troops, who had to ride around in soft-skinned vehicles or clinging to the outside of the tanks. Nothing much short of an artillery or tank round or an anti-tank mine could injure a tank crew, whereas the motor rifle troops suffered 32 per cent of their casualties through small-arms and machine-gun fire, as opposed to just 6 to 7 per cent of the tankmen. This drives home the lesson, which few armies have been willing to accept, that supporting infantry will always take disproportionately heavy losses until they are put into something about as well protected as a tank.

Special Forms of Operations

Combat Against Roving Cauldrons

As some of the pioneers of blitzkrieg had foreseen, when the armoured columns exploited deep into the enemy rear the character of the combat took on some of the characteristics of naval warfare, with the forces clashing in 'meeting engagements,' and cut-off formations and units trying to fight or infiltrate their way back to their parent armies. The Germans showed great persistence and resourcefulness in this respect, as Konev admits (Konev, 1969, 75), and Katukov writes about one of the actions of the XI Guards Tank Corps in East Pomerania that

> what saved us more than anything else was the fact that every officer of the staff had a full understanding of military realities. Now that our tank forces had driven deep into the enemy rear the fighting could develop at any hour or minute—and not just to our front, but on the flanks and around the whole arc of the circle. The only thing that mattered was not to lose your presence of mind. (Katukov, 1976, 380)

Attacks on Towns, Cities and Fortifications

The Russians experienced two sequences of close-quarter fighting in their offensives in Poland and Germany in 1945. The first, comparatively short, was when they ground through the German tactical zone of defence. The second developed later, when the Germans had recoiled to the Baltic, the Oder and the Sudetens, and they had to be winkled out of the cities and industrialised areas.

In most cases the Soviet procedure was to encircle the target city, then divide it into manageable segments by concentric thrusts through what they called the 'new town' (*novyi gorod*) of suburbs and factories, where the Germans usually held about two-thirds of their strength. (Strangely enough, the Russians failed to carry out this practice at Breslau, and the Germans were able to maintain a coherent defence until the very end.) The final blow was then dealt against the historic core.

The concentrations of force were gigantic. A division might be committed to an advance down a single street, and as many direct-fire weapons as possible were brought up to blast the defenders at close range. The Russians devoted no less than 41,600 guns to their grand offensive against Berlin in April and early May.

For the detailed business of fighting, the Russians constituted storm detachments of up to three companies of infantry, a machine-gun company, half a dozen tanks and assault guns, twenty pieces of calibres up to 152 mm, and a large complement of mortars, the whole amounting to about four hundred men.

The storm detachments were in turn divided into storm groups, such as those organised in the Forty-Seventh Army, which consisted of fifteen to twenty riflemen, three or four knapsack flame-throwers, a group of four or five sappers with demolition charges, one or two assault guns, and three or four light artillery pieces (45-mm and 76-mm).

The work of the units was highly specialised:

> After he had studied the intelligence concerning the enemy, the commander of the storm detachment or group used to set the various tasks: the supporting artillery was to suppress or destroy the enemy weapons positions and their isolated groups of infantry; the sappers prepared charges to break through walls or destroy individual buildings or strongpoints; the flame-throwers suppressed enemy weapons or units which could not be eliminated by our artillery; the rifle sub-units attacked designated targets in a specified sequence; the heavy and medium machine-guns concentrated their fire against the most accessible and least well-covered targets, and then, as necessary, swept the streets and alleys with their fire. (Zav'yalov and Kalyadin, 1960, 68)

Few of the Russians had any experience of this kind of action, and the veterans of Stalingrad and other episodes of urban combat were pumped for their experiences. The learning process continued during the fighting. Chuikov found that the best use for his tanks in Posen was to form them in pairs of double columns, which then drove down both sides of a given street simultaneously, protecting the infantry in the middle, and shooting up targets on the opposite sides of the road. On 7 April, when the assault on Königsberg threatened to bog down,

Marshal Bagramyan called on his officers for inspiration. General Shcheglov reported:

> We must alter the way we use direct fire against strongpoints and other masonry buildings. The attics and upper floors should be our first target—that's where the enemy have the observers and staffs who direct the combat. They are the 'eyes' of the strongpoint, and it's important for us to pluck them out. After that we direct the fire from the top downwards, as far as the half-basements and the cellars. (Beloborodov, 1978, 381–82)

The Russians experienced particular problems when they had to smash open a number of the tough old Prussian fortress-towns. Some of the core works were not particularly modern —those at Küstrin dated from the sixteenth century, at Graudenz from the eighteenth century, and at Posen and Königsberg from the middle decades of the nineteenth century, but all were built of hard brick with thick overhead coverings of earth, and they were endowed with pillboxes, minefields, belts of wire and other exterior defences.

The first step of the Russians was usually to rain down fire on the earthen overmantles of the forts, as at Königsberg on 2 April: 'The artillery fire gradually stripped away the cushioning of earth. Explosions with a characteristic grey smoke confirmed that the shells were bursting on concrete cover, while black smoke indicated bursts on brick masonry' (Beloborodov, 1978, 377). Not even direct hits from 280-mm shells could be guaranteed to crack open the concrete or brick scarps, but once the Germans had been driven from the exterior defences, the way was normally open for Russian sappers to rush across the ditches and make or expand practicable breaches (ramps of rubble) with explosive charges. The storm detachments then climbed the breaches and worked their way through the interior of the fort just as if they had been clearing a town.

The German Style

The German Forces Under the Storm

IT IS NOT DIFFICULT to present a passably comprehensive overview of the principles of Soviet warfare as they stood in 1945. The same is by no means true of the German conduct of war at that time. The coherence had largely broken down, partly on account of internal contradictions, and partly because the weight of the Soviet superiority in material. The Germans therefore reacted to events instead of dominating them.

The German performance in general was degraded by the fact that the Reich was fast coming to the end of its usable manpower. The Red Army was no better off in this respect, but it was able to compensate for human failings through the number and quality of its machines. The German decline is best illustrated with reference to some of its Panzer divisions, which were by definition counted among the crack forces. Under the pressure of operations a number of these formations suffered unmistakable breakdowns of discipline and morale, like the Panzer Division Holstein during its retreat with the von Tettau corps group on 8 March, or the 5th Panzer Division in the last days in Samland on 15 and 16 April. There was a cumulative decline in the 7th and 4th Panzer divisions, which were eventually pushed back through Pomerania into the Danzig-Gotenhafen Fortified Region:

- On 1 January the commander of the 7th Panzer Division reported that the division was hampered by a shortage of tanks and fuel. On the other hand, 'the *esprit de corps* of all personnel is good and there is confidence in our strength.'

- By 1 February heavy losses in vehicles and personnel had taken their toll, though the division was still capable of limited offensive action.
- By 1 March the losses were critical, and the new officers were 'inexperienced and not tough enough.' The division was equal to defensive operations only. (Glantz, 1986, 467)

In the companion division, the 4th Panzer, losses were so heavy that on 11 February the first battalion of the 33rd Panzer-Grenadier Regiment had just twelve combatants with which to hold a frontage of twelve kilometres. Drafts of service troops were being sent up from the rear, 'but some of them were wounded or disappeared before we had a chance to take their names. An old corporal with two or three soldiers could hold a trench better than thirty or forty scraped-together men of this kind, who were untrained and devoid of front-line experience.' By the final stages it

had become clear to the most stupid soldier that the war was lost. There was absolutely nothing more to gain—no military honours, no decorations, no promotion, no special leave, just a 'cold arse,' to use the apt expression of the *Landser* at that time. It had become a pitiless battle for sheer survival. (Schäufler, 1979, 85, 67)

Organisation and Weapons

Army Group

The German army group was the equivalent of the Soviet Front. It was Army Group A under Colonel-General Harpe which stood most directly in the path of the Soviet offensive in Poland in January 1945. It was comprised of

four armies, made up of 28 to 30 divisions
400,000 troops
318 tanks
616 assault guns and varieties of tracked anti-tank vehicles
4,000 artillery pieces and mortars

Army

This large formation had no stable organisation, and included everything from two to seven corps. In Army Group A in January the Fourth Panzer Army had a relatively powerful concentration of 474 tanks and assault guns and 597 artillery pieces on its frontage of 187 kilometres. The other army, the Ninth, was spread much more thinly, for it possessed only 323 tanks and assault guns and 586 artillery pieces on its sector of 220 kilometres.

Corps

The components once more varied considerably, and numbered between two and seven divisions.

Division

This was the basic level of German command. The German divisions were many fewer than the Soviet, but in partial compensation they were individually at least twice as strong. They came in the following categories.

Infantry Division

12,000 troops (six-battalion organisation), or
15,000 troops (nine-battalion organisation).

Panzer-Grenadier (Mechanised Infantry) Division

Two Panzer-Grenadier regiments of three battalions each, together with a tank or assault gun battalion and supporting troops:

14,000 troops
48 tanks.

Panzer (Armoured) Division

One or two tank battalions, one Panzer-Grenadier brigade, with supporting battalions of reconnaissance troops, motorised artillery and Jagdpanzers. The details varied considerably, but as an example we may take the 7th Panzer Division in East Prussia, which consisted of a tank regiment, two Panzer-Grenadier regiments, an armoured reconnaissance battalion, an armoured artillery regiment, an armoured engineer battalion, and a signals battalion. A full-strength Panzer Division had

14–17,000 troops
103–125 tanks.

However, a reliable Soviet source puts the average in 1945 surprisingly low:

11,400 troops
40 tanks
40 assault guns and Jagdpanzers
16 armoured cars
120 artillery pieces and mortars
90 armoured infantry carriers
350 motor cycles
115 tractors
2,171 other vehicles. (Radzievskii, 1977, 21)

Companies of Tiger tanks stood outside the Panzer divisions, but usually worked in close association with them. In addition, commanders of corps and armies held batteries of Jagdpanzers and assault guns, and battalions and sometimes regiments of tanks at their personal disposal quite outside the structure of the Panzer divisions.

Notes on Some Key Weapons

Tanks

The one tank to derive in basic design from the start of the war was the Mark IV. Originally conceived as an infantry-support tank, it was completely outclassed by the T-34 in tank-to-tank combat. The stubby 75-mm gun was replaced by a long-barrelled high-velocity version in 1942, and the armour was supplemented by various add-ons, but the Mark IV was undergunned and inadequately protected by the standards of 1945:

Mark IVJ

Weight:	25 tons
Armament:	one 75-mm gun, two machine-guns
Armour:	20–80 mm

The best all-round German tank, the Panther (Mark V) was inspired by the T-34, with its low silhouette, well-sloped armour and wide tracks. The Panther came into large-scale production early in 1943, and was equipped from the beginning with a long 75-mm gun which had great penetrating power. The Panther was speedy and manoeuvrable, though more complicated and less reliable than the T-34:

Panther (Mark VF)

Weight:	45.5 tons
Armament:	one 75-mm gun, two machine-guns
Armour:	50–100 mm

The Tiger was designed to mount the 88-mm gun, which had begun its career as an anti-aircraft weapon, and then proved remarkably effective against tanks. However, the Tigers never properly repaid the Germans for their investment in weight of armour, and even the top of the range, the T-VI King Tiger, was unable to withstand the 122-mm gun of the IS-2, or the devastating ISU-152 152-mm-tracked howitzer:

Tiger-VIE
Weight: 57 tons
Armament: one 88-mm gun, two machine-guns
Armour: 80 100 mm

Tiger-VIB (King Tiger)
Weight: 68 tons
Armament: one 88-mm gun, two machine-guns
Armour: 80–180 mm

Tracked Artillery, Assault Guns and Tank-hunters

By 1945 the Germans had produced a great profusion of types of tracked ordnance, ranging in type from conventional self-propelled artillery to specialised assault guns and anti-tank weapons—the rather makeshift Panzerjägers and the purpose-built and enclosed Jagdpanzers. These vehicles were cheaper to produce than conventional tanks, for they had no revolving turrets, and the gun projected straight from the front of the hull. In February 1945 one of the tank platoon commanders of the 4th Panzer Division, Sergeant-Major Bix, was initially disgusted to be issued with a Jagdpanther Pak 43/3 (a model of Jagdpanzer) instead of the promised Panther tank:

It was a hull without a traversing turret—you had to move the machine bodily in order to aim, and you exposed yourself somewhat in the process. On the other hand, it was a steel colossus, very low-lying, and it had a first-class 88-mm gun with enormous penetrating power, fabulous range and marvellous accuracy. We rapidly got over the Jagdpanther's unfamiliarity and threw ourselves into developing its good points. We very soon had an opportunity to display them to good advantage.

This proved to be in an action near Preussisch-Stargard on the morning of 25 February. Bix knocked out fifteen Russian tanks in three separate actions, and was making for the rear with two rounds left when he got stuck in the mud under the gun of a sixteenth tank. He was inching his Jagdpanther around in an attempt to bring his armament to bear, whereas the Russian turret was pointing in his direction. The enemy failed to open fire, and it became evident that the Soviet machine was slanting backwards into its own patch of mud, with the result that the gun could not be depressed sufficiently to hit the Germans. The tracks of the two vehicles churned away until Bix brought his machine around and had the Russians at his mercy:

All of a sudden the hatch flew open, and two hands extended and waved. Did the crew wish to surrender, or were they trying to fool us? By that time we were prepared for anything. No, I couldn't take the risk. To be absolutely certain, we shot our last but one round into the panel covering the running gear. The crew bailed out—one, two, three, four. *Alles in Ordnung!* Splendid! Our last shot hit the Russian tank full on, and it immediately took fire. (Schäufler, 1979, 48, 51–52)

Aircraft

Like many machines in the history of aviation, the Ju-87 (Stuka) dive-bomber proved surprisingly adept at new work, in this case as a tank-busting aircraft (Ju-87-G) armed with two 37-mm cannons. It was the weapon of Colonel Rudel's ground-attack wing, which was transferred from Hungary to the Oder at the culminating point of the Vistula-Oder Operation, and helped to stop the Russian drive on Berlin (see p. 118). Air support also proved very valuable in the fighting in East Pomerania and West Prussia, where the Luftwaffe alone had destroyed 120 tanks by 5 March.

Command and Control

It was perhaps too convenient for German veterans to blame the Führer for every misfortune which overtook Germany in the early months of 1945.

Certainly, it is difficult to find excuses for the way Hitler insisted on the kind of thin but rigid forward defence which left the Germans so vulnerable in Poland. He was also surely misguided to intervene as directly as he did as low as the divisional level of combat, in virtue of his decree of 21 January 1945 (see p. 38). Stalin was Olympian and detached in comparison.

However, someone will have to make deep investigations of the economy of the Reich before we can state outright that Hitler was altogether wrong to put so much effort into safeguarding the Hungarian oilfields. He was possibly correct in the long term when he insisted that Hossbach's Fourth Army must hold its salient deep inside East Prussia, for this may have been one of the considerations which induced STAVKA to turn the 2nd Belorussian Front away from its original axis across the lower Vistula, and so weakened the offensive on the Berlin axis.

On the matter of intelligence, Hitler was much nearer the mark than his professional advisers when he put the average strength of the Russian divisions at a paltry 7,000 troops each (when it was actually lower still). The trouble was that neither he nor Colonel Gehlen of the 'Foreign Armies East' branch of the OKH had any idea of the great number of such divisions which had been assembled for the offensive in Poland.

German military intelligence likewise failed to communicate

useful and up-to-date evaluations of the Russian military leadership. After Königsberg had fallen, the Russians were astonished to find that the German generals were almost totally ignorant of the new generation of Soviet commanders. Names like Konev, Zhukov, Rokossovskii and Vasilevskii conveyed no meaning to them:

> They exchanged glances but said nothing. After a moment's silence General Lasch said somewhat bashfully that he had not heard of Marshal of the Soviet Union Vasilevskii before his name was mentioned in the ultimatum to the Königsberg garrison. This meant that hardly any of the German generals had access to the information collected by the Reich's intelligence services, since we had no doubt that dossiers on Soviet commanders were filled with such details. (Bagramyan, in Erickson, 1987, 243)

Another curious failing of German staff work was in the matter of maps, which were generally inferior to those of the Soviets. German officers on the Bight of Danzig were puzzled to find that the Hela peninsula was called by the unfamiliar old name of the 'Putziger Nehrung':

> The explanation is simple. The maps were *Published by the Cartographical Section of the Royal Prussian Survey of the Year 1911*, and printed in 1914. We had to be on the watch for the subsequent changes in topography, especially as they affected the towns. It was noticeable that Gotenhafen was called 'Gdingen,' and was depicted as a sea resort, not a harbour. (Husemann, 1971–73, II, 431–32)

Finally, it is legitimate to ask whether at the level of army and below the tradition of *Auftragstaktik*, or 'mission-directed command' (see p. 55), which had served Germany so well, did not finally become a recipe for general disintegration, however well suited it was for guiding cut-off groups. Hitler and the OKH had fallen all too easily into the habit of retrieving generals and staffs from the wreck of one army or another and reassigning them to the command of entirely separate armies, with results which could be extremely disruptive (Plato, 1978, 406). There were divisions which did not have their components together for months on end (Neidhardt, 1981, 375), and SS Colonel (Standartenführer) Harzer cursed the near-paralysis which overtook his 4th SS Police Panzer-Grenadier Division in Pomerania in late February. It took four days instead of five hours to move the division from Konitz to Rummelsburg, 'and we squandered further precious time there, for most of the tank and mechanised units stood under the command of infantry-trained officers, who did not always employ them properly in the tactical sense and were not alive to their potential' (Husemann, 1971–73, II, 487).

Mobile Warfare

The Nature of German Blitzkrieg

The development of German mechanised warfare did not differ in kind from that of the Soviets. Indeed, German and Soviet officers and technicians cooperated directly in exercises and weapons development at Kazan, in southern Russia, from 1928 until Hitler put a stop to the practice in 1933.

The German version of blitzkrieg, like the Soviet, emerged naturally from concepts of mobility and inter-arms cooperation, in this case the notion of Combined Arms Warfare (*Gefecht der verbundenen Waffen*) which was advocated with great passion by Colonel-General Hans von Seeckt, the head of the *Truppenamt* (a substitute General Staff) in the 1920s. Significantly, the driving force behind the establishment of the Panzer arm was not a former officer of tanks but Heinz Guderian, whose specialities had been in light infantry, radio, motor transport, and the teaching of tactics and military history (see p. 46). Major Guderian did not see the inside of a tank until 1929, but in that year he formulated his concept of the Panzer division as a balanced force of tanks, infantry and supporting arms. Guderian caught the attention of Hitler, who assumed supreme power in 1933, and the first three such Panzer divisions were set on foot in 1935. In 1938 three more divisions came into being (the total finally reached twenty-one designated Panzer divisions and fourteen equivalents) and Guderian was made chief of mobile troops. He commanded less authority than the title might suggest, for he faced opposition from conservative circles in the Wehrmacht, and, more seriously still, he was unable to persuade Hitler that the new style of mechanised warfare demanded a large commitment of resources. For the Führer the Panzer forces represented an attractively economical means of snatching at victory in a short war.

The horse remained the motive power of the great majority of the German forces. In 1945 the Panzer and Panzer-Grenadier divisions accounted for only about one of out ten divisions on the Eastern Front, and the Panzer divisions themselves had just one-thirteenth of their troops actually in the tank forces. Blitzkrieg warfare was much more than just an affair of tanks, as has been stressed repeatedly, but by 1945 the Germans had reached a point where their tank forces could scarcely be considered as the kernel of their armoured formations. The Soviet superiority in numbers of tanks was now on the order of 6:1, and, as a rule of thumb, one German Panzer division was pitted against the equivalent of one Soviet tank army.

Strategic and Operational Mobility

In his memoirs, General Chuikov was dismissive of Colonel-General Guderian's proposal to strip the theatres of war in the Balkans, Italy, Norway and the Baltic so as to create a force to throw against the flank of the Russian armies on the Berlin axis:

It was totally unrealistic, because it could not be implemented at short notice and would have required roads, trains and ships. It should be remembered that at the time the Allied air forces had complete air supremacy, flying freely throughout the length and breadth of Germany. Such troop movements as did get under way, according to Guderian, 'proceeded very slowly, and the enemy air supremacy completely paralysed not only troop transportation, but also the will of the Command.' (Chuikov, 1978, 163)

The shortage of petrol restricted the use which could be made of roads for approach marches, and not just by the tanks, with the limited duration of their tracks, but by all kinds of vehicles. This limitation impeded the buildup of forces for Operation Sonnenwende towards the middle of February. Again it was principally to regain the full use of the perpendicular railway between Lusatia, Lower Silesia and Upper Silesia that the Germans thought it worth their while to undertake their offensive at Lauban at the beginning of March.

Lateral movement behind the Eastern Front was a truly desperate affair, in which the pace was dictated by the Russians. As Goebbels explained, 'We have to shuffle our units about to the hot spots like a fire brigade in order to plug the holes as best we can, suffering severely in the process' (Goebbels, 1977, 32).

There was no guarantee that the tanks would be able to detrain before they reached the scene of the fighting. On the snowy 6 March the 4th Panzer Division was dispatched from Bütow in the direction of Neustadt in West Prussia, and

we travelled . . . into the milky unknown with mixed feelings. The situation was unclear. We knew absolutely nothing about the enemy. There was no more aerial reconnaissance, and not even any kind of short-range reconnaissance by our recce detachments, because we did not have the requisite fuel. For this reason all the crews were ordered to occupy their tanks during the rail journey, with guns cleared for action, since we might have to go into combat directly from the train. All the radios were on 'receive,' but strict radio silence had been ordered. . . . Our goods train groped its way slowly northwards, sometimes only at a walking pace. Not a living soul was to be seen left or right of the track. Our train, all bristling with weapons, slid through the snowstorm almost like a ghost. We had placed the locomotive in the middle. The tanks stood on open flat cars and each machine had been assigned its own arc of observation and fire. Improvised ranks were ready on every car to help us to go straight into action in the open field. (Schäufler, 1979, 59)

On 17 January the nightmare had become reality for the tanks of the Grossdeutschland Panzer Corps, when they were compelled to detrain near Lodz in the face of Zhukov's armoured columns (see p. 80).

The Commitment of the Panzer Reserves

Long before the Vistula-Oder Operation opened, the commander of Army Group A, Colonel-General Harpe, and his chief of staff Lieutenant-General von Xylander, had given careful consideration as to how to deploy their scanty operational reserves, the XXIV and XL Panzer Corps (*Weisungen für die Vorbereitung der Abwehrschlacht zwischen Beskiden und Warschau*, 26 November 1944). They recognised that within the limits imposed by a shortage of fuel, and the superiority of the Russian air forces, it was still possible to retain these formations just far enough back to preserve freedom of manoeuvre, holding them safely out of reach of the enemy's initial bombardment. Even these slender margins, however, were sacrificed to the demands of Hitler, who insisted that the two corps must be emplaced close behind the tactical zone of defence.

Possibly such matters of detail—which come down to a matter of kilometres—were irrelevant in view of the weight and speed of the Russian attacks. It is in fact difficult to conceive what sort of measures might have stopped the Soviets once they had the bit between their teeth. The Grossdeutschland Panzer Corps was scattered to the winds when it sought to deploy across the Russian axis. Perhaps the powerful Sixth SS Panzer Army itself would have done little better, even if Hitler had launched it head-on against the Russians in Poland instead of sending it to Hungary. What finally halted the Soviets on the Oder was not a brilliant manoeuvre, but the cumulative effect of logistic difficulties, frontal barriers, and the buildup of unengaged forces on the Pomeranian flank.

Defensive Tactics in the Field

The old Reichswehr had studied the technique of the delaying action in the 1920s, but the Germans in Russia neglected this way of fighting until they were forced to relearn it during the retreat after the battle of Kursk in 1943. The Germans now fell back by bounds, sending the infantry and soft-skinned vehicles on ahead, and extending their tanks, assault guns and 88-mm guns in a screen which, they hoped, would knock out enough Russian tanks to win them the time to withdraw to their next position.

When they faced superior forces, the classic method of un-supported German infantry had been to lie low, let the Russian tanks roll over their trenches and foxholes, and then emerge to engage the enemy infantry coming up behind. This heroic tactic proved inadequate at the outset of the Vistula-Oder Operation in the middle of January 1945, for the initial artillery strike was crushing, and the Russians swamped the shattered defenders with their 'forward battalions.'

The German infantrymen began to fight back much more effectively once the battle reached their own country. They were helped by the thaws which set in from early February, and which canalised the Soviet armoured thrusts along the roads. No longer were the Germans contesting the open country of central Poland. They now fought along coherent river lines like the Oder, the Bober and the Lausitzer Neisse, and they could take full advantage of the cluttered terrain. On the southern flank the Germans put up a foot-by-foot defence of the remnant of the Upper Silesian Industrial Region which extended in the direction of Mährisch-Ostrau. Up in the north the Germans spread out among the lakes, marshes and extensive forests of Pomerania:

> Formerly, the Germans had striven to avoid combat in woods, preferring to outflank the forests out of fear of partisans and the local population. But now our forces were the ones fighting in enemy country. The Germans had no particular reason to apprehend hostility from the countrypeople [i.e. apart from ethnic Slavs in areas like the Tucheler Heide], and the forests helped them to put up a stubborn defence. (Zav'yalov and Kalyadin, 1960, 48–49. See also Shatilov, 1970, 170.)

Above all, the German infantrymen had a weapon which enabled them to operate as small groups or individuals and still knock out tanks. Up to about the middle of the war the only way to destroy tanks had been by air strikes, anti-tank mines, or through 'kinetic energy'—firing a shell or shot from a sizeable gun, in other words a weapon which was the preserve of the tank or artillery forces. The new principle of hollow or shaped charge, however, depended on 'chemical energy,' whereby the explosion of the warhead or grenade melted a hole through tank armour by a narrowly focussed jet of very hot gas. The velocity with which the charge could be delivered was irrelevant (indeed the Russian anti-tank grenades were applied by hand), except as far as it was needed to carry the warhead from the launcher to the target, and the German, American and British armies deployed a variety of light but effective anti-tank missiles. The German versions were the Panzerfaust, and the heavier but still man-portable Panzerschreck.

Courage and motivation were needed to make use of the new missiles, and these qualities were to be had in plenty in Germany in 1945. The Volkssturm (at least on the Eastern Front) provided dogged old men, and also the nimble and fearless *Hitlerjugend*, who were as dangerous to tanks as the lads of the PLO were going to be with their RPG-7s in Lebanon in 1982.

The contributions of the Wehrmacht were of two kinds. On 26 January Hitler ordered the setting up of a ferocious-sounding tank-hunting division (*Panzer-Jagd-Division*), which was composed of a host of little bodies of cycle troops, each commanded by a lieutenant, and carrying Panzerfausts in their front panniers: 'It was too bad about the men involved' (Guderian, 1952, 411). In addition, the Panzer divisions formed tank-killing companies (*Panzervernichtungs-Kompagnien*) out of tank crews who had lost their tanks. The one-armed Lieutenant Klaus Schiller commanded one such company in the 4th Panzer Division in front of Danzig. He was with one of his platoons when sounds of Russian armour were heard on the main road on the night of 23–24 March. The noise of the tracks stopped, and the waiting Germans saw that a T-34 had halted by the roadside and was revolving its turret in search of a target. No Russian infantry could be detected, and

> we worked our way cautiously towards the steel monster—fifty metres, forty, thirty, and then we found a shell hole. From this viewpoint the greyish form of our armoured enemy stood out clearly against the night sky.
>
> The fiery trail of our Panzerfaust ripped through the darkness. Our hearts stood still for two seconds, and then there was a bright flash and a shattering detonation—a direct hit!
>
> There were some screams, a hatch flew open, and panic-stricken forms fell out and staggered into the darkness. We did not open fire. The tank caught alight and blazed with deafening detonations. (Schäufler, 1979, 92)

There is clear evidence that the advantage in tank-infantry combat had swung back in favour of the Germans. With reference to the slow Russian progress in Upper Silesia, Konev writes that 'in analysing the causes of increased vulnerability of our tank units, we must not forget that . . . we had come up against such mass use of Panzerfausts for the first time during the war, and that we did not as yet know how to fight them properly' (Konev, 1969, 73).

Colonel-General Erhard Raus, commander of the Third Panzer Army, testifies concerning the fighting on the northern flank that 'one feature of the combat in Pomerania deserves to be emphasised, namely that out of the 580 enemy tanks we destroyed, two-thirds fell victims to Panzerfausts, in other words to brave individual soldiers. Never before had such a high proportion of kills been credited to Panzerfausts within a single army' (Murawski, 1969, 181).

Battle Groups and Roving Cauldrons

When the pressure was such that normal hierarchies of command collapsed, instinct and training told the Germans to accept the direction of the most senior commander on the spot, and coalesce into improvised fighting bodies which corresponded in size to any unit or formation from company to corps. With such a force it might be possible to escape from immediate encirclement. One of the feeders of Nehring's 'roving cauldron' in Poland was a battle group which Major-General Max Sachsenheimer had formed around the 17th Infantry Division. Five days of fighting had reduced Sachsenheimer's strength to less than a thousand men, and the Germans had to blow up gun after gun after their ammunition became exhausted: 'A final infantry gun under Captain Reinhardt had shot off its last shell and tried to gallop with its team of six horses through the closing pincers. The horses and the gun collapsed in a heap under the concentrated enemy fire, but the men were able to escape' (Sachsenheimer, in Ahlfen, 1977, 52).

The desperate straits to which the Germans could be reduced were illustrated by the provisional orders which were drawn up by the 5th Panzer Division on 11 April, for the case of a breakout through East Prussia from Samland. All the vehicles destined for the expedition were to be fully fuelled before departure, and the ammunition and medicaments distributed among the troops. Everything else was to be destroyed:

> The breakout will be put into effect at nightfall. It will be fought through according to the normal principles of combat, using all arms and all categories of ammunition.
>
> If we break through to the enemy rear, the division will seek to avoid all combat relying on the choice of suitable routes, the sending-out of reconnaissance parties, and flexible leadership. . . . We must protect the flanks and rear by flank guards and by deploying obstacles.
>
> In order to accomplish this task, the marching groups must be small, nimble and able to move cross-country. We cannot take with us any weapons or equipment which do not make a direct contribution to our striking power. What matters is to cover as much ground at maximum speed during the first night. If the division is held up by enemy resistance or impassable topographical obstacles, the vehicles are to be destroyed and the march will continue on foot. In that case we might have to disband the divisional structure and rely on the independent action of the commanders. (Plato, 1978, 411)

In the event, the 5th Panzer Division never emerged from Samland, where it was broken up and largely destroyed.

Most of the roving cauldrons failed to reach friendly lines, but the two corps groups of Nehring and von Tettau survived in epics of endurance. The Russians, however, claim to be unimpressed by these examples of 'shameful flight':

I don't know whether those 'valiant' generals are living. If they *are* still alive, they ought to thank Almighty God for saving their dishonourable skins. What did they do after all? With the remnants of their shattered corps they scuttled from one little wood to the next at night-time, and they got through to their own army simply because our forces could not keep up with them. (Babadzhanyan, 1981, 239)

This certainly accords with the memories of some of the survivors of the 16th Panzer Division. They were singularly uninspired by Nehring, and they followed in his tracks simply because they knew that their best hope of survival lay in that direction.

Positional Warfare

The Testimony and the Work of Guderian

Generally speaking, the importance of fixed defences in modern military history has been greatly underestimated. They offer little narrative interest to the reader, and they are of no great career concern to most professional soldiers, who prefer the éclat and aggression of mobile operations. For these reasons it is perhaps worth pausing a little to consider the great, if not fully realised, potential of positional warfare on the Eastern Front in 1945. For Guderian the fortifications fell well short of what they should have been, but they played

no small role in influencing the course of events, providing the troops with support and slowing down the Russian offensive to such a great extent that the demarcation line between the Western powers and the Soviet Union became the Elbe and not some other line still further back.

This is remarkable testimony from the foremost of the pioneers of blitzkrieg. The beginning of 1944 had nevertheless found Germany devoid of defences in depth on both the Western and Eastern fronts: 'In the former theatre Hitler had believed that he could rely on the Atlantic Wall, in the latter he was obsessed with the idea that if a fortified line existed the generals would conduct a less energetic defence and would be inclined to withdraw prematurely' (Guderian, 1952, 359).

Now that the war was approaching the Reich in the East, Guderian urged Hitler to restore the permanent positions along the pre-1939 German-Polish border, and built intermediate positions between there and the fighting front. Guderian worked out the necessary programme of construction with General Alfred Jacob, chief of engineers at the OKH, and he revived the recently dissolved Fortifications Department of the General Staff in order to evaluate fortifications in general.

It was also Guderian who was responsible for setting up one hundred battalions of fortress infantry and one hundred batteries of guns in order to defend the intermediate positions. From September 1944, however, seventy-eight of those battalions and all the captured Russian guns of a calibre of 76 mm or more were whisked away. Nobody is quite certain where they went. Guderian in his memoirs claims that they were diverted to the Western Front, though it is more likely that they were simply thrown piecemeal into the fighting against the Russians. In the event, 'the handsome fortifications and strongpoints remained ungarrisoned' (Guderian, 1952, 361).

Guderian seems to have hoped that the Volkssturm would provide a substitute (see p. 52), but most of these boys and old men were caught up willy-nilly in open combat or ended up in the defended cities.

So much for the issue of fortification in general. The fortifications themselves fell into a number of categories.

* * *

Front-line Field Positions

These comprised the positions which were held by the forces which were in immediate contact with the enemy—the trenches, dugouts, weapons positions, batteries and belts of wire and mines. In neither detail nor overall could this 'tactical zone of defence' be considered particularly strong. One of the fundamental reasons was identified after the war by Major-General Hans von Ahlfen, from his experiences in Silesia. He remarked that in the Great War the German army developed great skill in building shell-proof positions:

> In the Second World War, by way of contrast, this skill declined year by year among all the arms of the service, and even among the pioneers, who are supposed to instruct us in field fortifications—and yet the troops themselves were not to blame. It just came from Hitler's way of conducting war, which hurried the forces from 1941 from battle to battle, from one theatre of war to the next, from unexploited victory to unexploited victory, and finally from defeat to defeat, losing our best forces at an increasing rate. As a result, we lacked the time, opportunity and instructors to teach, learn and improve in this speciality. (Ahlfen, 1977, 26)

Although the Germans had been fighting fundamentally on the defensive from the late summer of 1943, their concept of positional warfare was confined for more than a year to a single *HKL* (*Hauptkampflinie*, or main battle line). In the autumn of 1944 Guderian was at last able to persuade Hitler that the Reich was in immediate danger, for the Russians had advanced to within two hundred kilometres of the Upper Silesian Industrial Region, and had already crossed the East Prussian border near Goldap. Guderian concluded that the Germans could fight confidently and effectively only if they were bolstered by fortified lines extending in depth towards the Oder. The lines in the deep rear will be considered shortly, but as a close support for the front-line troops Guderian proposed building a *Grosskampf-HKL* (Major Battle-*HKL*) situated about eighteen kilometres behind the *HKL*, in other words out of range of the initial Russian artillery strike. Hitler agreed with the idea of the *Grosskampf-HKL* in principle, but destroyed most of its effect by drawing it just two or three kilometres to the rear. The consequences were felt in Poland on 12 January 1945:

> Main line of defence, major defensive positions, reserves —all were buried beneath the tidal wave of the initial Russian breakthrough and lost to us. Hitler's rage was turned against the men who had built the defences and—since I had stood up to him—against me. He ordered that the minutes of the conferences held in the autumn of 1944 on the subject of a major defensive line be sent for, maintaining now that he had always wanted an eighteen-kilometre gap. 'Who was the half-wit who gave such idiotic orders?' I pointed out that it was he himself who had done so. The minutes were brought and read aloud. After a few minutes Hitler broke off the reading. (Guderian, 1952, 378)

The casualties were greater still because Army Group A held most of its forces in the *HKL*, and did not exercise the freedom it had been given to pull back to the *Grosskampf-HKL*, a measure which would have done a little to soften the impact of the Russian artillery strike.

Only in the final weeks of the war did the Germans apply the principle of defence in depth to any great effect. This was in virtue of an order which Hitler sent on 30 March to Army Group Vistula for the defence of the Oder line:

> A *Grosskampf-HKL* is to be determined and built some three to six kilometres behind the present front line. When the enemy attack is recognised to be imminent, the commander of the army group is to occupy that position in good time. It

is essential to avoid the effect of the enemy massed artillery destroying our entire defensive system. (Magenheimer, 1976, 135–36)

General Chuikov, the commander of the Eighth Guards Army, testifies how effective the new German way of fighting proved to be on 16 April, the first day of the Berlin Operation, when the offensive of the 1st Belorussian Front was halted at the foot of the Seelow Heights. Formerly, the main force and the operational reserves of the Germans had been destroyed or broken up by the first strike:

> Now the Germans were wiser. They occupied not only the first line but placed large numbers of infantry, artillery and Panzers in the second and third lines too. On top of that, strong reserves were deployed in the rear of the defence lines. . . . We also underrated the specific features of the terrain, which abounded in canals, streams, lakes and other natural obstacles. Lack of roads restricted our freedom of manoeuvre and made it impossible to commit large forces during the attack. (Chuikov, 1978, 181–82)

Chuikov's last point emphasises indirectly how much the Russian freedom of manoeuvre during the Vistula-Oder Operation had depended on the ground being hard frozen.

Intermediate Postions—the *a-*, *b-* and *c-Stellungen*

These lines were designed by the OKH and built from the autumn of 1944 from civilian labour under the direction of the gauleiters. They extended to a depth of two to three hundred kilometres and covered the area between the lower Vistula, Pomerania and the Carpathians. The outermost line, the *a-1 Stellung*, exploited the barriers of the Dunajec and the Nida on its southern and central sectors, and ran from Tarnow across the Pilica to Tomaszow, and on through Sochaczew to the Vistula; the *b-1 Stellung* was the main rearward position, screening the Upper Silesian Industrial Region and the Warthegau, and ran west of Krakow and east of Czestochowa to the Warthe at Sieradz, then on to the Vistula at Thorn, from where it followed the general axis of the river from Bromberg to Graudenz.

The Soviet spearheads learned to treat the potential of the intermediate lines with great respect:

> The experience of our operations proved that in the course of the pursuit it is very important not to give the enemy the opportunity to occupy prepared lines. Whenever the enemy was able to take up such a position, it was impossible for our corps [XI Tank Corps] to overcome them completely until the infantry formations arrived to help. (Yushchuk, 1962, 138–39)

Here we have a clue as to what the intermediate positions might have accomplished if they had been properly defended. This, however, was rendered almost impossible by the lack of liaison among the German authorities.

German reserves were so badly mismanaged that Army Group A had only six battalions of fortress infantry with which to hold the *a-1 Stellung* when the Russian offensive opened on 12 January. By 18 January the commander of the Posen Military District (No. XXI) had twenty-one battalions of Volksstrum to hold his sector of the *b-1 Stellung*, but this was a task which demanded fourteen divisions, and the Russian armoured forces had already broken across the line in a number of places on the day before. Still further to the rear the Upper Silesian Volksstrum was released by the Party only on 13 January—too late to allow it to be incorporated into the defence of the Upper Silesian Industrial Region.

The interference of the gauleiters extended as far as technical design. From July 1944 'Fire Brigade General' Fiedler planted the borders of East Prussia with great numbers of the Koch Pots *(Koch Töpfe)*, which were named after the notorious gauleiter, and consisted of concrete tubes which were partially sunk in the earth and furnished with two machine-guns each. Escape from the pots was out of the question once combat had begun, and the concrete broke up the first hit from artillery, which was profoundly discouraging. Closer to Königsberg the 14th Panzer-Grenadier Regiment of the 5th Panzer Division found it impossible to hold the village of Gutenfeld, because the Russians had infiltrated themselves into trenches which had built on the orders of Koch. Captain Jaedtke complained that 'right from the beginning of the actions in East Prussia those bloody trenches did us more harm than good. We were a Panzer division, and as we were weak in infantry, we could not make use of the trenches ourselves. If the Russians got into the trenches first, it was difficult for us to get them out again' (Plato, 1978, 382).

Permanent Frontier Lines

It is just the same story when we turn to the powerful fortifications which had been built along the frontiers of Germany before the war. In East Prussia work on the Heilsberg Triangle (*Heilsberger Dreieck*) had begun while Germany was still labouring under the restraints imposed by the Treaty of Versailles. The scope was expanded gradually, when the provisions lapsed, and the positions ultimately formed a broad curve which extended for nearly two hundred kilometres from the Frisches Haff to the Kurisches Haff. The triangle was studded with 1,100 main installations, and covered one-third of East Prussia, including Königsberg and the most economically important regions. Too late the Germans discovered that nobody had bothered to update the scheme of defence in accordance with the recent developments on the Eastern Front. Early in February the 24th Panzer Division was ordered to occupy the westward-facing positions, but

the fact that it was impossible to procure maps of these defensive installations or even keys for the bunkers was typical of the confusion which characterised this phase of combat. Apart from this the installations, which had been built in the twenties, were unsuited for the use of our weapons. The firing lanes had not been cleared for years and were thus unsuited for the use of modern anti-tank weapons. Hence, it was impossible to execute this order which had been issued in absolute ignorance of the real situation. (Major Hans von Knebel Döberitz, in Glantz, ed., 1986, 419)

Technically, the positions of the Meseritz Fortified Region (Tirschtiegel Riegel) were considerably stronger, for they covered the direct approaches to Berlin and ran behind the pre-1939 border with Poland in the rear of the recently annexed Warthegau. They formed multiple lines, and were anchored on the Netze and the Warthe in the north and on the Oder bend in the south. As things turned out, the Russian spearheads arrived there before the German field troops, and on 31 January the Eighth Guards Army secured most of the region in spite of an encounter battle with a German division which had been rushed up from the rear. The Russians had arrived in a hurry, but

luckily the men of the fresh German division were in a similar predicament. Evidently, they had poor knowledge of their own fortifications and consequently could not make the most of their fire-power and advantageous positions. They fought with determination but were lacking in skill. Of course, if the German divisional command had a better knowledge of the fortified area and had had just two days to study the situation and organise the fire system and co-operation with other German forces, it is difficult to say how the events would have developed. I am inclined to think that in that case we would have had to fight a long battle and sustain heavy losses. (Chuikov, 1978, 151)

Defended Towns and Cities

Incomparably the toughest and most successful kind of positional defence which the Germans offered was the one they put up in the towns. An important model was set by Posen, which fell only on 22 February, after nearly five weeks of resistance.

Pre-existing fortifications were useful to the defenders, as at Königsberg or at Posen itself, but less vital than a spirit of resourcefulness. The Germans typically broke open cellar walls to secure underground communications along whole rows of buildings. Carpets and curtains were suspended across the streets to screen the defenders from view. Thousands of mines were manufactured daily, using fillings extracted from naval mines or torpedoes, as at Königsberg, or from unexploded Russian bombs, as at Breslau.

The Germans were every bit as inventive as the Russians when it came to applying solutions to unexpected problems. At Breslau the whip-like crack of the well-camouflaged Soviet anti-tank guns got on the nerves of the German infantry. Lieutenant Hartmann, as commander of an assault gun, worked out a procedure of his own:

> This was not particularly easy, because these were low-trajectory weapons and the noise of the discharge was readily confused with that of the impact. I used to creep out to some suitable corner, often detaching my periscope and taking it with me, and if I was able to detect the target, I would bring my gunner and show him exactly where to aim. Then we would load the gun, charge around the corner like a fire engine and within a few seconds send our first shell tearing down the street. No Russian gunner would stand by his piece at the sight of our assault gun, all spitting fire, and we could then knock out the enemy anti-tank guns at our leisure. (Ahlfen and Niehoff, 1978, 65)

Supporting Arms and Services

The Kriegsmarine and the Luftwaffe

The contributions of the German navy and air force have been treated in detail in the main body of the text. As commander-in-chief of the navy, Grand-Admiral Doenitz made a 'fine imposing impression' (Goebbels, 1977, 1), and stood high in the esteem of the Führer. The OKH reproached him for insisting so long on keeping German forces bottled up in Kurland, to help the U-boats to train and operate in the eastern Baltic. However, the Kriegsmarine performed magnificently in lifting 2 million soldiers and refugees from the shores, and through the fire of the *Prinz Eugen* and other celebrated warships, it offered powerful fire support to the soldiers well inland.

The Luftwaffe, unlike the German navy, did not enjoy the overall superiority in its element. It nevertheless offered the Germans the one speedy means they had of striking at Soviet breakthroughs, and in 1945 the tank-killing role emerged as probably the most important contribution of the air forces. Exploiting local and temporary superiorities, the Luftwaffe helped to contain the Russian bridgeheads in front of Berlin and to make the fighting in Pomerania so costly for the enemy.

Logistics and Mechanical Repair

The Germans had no uniform logistic system as such, and the expedients by which they had kept themselves going now underwent a near-total collapse. At the most fundamental level, the Germans no longer had the industrial and transport base to forward the most necessary commodities to the various theatres of war. Lack of fuel precluded brilliant sweeping movements by the mechanised forces, just as the near-universal lack of ammunition for the artillery, tanks and assault guns had a crippling effect on all arms in nearly every action (see the report by the Second Army in Pomerania, 25 February, in Murawski, 1969, 92).

And yet affairs could have been managed better than they were. Some revealing comments are made by Lieutenant Schäufler, from what he saw of the campaign in Pomerania. In his experience the lack of fuel and ammunition was relative—stocks indeed existed, but it was not always easy to obtain the necessary release, the transport of these highly explosive loads was a 'suicide mission,' in view of the enemy air superiority, and the strict traffic controls imposed further delay (Schäufler, 1979, 87).

Schäufler likewise attributes the high rate of mechanical losses to a failure of command and organisation. Tanks were complicated and surprisingly delicate machines which demanded constant care and attention, and they were vulnerable to

> technical ignorance, lack of knowledge as to how tanks operated and fought, and what their limitations were. Together with a big-headed but narrow-minded way of thinking, and occasional applications of brute force, this led to frequent losses and misfortunes when we were assigned to non-mechanised units. Later all the blame was heaped on the tank crews. For that reason every tank commander shuddered when he heard that he might be detached to the infantry. (Schäufler, 1979, 46)

The German experience in East Prussia may serve as a microcosm of the Reich. The depots of the Kriegsmarine were managed by an office in distant Kiel. The Volkssturm were supplied both by the Wehrmacht and the SS. In addition, there was separate logistic support for the SS, the Luftwaffe, the gauleiter in his capacity as *Reichsverteidigungskommissar*, and the two labour and construction outfits—the Reichsarbeitsdienst and the Organisation Todt.

The Third Panzer Army met the Russian attack in January with fuel and ammunition for scarcely three days, and the combat was so intense that one of its corps was expending ammunition at a rate of three train-loads a day—which far outstripped the capacity of the transport system. Mechanical repair workshops were unable to operate sufficiently long in a single place to do any useful work, even if there had been any way of rescuing damaged vehicles from the battlefield. In the 5th Panzer Division Major von Ramin reported how his 53rd Panzer-Jäger Detachment was virtually crippled in the course of the month:

> The roads were completely jammed by the columns of refugees, and the detachment did not have the means of retrieving all of the damaged Jagdpanzers in good time. Out of our fourteen complete write-offs, only three were lost through enemy action—the other eleven had to be blown up, for we did not have the tractors to save them from the enemy. (Plato, 1978, 383)

When the composite Armee Ostpreussen was finally driven back to Pillau, the officers were outraged to discover that the Samland woods concealed immense underground depots belonging to the Kriegsmarine and the Luftwaffe. The contents now had to be blown up, burnt, or, in the case of the stores of fuel, pumped away like the hopes of Germany into the sand.

BIBLIOGRAPHY

Abbreviation *VIZh* = *Voenno-Istoricheskii Zhurnal*, Moscow.

Adair, P. (1986), 'The German Army in 1945,' in Glantz, ed. (1986).

Ahlfen, H. (1977), *Der Kampf um Schlesien 1944–1945*, Stuttgart.

Ahlfen, H., and Niehoff, H. (1978), *So Kämpfte Breslau*, Stuttgart.

Antonov, V. S. (1975), *Put' k Berlinu*, Moscow. Fifth Shock Army.

Babadzhanyan, A. Kh. (1981), *Dorogi Pobedy*, Moscow. XI Guards Tank Corps of First Guards Tank Army.

Bagramyan, I. K. (1987), 'The Storming of Königsberg,' in Erickson, ed. (1987).

Bartov, O. (1985), *The Eastern Front, 1941–1945: German Troops and the Barbarisation of Warfare*, London.

Beloborodov, A. P. (1978), *Vsegda v Boyu*, Moscow. Eleventh Guards, Thirty-Ninth and Forty-Third Armies.

Bidlingmaier, I. (1962), *Entstehung und Räumung der Ostseebrückenköpfe 1945*, Neckargemünd.

Binder, M. (1986), 'Armoured Group of 5th Panzer Division in the Defensive Operation,' 'Operations of XX Army Corps,' and 'Views of a Red Army Officer,' in Glantz, ed. (1986).

Bokov, F. (1974), 'Nastuplenie 5-i Udarnoi Armii s Magnushevskovo Platsdarma,' *VIZh*, 1974, No. 1.

Bokov, F. (1979), *Vesna Pobedy*, Moscow.

Bongartz, H. See 'Thorwald, J.'

Chuikov, V. I. (1978), *The End of the Third Reich*, Moscow. Eighth Guards Army.

Condne, Brigadier-General (1986), 'Employment of 7th Panzer Division with Emphasis on its Armoured Group,' and 'Terrain and Weather Conditions,' in Glantz., ed. (1986).

Danilov, F. V. (1958), *Radom-Lodzinskaya Operatsiya*, Moscow. Sixty-Ninth Army.

Del'va, V. A. (1983), *My shli syuda dolgo*, Kharkov. A soldier's diary.

Dick, C. J., 'The Operational Deployment of Soviet Armour in the Great Patriotic War,' in Harris, J. P., and Toase, F. H., eds., (1990), *Armoured Warfare*, London.

Dieckert, K., and Grossmann, H. (1960), *Der Kampf um Ostpreussen*, Munich. Good solid history.

Dragan, I. G. (1977) *Vilenskaya Krasnoznamennaya*, Moscow. 144th Rifle Division.

Dupuy, T. N., and Martell, P. (1982), *Great Battles on the Eastern Front*, London.

Edwards, R. (1989), *Panzer: A Revolution in Warfare, 1939–1945*, London.

Efimov, A. (1985), 'Primenenie Aviatsii pri Vedenii Operatsii v vysokikh Tempakh i na bol'shuyu Glubinu,' *VIZh*, 1985, No. 1.

Ellis, J. (1990), *Brute Force: Allied Strategy and Tactics in the Second World War*, London. Good on material superiorities, but underestimates Soviet skill in the conduct of operations.

Erickson, J. (1975–83), *Stalin's War with Germany*, 2 vols., London. An indispensable source book.

Erickson, J., 'Koniev' and 'Zhukov' in Carver, M., ed., (1976), *The War Lords*, London.

Erickson, J., ed., (1987), *Main Front: Soviet Leaders Look Back on World War II*, London.

Evans, R. J. (1989), *In Hitler's Shadow: West German Historians and the Attempt to Escape from the Nazi Past*, London.

Frolov, G. D., et al. (1982), *Vyshli na Front Katyushi*, Moscow.

Gaunitz, L. O. (1987), *Die Flucht und Vertreibung aus Ostpreussen, Westpreussen, Pommern, Schlesien und dem Sudetenland*, Bad Nauheim.

Getman, A. L. (1982), *Tanki idut na Berlin*, Moscow. XI Guards Tank Corps of the First Guards Tank Army. A useful supplement to Babadzhanyan.

Glantz, D. M., commentator and ed. (1986), *1986 Art of War Symposium. From the Vistula to the Oder: Soviet Offensive Operations, October 1944–March 1945*, Carlisle (Pa.). A triumph of scholarship. The daily situation maps are particularly useful.

Glantz, D. M. (1989), *Soviet Military Deception in the Second World War*, London.

Glantz, D. M. (1990), *Soviet Military Intelligence in War*, London. Esp. pp. 284–354 on the Vistula-Oder Operation.

Goebbels, J. (1977), *The Goebbels Diaries: The last Days*, London.

Golovnin, M. I. (1988), 'Uroki dvukh Operatsii,' *VIZh*, 1988, No. 1.

Gorb, M. G. (1976), *Stranu zaslonyaya Soboi*, Moscow. 239th Guards Rifle Regiment.

Guderian, H. (1952), *Panzer Leader*, London. The vital testimony of the chief of the OKH.

Gurevich, S. R., et al. (1979), *S Boyami do El' by*, Moscow. 60th Rifle Division of the Forty-Seventh Army.

Hartelt, Colonel (1986), 'Battle Report of a Panther Tank Company of Panzer Division "Hermann Goering," ' in Glantz., ed. (1986).

Hartung, H. (1976), *Schlesien 1944/45*, Munich.

Haupt, W. (1968), *Heeresgruppe Mitte 1941–1945*, Dorheim.

Haupt, W. (1970), *Das Ende im Osten: Chronik vom Kampf in Ost- und Mitteldeutschland*, Dorheim.

Haupt, W. (1980), *Kurland: Die vergessene Heeresgruppe 1944/1945*, Friedberg.

Haupt, W. (1987) *Die 8. Panzer-Division im Zweiten Weltkrieg*, Friedberg.

Heinemann, W., 'The Development of German Armoured Forces 1918–40,' in Harris, J. P., and Toase, F. H., eds., (1990), *Armoured Warfare*, London.

Hiden, J., and Farquharson, J. (1989), *Explaining Hitler's Germany*, London.

Hillgruber, A. (1986), *Zweierlei Untergang: Die Zerschlagung des Deutschen Reiches und das Ende des europäischen Judentums*, Berlin.

Humboldt, Lieutenant-Colonel (1986), 'View from OKH,' in Glantz, ed. (1986).

Husemann, F. (1971–73), *Die guten Glaubens waren: Geschichte der SS-Polizei Division (4. SS-Polizei-Panzer-Grenadier-Division)*, 2 vols., Osnabrück.

Irving, D. (1977), *Hitler's War*, London. Important and very well written.

Ivanov, V. (1980), 'Iz Vostochnoi Prussii—v Vostochnuyu Pomeraniyu,' *Voennyi Vestnik*, 1980, No. 2, Moscow.

James, H. (1989), *A German Identity 1770–1990*, London.

Kalutskii, N. (1977), 'Boi Strelkovogo Batal'ona za Zakhvat i Uderzhanie Platsdarma na Visle,' *VIZh*, 1977, No. 1.

Karpov, V. V. (1987), *The Commander*, London. On General I. E. Petrov.

Kartashev, L. S. (1980), *Ot Podmoskov'ya do Kenigsberga*, Moscow. 83rd Guards Rifle Division of the Eleventh Guards Army.

Katukov, M. E. (1976), *Na Ostrie Glavnovo Udara*, Moscow. XI Guards Tank Corps of the First Guards Tank Army.

Keilig, W. (1983) *Die Generale des Heeres*, Friedberg. Very useful.

Kershaw, I. (1989), *The Nazi Dictatorship: Problems and Perspectives of Interpretation*, London.

Khetagurov, G. I. (1977), *Ispolnenie Dolga*, Moscow. 82nd Rifle Division of the Eighth Guards Army.

Kireev, N. (1985), 'Primenenie Tankovykh Armii v Vislo-Oderskoi Operatsii,' *VIZh*, 1985, No. 1.

Kir'yan, M. M. (1960), *S Sandomirskogo Platsdarma*, Moscow.

Kir'yan, M. M. (1982), *Voenno-Tekhnicheskii Progress i Vooruzhennye Sily SSSR*, Moscow.

Kissel, H. (1962), *Der deutsche Volkssturm 1944/45*, Frankfurt-am-Main.

Kobrin, N. (1984), 'Advance Detachment,' *Soviet Military Review*, 1984, No. 11, Moscow.

Kolibernov, E. (1985), 'Kharakternye Osobennosti Inzhenernogo Obespecheniya Voisk Frontov v Vislo-Oderskoi Operatsii,' *VIZh*, 1985, No. 1.

Konev, I. (1969), *Year of Victory*, Moscow. By the commander of the 1st Ukrainian Front. Important and wide-ranging.

Konichev, N. (1985), 'Organisatsiya Svyazi pri Podgotovka i v Khode Vislo-Oderskoi Operatsii,' *VIZh*, 1985, No. 1.

Kon'kov, V. (1983), 'Tak kovalsya Uspekh: Tylovoe Obespechenie 1-i Gvardeiskoi Tankovoi Armii v Vislo-Oderskoi Operatsii,' *Tyl i Snabzhenie Sovetskikh Vooruzhennykh Sil*, 1983, No. 2, Moscow.

Koriakov, M. (1948), *I'll Never Go Back*, London. Experiences with the 1st Ukrainian Front.

Korovnikov, I. T. (1975), 'Udar na Krakov,' *VIZh*, 1975, No. 1. Fifty-Ninth Army.

Koyander, E. V. (1978), *Ya "Rubin" prikazhyvayu*, Moscow. By the commander of an aviation group in East Prussia.

Kozlov, L. (1975), 'Nekotorye Voprosy Voennogo Iskusstva v Vislo-Oderskoi Operatsii,' *VIZh*, 1975, No. 3.

Kozlov, L. (1980), 'From the Vistula to the Oder,' *Soviet Military Review*, 1980, No. 1.

Krainyukov, K. (1979), 'Special Weapon,' *Soviet Military Review*, 1979, No. 9. On party-political work.

Krylov, N. I.; Alekseev, N. I.; and Dragan, I. G. (1970), *Navstrechu Pobede: Boevoi Put' 5-i Armii Oktyabr' 1941 g.–Avgust 1945 g.*, Moscow.

Kurowski, F. (1987), *Endkampf um das Reich 1944–1945: Hitlers letzte Bastionen*, Bad Nauheim.

Larionov, V., et al. (1984), *World War II: Decisive Battles of the Soviet Army*, Moscow.

Laoch, O. (1977), *So fiel Königsberg*, Stuttgart. By the commandant of Königsberg.

Lelyushenko, D. D. (1970), *Moskva-Stalingrad-Berlin-Praga*, Moscow. By the commander of the Fourth Tank Army.

Liebeskind, Brigadier-General (1986), 'Operations of the 21st Panzer Division in the Kuestrin Area and between the Oder and Neisse Rivers,' and 'The Soviet Soldier in World War II,' in Glantz, ed. (1986).

Liebisch, Colonel (1986), '17th Panzer Division Operations to 27 January 1945,' and 'Second Phase of 17th Panzer Division Retrograde Operations East of the Oder River,' in Glantz, ed. (1986).

Lisitsyn, F. Ya. (1978), *V te groznye Gody*, Moscow. Third Shock Army.

Magenheimer, H. (1976), *Abwehrschlacht an der Weichsel 1945*, Freiburg.

Magenheimer, H. (1985), 'Das Kriegsende 1945 in Europa,' *Oesterreichische Militärische Zeitschrift*, 1985, No. 3, Vienna.

Maryshev, A. P. (1988), 'Proryv Oborony Protivnika,' *VIZh*, 1988, No. 3.

Matsulenko, V. (1975), 'Operativnaya Maskirovka Voisk v Vislo-Oderskoi Operatsii,' *VIZh*, 1975, No. 1.

Middeldorf, E. (1953), 'Die Abwehrschlacht am Weichselbrückenkopf Baranow', *Wehrwissenschaftliche Rundschau*, III, No. 4, West Berlin and Frankfurt-am-Main.

Mitcham, S. W. (1988), *Hitler's Field Marshals and Their Battles*, London.

Murawski, E. (1969), *Die Eroberung Pommerns durch die Rote Armee*, Boppard. A most professional military history.

Neidhardt, H. (1981), *Mit Tanne und Eichenlaub: Kriegschronik der 100. Jäger-Division*, Graz.

Nersesyan, N. G. (1964), *Fastovskaya Gvardeiskaya*, Moscow. 53rd Tank Brigade of the Third Guards Tank Army.

Nes, Colonel (1986), 'German Intelligence Appreciation,' in Glantz, ed. (1986).

Oven, W. (1974), *Finale Furioso: Mit Goebbels bis zum Ende*, Tübingen.

Pankov, F. D. (1984), *Ognennye Rubezhi: Boevoi Put '50-i Armii v Velikoi Otechestvennoi Voine,'* Moscow.

Paul, W. (1978), *Der Endkampf um Deutschland 1945*, Esslingen.

Peredel'skii, G., and Khoroshilov, G. (1985), 'Artilleriya v Srazheniyakh ot Visly do Odera,' *VIZh*, 1985, No. 1.

Plato, A. D. (1978), *Die Geschichte der 5. Panzerdivision 1938 bis 1945*, Regensburg.

Polushkin, M. (1977), 'Achieving Continuity of an Offensive by All-Arms Armies,' *VIZh*, 1977, No. 1 (Consulted by this author only in NATO translation).

Radzievskii, A. I. (1977), *Tankovoi Udar*, Moscow.

Radzievskii, A. I. (1979), *Proryv*, Moscow. Radzievskii's works are characteristic of the best Soviet military historiography, with its firm statistical base.

Rokossovskii, K. (1985), *A Soldier's Duty*, Moscow. By the commander of the 2nd Belorussian Front. Not particularly informative or exciting.

Roos, G. (1953), 'Die Problematik ständiger Befestigung im Licht der Erfahrungen des II. Weltkrieges,' *Wehrwissenschaftliche Rundschau*, 1953, X, West Berlin and Frankfurt-am-Main.

Rudel, H. U. (1952), *Stuka Pilot*, Dublin.

Rudenko, S. (1985), 'K 40-letiyu Vislo-Oderskoi Operatsii,' *VIZh*, 1985, No. 1.

Ryan, C. (1980), *The Last Battle*, London.

Sajer, G. (1971), *The Forgotten Soldier*, London. By a native of Alsace, serving with the Grossdeutschland Panzer Corps. Possibly the best of all the private-soldier reminiscences from the Eastern Front.

Samchuk, I. A. (1971), *Trinadtsataya Gvardeiskaya*, Moscow. 13th Rifle Division of the Fifth Guards Army.

Schäufler, H. (1973), *Der Weg war weit . . . Panzer zwischen Weichsel und Wolga*, Neckargemünd.

Schäufler, H. (1979) *1945 . . . Panzer an der Weichsel*, Stuttgart.

Schieder, R., ed., (1953–61) *Dokumentation der Vertreibung der Deutschen aus Ost-Mitteleuropa*, 5 vols, Wolfenbüttel.

Schramm, P. E., ed., (1982), *Kriegstagebuch des Oberkommandos der Wehrmacht (Wehrmachtführfungsstab)*, 4 vols, Munich.

Seaton, A. (1971), *The Russo-German War 1941–1945*, London.

Seaton, A. (1976), *Stalin as Warlord*, London.

Semenov, G. G. (1970), *Nastupaet Udarnaya*, Moscow. Third Shock Army.

Shatilov, V. M. (1970), *Znamya nad Reikstagom*, Moscow.

Shcherbakov, B. (1979) 'Material'noe Obespechenie 4-i Tankovoi Armii v Vislo-Oderskoi Operatsii,' *VIZh*, 1979, No. 6.

Shtemenko, S. M. (1985), *The Soviet General Staff at War (1941–1945): Book One*, Moscow. Esp. on the planning for the January 1945 offensives.

Skorobogatov, D. I. (1976), *Odnopolchane*, Moscow. Artillery support in the Baltic theatre.

Smirnov, E. (1978), 'Deistviya 47 Gv. TBR v Peredovom Otryade Tankovogo Korpusa,' *VIZh*, 1978, No. 1.

Speer, A. (1969), *Erinnerungen*, Frankfurt-am-Main.

Syropyatov, V. (1985), 'Nekotorye Voprosy Tankotekhnicheskovo Obespecheniya v Vislo-Oderskoi Operatsii,' *VIZh*, 1985, No. 1.

Tarassuk, Mr. (1986), 'Views of a Red Army Soldier,' in Glantz, ed. (1986).

Thorwald, J. (pseudonym of Bongartz, H.) (1950), *Es begann an der Weichsel*, Stuttgart.

Thorwald, J. (1951), *Das Ende an der Elbe*, Stuttgart.

Tippelskirch, K. (1976), *Geschichte des zweiten Weltkrieges*, Bonn.

Van Creveld, M. (1983), *Fighting Power . . . German and U.S. Army Performance, 1939–45*, London.

Volkogonov, D. (1991), *Stalin, Triumph and Tragedy*, London. The classic revisionist study.

Vysotskii, F. I. (1974) *Gvardeiskaya Tankovaya*, Moscow. Second Guards Tank Army.

Werthen, W. (1958), *Geschichte der 16. Panzer Division 1939–1945*, Bad Nauheim.

Yushchuk, I. I. (1962), *Odinnadtsatyi Tankovyi Korpus v Boyakh za Rodinu*, Moscow. XI Tank Corps of the Sixty-Ninth Army.

Zav'yalov, A. S., and Kalyadin, T. E. (1960), *Vostochno-Pomeranskaya Nastupatel'naya Operatsiya Sovetskikh Voisk*, Moscow. Contains a wealth of instructive detail.

Zhilin, P. A. (1986), *Istoriya voennogo Iskusstva*, Moscow.

Zhukov, G. K. (1971), *The Memoirs of Marshal Zhukov*, London.

Ziemke, E. F. (1984), *Stalingrad to Berlin: The German Defeat in the East*, Washington D.C. (U.S. Army Center of Military History). Readable and balanced.

INDEX

391

Other titles of interest

Available at your bookstore